THE ENGLISH VERB

Form and Meanings

Martin Joos

The English Verb

FORM AND MEANINGS

The University of Wisconsin Press

Madison and Milwaukee, 1 9 6 4

Published by the University of Wisconsin Press
Madison and Milwaukee
P.O. Box 1379, Madison, Wisconsin 53701

Copyright © 1964 by the Regents of the University of Wisconsin

Excerpts from *The Trial of Dr. Adams*
Copyright © 1958 by Sybille Bedford
Reprinted by permissions of Simon and Schuster, Inc., and the author

Printed in the United States of America
by George Banta Company, Inc., Menasha, Wisconsin

Library of Congress Catalog Card Number 64-7723

The Hatter was first to break the silence. "What day of the month is it?" he said, turning to Alice: he had taken his watch out of his pocket, and was looking at it uneasily, shaking it every now and then, and holding it to his ear.

Alice considered a little, and then said, "The fourth."

"Two days wrong!" sighed the Hatter. "I told you butter wouldn't suit the works!" he added, looking angrily at the March Hare.

"It was the *best* butter," the March Hare meekly replied.

"Yes, but some crumbs must have got in as well," the Hatter grumbled: "you shouldn't have put it in with the bread-knife."

The March Hare took the watch and looked at it gloomily: then he dipped it into his cup of tea, and looked at it again: but he could think of nothing better to say than his first remark, "It was the *best* butter, you know."—Charles Lutwidge Dodgson, Lecturer in Mathematics, Christ Church College, Oxford, *Alice's Adventures in Wonderland*.

Why then this sagging feeling, of dust and ashes, this letdown as though the case were done and dead? Is it curiosity cheated? It is. Yet this curiosity, as we call it, is it not one of man's oldest, deepest longings? the desire to hear the tale, to know the truth and meaning, the solution and the cause? The wanting to see the wheels go round, the little boy and the watch, man and his maker, the need for pattern and design: only connect. And with it there is that other longing for what the pattern seen, the design revealed should be—must be! that longing, too, is as young as hope—the desire for symmetry, sense and justice, the absolute and the answer. The machinery of law, such as we have evolved it, is perhaps a tribute to civilised restraint and melancholy realism; it is not always wholly to the taste of our instincts.—Sybille Bedford, *The Best We Can Do*, Day Thirteen.

Euclid alone . . . —Edna St. Vincent Millay.

Preface

All languages are equally hard, and equally easy, taken as wholes; but each has its greatest difficulties located in its own place. German, for instance, is especially difficult in its nouns, where English is easy. Native children learn substantially all there is to learn about English verbs before first going to school; fortunately, we say, but then that is only what we must expect, for the complete grammar of any language is all within the capacities of an eight-year-old child, and the most important (the hardest) parts of it are learned in the middle of that range of years.

That is what makes a technical description of that hardest part so difficult to write, or indeed to work out by scientific investigation so that it can be written. Our children learn to tie their shoe-laces (with a bow-knot!) before they start school; fortunately, we say, but then that is only what we must expect, for the complete system of all the knots that sailors used to tie is all within the capacities of an eight-year-old child, and the hardest of them were learned in the middle of the sailor's apprenticeship.

Just sit down and try to write a usable description of how bow-knots are tied, and you will see exactly what I mean. Even so, it will be easier than the task I have undertaken in this book, because no reader will expect you to base it on the theory of how a necktie gets knotted into a four-in-hand, as our school grammars are based on Latin and on traditions of correctness. A person who has learned how to describe a language by itself is a professional linguist.

He is comparable to a person who has learned how to write technical descriptions of all those sailor's knots, and to do it from watching the sailor without listening to him. No sailor's knot is the same as the bow-knot for shoe-laces; but after that experience he can do this too. It took me a quarter of a century to do it for the English verb. The knot expert could write the bow-knot description (for other experts to read) in the message-space of a picture-postcard; if he wrote it for me to read, he would have to fill a sixteen-page pamphlet. But once I have understood his pamphlet, I think I could put it all on a government postcard. The English verb is a little bit harder than that. I have described it here in a moderately thick book; for professional linguists I could have put it all into one typewritten page—I know this because I have done it —but my book can be understood by anyone who reads University Press books at all, and such a reader can put it into a few pages.

It was in 1939, when I was asked to help with the orientation of Sudetenland adults in Toronto, that I came to see how unaccountable the English verb must seem to speakers of more ordinary European languages like German and Czech. Books were of little use, and I had to improvise; and quite soon I came to see what I must try to do. It was fortunate that I have always had a good many other things to do, for the work on the English verb had to be cut-and-try, with long periods of occasional, rather vague, pondering before I cut the next pattern.

The final description is approximately the fifteenth of them all. The first three took seventeen years. The greatest progress came within one month in the summer of 1960, at the University of Texas during the Linguistic Institute; that was because I was in a working group including Ian Catford, David DeCamp, W. Nelson Francis, Mary Lu Joynes, and W. Freeman Twaddell. I owe details to each of them, but what I owe them most for is the requisite wrangling. After that I worked alone again. In 1962, an adequate sample of authentic English fell into my hands; and in 1963, May to July, I worked out a prospectus. The present book, completely rearranged and more than twice that long, was written complete since the beginning of this year.

MARTIN JOOS

Madison, Wisconsin
25 April 1964

Contents

i Introduction 3

Purpose 3, Data 6, Citation 10,
Stress 12, Plan 13

i i Non-Finite Verbs 14

Finite Verbs and Their Subjects 14,
Non-Finite Citations 15, Infinitive 16,
Quasi-Auxiliaries 20, Infinitive: Conclusion 30,
Presentative 31, Presentative Citations 32,
Citations for Other Non-Finites 38, Gerund 40,
Present Participle 46, Past Participle 47

i i i The Finite Schema 53

Simplified Schema 54, Finite Subjects 56,
Meaningless DO 59, Insistence 61, Negation 62,
Propredicates 65, Extended Propredicates 68,
Finite Predication 71, Summary 72,
Complete Schema 73

i v Basic Meanings and Voice 81

Meanings and Markers 81, Base Meaning 82,
The Copula 85, Passive Voice 91,
Unmarked Passive 96, Privative Marking 98

v Aspect, Tense, and Phase 101

Citations 102, Temporary Aspect 106, Generic Aspect 109,
Privative Aspect Marking 112, Choice of Aspect 113,
Status Verbs 116, Tense 120, Past Tense 125,
Narative Aspects 126, Narrative Actual Tense 131,
Aspect, Tense, and Time 133,
Phase 138, Privative Phase Marking 145

v i Assertion 147

Modal Summary 149, Verification 154,
Casual Assurance 156, Remote Assurance 165,
Remote Adequate Assurance 172, Casual Potentiality 179,
Contingent Casual Potentiality 185,
Stable Modals 190, Modal Negation 197

Appendix 205

On Formal Criteria 205, On Contractions 208,
On Journalistic Inversion 210,
Graphs for Aspect and for Phase 211,
On Busybodies 212, Citations for the Modals 214,
On Documentary *Shall* 231, On Scarecrows 233

Index 241

Collation Table 251

THE ENGLISH VERB

Form and Meanings

I

Introduction

This preliminary chapter is a rather loose collection of background pieces intended to set the stage for the rest. Some parts of it can be left behind after a single reading, but others will be relied on throughout the remaining chapters and even referred to on occasion. This arrangement will save the later chapters from carrying any heavy load of footnotes.

Purpose

Two complementary purposes are worth distinguishing to begin with. They are stated here in arbitrary sequence; neither is more important than the other.

The forms of English verb-phrases, and the associated meanings, are common property. The statements about them here will seldom go beyond what every eight-year-old native English speaker already knows, at least in the sense of 'knowing' that is most important for ordinary people in normal life—that is, when they are not being harassed by grammarians. Now one purpose of this book is to show what happens when familiar things are analysed and laid out so as to display all the system within them—all the parts that can be distinguished, and all the relations between parts that can be discerned.

In this purpose, the book appeals to a reader interest as old as what we may fairly call modern times; it can be dated by the emergence of the term *natural history*, which the Oxford Dictionary reports from 1555. Two centuries later this reader interest supported the Diderot encyclopedia; after another century it was responsible for the notoriety of Darwin's works; today the young science of linguistics claims a share of this reader interest. It is a small share;

but readers of that sort are more numerous than ever, so that even a small fraction of them still constitutes an audience large enough, with an intelligent enough interest, to earn the respectful concern of writers in linguistics.

Linguistics today has in common with Darwinism a century ago the interesting trait—or fate—that it annoys, shocks, or even outrages a large number of people. There are several reasons. Here it is enough to mention the reason that is most intimately associated with the purport of this book. Above I spoke of "all the parts that can be distinguished, and all the relations between parts that can be discerned." In describing English verbs, I am going to distinguish a countable set of parts, and discern a countable set of relations. And the shocking aspect of it is that I am going to say—sometimes state and always imply—that when that has been done there will be nothing left. I am going to discuss the English verb system in that mode of discussion which is called descriptive linguistics, whose cardinal principle is that the topic under discussion can be totally exhausted by giving a list of parts and relations that is not an endless list.

More briefly: language is finite, its elements can be counted. When the parallel atomic theory emerged in chemistry in 1810, that was equally shocking; yet the world finally became reconciled to it. But then, chemistry deals with dead matter; language is human, and that makes any atomic theory of language essentially more shocking, and distressing for a longer time. For one thing, it seems to be a denial of Free Will. No doubt there will always be wise and well-informed people who reject descriptive linguistics for just that reason; in contrast to the fate of chemistry, where the atomic theory—corrected and brought up to date, in which respect there is still a lot left to do in chemistry and more in linguistics— is rejected by nobody who is either wise or well informed.

One purpose of this book, then, is to please some readers and annoy others by showing what happens when the philosophy of natural history is applied to the native language. And there is this advantage over any other subject-matter of science, that the material being dissected is plentiful and found everywhere. No laboratory is needed for linguistics, and no expedition to Antarctica.

The other purpose is to serve readers who either are already linguists or are accustomed to use linguistic results for their various practical purposes. Problems of translating between English and other languages, problems of teaching English as a foreign language or teaching other languages to native speakers of English, and finally, with increasing conspicuousness in recent years, the problems of dealing with the peculiar nature of English in American and other English-speaking schools—all such problems call for clear and thorough descriptions of constituent systems within English. This book undertakes to provide one for the verb. And for the professional linguist there will be, I hope, the interest that naturally attaches to any treatise which tries to make contributions to general linguistic theory while describing a body of data in one professional way.

For the professional readers there is no need for me to explain in advance just what style of description has been adopted here; it is enough to name it with a few technical terms which will remain undefined so as not to burden other readers. My method is eclectic. This is a treatise in signals grammar. I avoid problems of immediate constituency by using the slot-and-filler display and relegating morphophonemics to the lexicon except for the auxiliaries. I assume that signals will have consistent meaning when the boundaries of each signal have been well chosen, and that is my criterion for delimiting the signals. For sorting out meanings, I occasionally draw upon transformational grammar. Finally, I assume that the meanings of grammatical signals are as strictly organized as morphology is; and even more strictly by preference.

For other readers I have one warning. This is not the only way it is done among professional linguists, so please don't jump to conclusions about the methods of linguistic description. A professional linguist could show you how to convert this description into other modes of describing, perhaps even into the one mode which he considers alone respectable.

Data

It is notoriously impractical to decide in advance just what kind of English is to be described and then go in search of a fair sample. By a fortunate accident, there has recently become available a large sample of a kind of English that is very much worth describing. For one thing, it is a kind of English that can be taught to foreign learners with perfect safety—the kind that is spoken when in the presence of strangers but without a script; roughly, semi-formal English, and in this sample it is spoken by natives with educations ranging from superior to moderately good.

Serious readers will want to procure a copy of that sample and do their own checking-up. Masses of examples from it are reprinted here, but one must always wonder whether they were quoted with adequate context, and also whether inconvenient counter-examples have been suppressed. Besides, the sample is a book worth reading for its own sake. For the present it is enough to know that it is a report of a murder trial, and in British English.

This sample is here analysed by an American, and by the same token the research worker who analyses a comparable sample of American English ought to be an Englishman. In either case, the text can always be understood if scrutinized with great care; and the constant reminders of its foreignness will insure that great care is taken all along. Further, there is the advantage that in such a report as the present one the reporter will, in self-defense, restrain himself from making any statement that can't be backed up by citing the data, statements such as he might be tempted to make about the idiom of his home region with unjustified confidence that the data would back up him if ever collected and examined.

British and American English of educated speakers, when confined to what I have called semi-formal usage, differ very little with regard to our present topic: form and meaning in the verb. To make this book a fair representation of English as a whole would require multiplying the research by a hundred times. What I mean to do is simply to report also on American semi-formal English wherever it differs from the British sample; for the reason already given, those reports will be less reliable, but they will be all I can offer within our limitations.

One systematic difference needs comment in advance. British semi-formal style is notably more relaxed, much closer to casual style, than American semi-formal style is. Thus the Judge's charge to the jury, thirty pages of our sample, strikes an American reader as almost conversational in tone—nothing like the way an American judge would address his jury. Interested readers would do well to compare an American judge's charge—not taken from a transcript, to be sure, but composed by a competent novelist after long observation—in James Gould Cozzens, *The Just and the Unjust*, pages 370 to 378 [New York: Harcourt, Brace and Co., 1942]. It would certainly be far more difficult, if not impossible, to find a printed sample of American English which would represent normal speech as authentically as our British one.

The provenience of the sample is this. In March of 1957 there was held at the Old Bailey the longest murder trial—seventeen days—in the history of British justice up to then. By the standards of Great Britain, where press and radio are legally bound to be reticent in all matters touching upon the chances of a fair trial, there had been an extraordinary amount of advance publicity arising out of many months of gossip before the accused was arrested and thereby brought under the protection of the courts, and the publicized details promised a fascinating trial. A change of venue moved the trial to the most populous area in Great Britain; but still, fortunately for us, the novelist Sybille Bedford, already famous as the author of *A Legacy*, wangled a seat in the press box for the duration, even though she had not been commissioned by any publisher to cover the trial.

From her point of vantage Mrs. Bedford took voluminous notes, recording especially the tones of voice and other similarly pertinent details accompanying the speech which she knew she could eventually find recorded complete in the official transcript. Ultimately she was to insert some of these notes into her printed report, often in square brackets, and these are preserved in my citations: examples appear under my next heading, *Citation*. They give extraordinarily life-like realism to her book, and are often crucial to the linguistic analysis.

In my view of this point, I am supported by the American linguist Henry Lee Smith, Jr., who has for years been professionally concerned with these expressive hitchhikers upon spoken language, cooperating with psychiatrists to their advantage as well as to ours: "In my opinion Sybille Bedford's *The Trial of Dr. Adams* is unique in English writing. There is no other work to my knowledge that so carefully mirrors actual English speech; and the devices she uses in her painstaking rendition of all aspects of the trial enable the reader to catch every nuance of the entire interactions involved. Her indications of what are technically called paralinguistic events —certain structured tone-of-voice phenomena that accompany language itself—are masterful and leave the reader in no doubt as to not only what was said but also how it was said."

Professor Smith included this in a letter to me because I had asked him for a quotable formulation of his appraisals previously contained in a long conversation. In his letter he says he "also would subscribe most heartily" to my contrasting of American and British semi-formal styles, and he agrees to the label *semi-formal*.

In writing for book publication, Mrs. Bedford dropped out a great deal of what appears in the transcript, trusting in her skill as a novelist; but for the same reason she would not have misrepresented what she does include. She does not repair the mutilations which court reporters routinely commit. For example, she evidently follows the transcript, rather than her notes or memory, in writing *do not* or *don't*, *does not* or *doesn't*. There is hardly an example of *can't* in her book, apart from what she takes from her notes or memory of overheard corridor conversation; she always copies the official *cannot* of the court reporter, so that we are left to guess between *can't* and *cannot* from our knowledge of English and from her stage-directions. When we remain unable to repair the damage, the evidence will be used with great caution if at all. Incidentally, I take what she composed herself—a substantial minor fraction of the book—as authentic written English. For some purposes it would be worth while to segregate the data according to the three types mentioned above, plus her quotations from other print (notably the bits from *The Times*), the passages read aloud from the nursing records, and a few other minor categories. All I have done about that is to name the category whenever it is not clearly transcript material, and to be very careful about merging heterogeneous evidence. Finally, all my leading conclusions derive from the presumed transcript material.

Sybille Bedford's book is read mostly as a novel; the Library of Congress classes it under Criminology, and our law schools shelve it with the reports of criminal trials. It is published in the United Kingdom under the title *The Best We Can Do*, but in the United States as *The Trial of Dr. Adams*. In my discussions I cite it as *Trial* and refer by page-number to the two easily accessible printings: there have been four printings with different paginations, but the others are difficult of access, especially the out-of-print first edition: Collins, 1958.

The first American edition, Simon and Schuster, 1958, was put into type straight from the Collins edition according to the rule 'follow copy!' The proofreading was perfect by shop standards, but it was not critical. Every British hyphen, as in *wheel-chair*, was (*a*) saved if the word was within the line in both printings, but (*b*) thrown away to make *wheelchair* if the hyphen ended the Collins line and the word came within the Simon and Schuster line. The resultant inconsistencies were not noticed even when the same word, hyphenated in Collins, was treated both ways in the same paragraph in Simon and Schuster. The Simon and Schuster edition is out of print as such; but the Grove Press paperback, Black Cat Book BA-21, is identical for citation: it is a photographic reproduction. This gives the first of the twinned page-numbers that I offer with a colon between them: [183:169] and the like.

The second number of such pairs refers to the current edition outside the United States, which is Penguin Book No. 1639, since

1961. This is not only respelled for international sale, and somewhat repunctuated; it is blemished by several pedantic corrections, for instance *did* for *does* at the end of the 18th line on page 139.

From the Simon and Schuster pages, of course with further attrition of hyphens, the handsome paperback of the Time Reading Program was put into type in 1962. After the original distribution to subscribers, there has been no further sales effort as far as I know; but of course there is the usual surplus stock, from which several copies were graciously presented to us for editorial purposes.

My citations cover 20 percent of the whole text of *Trial*. The collation-table printed at the end of the book will make the pages of the Collins and the Time editions easily usable too.

Citation

[Measured toll] "I am asking for your opinion."
[Noticeably determined to stick it out] "She certainly could have survived those doses."
"Of that quantity?"
"I think it is possible."
"Do you think it is *likely?*"
Dr. Harman: "Yes, I think it is likely."
The Attorney-General: "Would you have expected these doses to do her any good?"
[Cocky] "They might have done."
The Attorney-General: "If she had those prescriptions given her in that short period, *that* would have formed a topic of medical shop?"
"Yes, those doses would."

Now if this were to be cited to exemplify the two verb-phrases 'would have expected' and 'might have done,' without calling attention to any of the others, the citation could be in this form:

[Measured toll] "I am asking for your opinion." — [Noticeably determined to stick it out] "She certainly could have survived those doses." — "OF THAT QUANTITY?" — "I think it is possible." — "Do you think it is líkely?" — "Yes, I think it is likely." — *"Would* you *have expected* these doses to do her any good?" — [Cocky] "They *mĭght hăve dòne*." — "If she had those . . . in that short period, thát would have formed a topic of medical shop?" — "Yes, those doses would." [183:169]

The dashes in the citation, each with spaces before and after it—unlike the dashes in this sentence—replace the paragraph indention in *Trial*. Usually this marks a change of speakers; the novelistic practice of using paragraphing for that purpose is too extravagant of space for our citations, and these dashes allow us to use our own paragraph indention to assemble a number of citations into one block. In the sample above, unneeded speaker identifications are omitted without warning, and the dots . . . indicate other omissions. My own insertions into *Trial* text will be enclosed in braces { } to avoid confusion with Mrs. Bedford's brackets.

I have technical uses for italics. Thus the *Trial* italics have got to be represented otherwise here. Now there are two kinds of emphasis customarily italicized in books, with a difference which native addressees always hear and employ for understanding, and our data would be confused if they were cited alike.

I cite in small capitals to indicate that two or more words were presumably spoken together with some extra expressive signalling, generally in the manner which novelists and dramatists call 'weighty.' Further details are of course interesting for certain purposes, among others the studies referred to above, where I quoted H. L. Smith, Jr. Here they can be disregarded, since I have found no instance where they would alter the grammatical interpretation; the fact that there was such signalling is of importance to us, but not the choice of signals.

I change italicized single words back to roman, but I add an acute accent-mark to indicate what the italics presumably meant—the word is the loudest in its neighborhood and is furthermore spoken with extra-high musical pitch, a well-known English signal which means 'prominence' of the single word without necessarily implying the weightiness mentioned above.

Now I have another use for that acute accent-mark, namely the way I use it in this citation in the second verb-phrase that I italicize. The two uses are not in conflict. This last use simply locates the primary stress—see next—without implying (or excluding) extra-high pitch.

Stress

An essential part, never absent and always significant, of native English speech is the choice and placement of the four degrees of stress. When I need to call attention to them, I write them on convenient letters of the usual spelling; thus: *ĕlĕvàtŏr ŏpĕràtŏr* for the way this is fluently spoken unless the operator is being insisted on in opposition to the starter or the door or whatnot. The stresses are named primary *ó*, secondary *ô*, tertiary *ò*, weak *ŏ* (the four *o* letters are here only for convenience in printing and reading); they run here from loudest to softest, other things being equal. Note that primary stress does not necessarily mean emphatic speaking; the mark simply shows *where* the primary stress is located—for there must be one *somewhere* if this is native English, no matter how softly spoken as a whole, or on how low a pitch.

For grammatical purposes, *ó* and *ô* constitute the category of major stress, and *ò* and *ŏ* belong to the category of minor stress. The latter category also grammatically includes the elimination of a syllable—its vowel drops out together with any preceding consonants, while its following consonants are still spoken but attached to the preceding syllable—and I write this with a little zero pretending to be a stress-mark. Then for example any spoken *he'd* can be cited on occasion as *he hăd* or as *he wôuld* to signify two things at once: that *Trial* prints *he'd*, and that *'d* is this or that word but weakened. Furthermore, I can take advantage of this device to transfer crucial information from the context to the citation itself, thus:

"Now let ûs go through your entries." [22:30]
"Let ŭs not fall into confusion about this." [199:183]

In the first sentence, we can be sure that Mr. Lawrence said *let's* despite the *Trial* spelling; we know this as native speakers of English because Mrs. Bedford has told us with a slightly earlier remark: "Quite sharp suddenly"; and now I provide my readers with this crucial information right where it becomes effective by printing the zero-sign on her (or the printer's or the court stenographer's) dishonest but conventional letter *u* standing for an honest vowel-omission mark in *let's*. In the second sentence, the vowel is spoken but of course weak; by this time we are well acquainted with how Mr. Lawrence addresses the jury, and Mrs. Bedford has told us how he is speaking just now: "With forceful common sense."

Finally, let me remark that readers who are not native speakers of *British* English need the stress-marking which I have provided on 'They might have done'; without it, I could not clearly explain this point of grammar, for it is foreign to American English.

Plan

Technical terms can sometimes mislead a reader who takes them for words used in ordinary senses, for instance the term *work* as it is used in physics. In this book the leading cases of that sort are probably the following, all easily cleared up with the aid of the Index: *actor, assertion, casual, event, factual, form, formal, progressive, stress, style, victim.*

The arrangement may often seem unsystematic. The reason is that it always is meant to progress from the known to the novel. Excessive interlacing is avoided by squeezing out some excursus from time to time, and printing it in the Appendix; careful cross-reference by page-number will make everything easy to find.

II

Non-Finite Verbs

The greater part of this treatise will be devoted to the finite verb of English, which constitutes a system of great complexity but also of almost equally great symmetry. First, however, I must deal with the separation of the finite verbs from the non-finites in the total mass of data, and with all those details of the non-finites which are of sufficient interest to compete with the finite verbs. The separation is here accomplished by means of a single criterion: the form of the verb's subject. One result is that a few verb-uses will be called 'non-finite' that are called 'finite' in more traditional treatments of English grammar; that is a small price to pay for the very great improvement in clarity in the over-all description accomplished by that criterion.

Finite Verbs and Their Subjects

For our purposes, a finite verb is one that requires a subject and can take a subject chosen from the list *I, we, he, she, they*, or else a verb that is in all other respects similar but has *it* instead: 'He looked at them' and 'It rained on them.'

The categorical meaning of finite verbs—that is to say, that 'grammatical' meaning which belongs to the whole category, no matter what may be the lexical meaning that changes when we change from *resembles* to *rains* or *shows* and so on—will be called *assertion*. By definition, then, assertion is exclusively a function of finite verbs; and whatever is done by non-finites—e.g., by that non-finite called 'infinitive,' such as *to leave, to rain*—will not be called assertion: other descriptions will be found for what they do. For the present chapter it will be unnecessary to inquire further into what is accomplished by finite verbs in their assertion function.

Therefore, in the citations which follow next, the *finite* verbs are, for our present purposes, eliminated by printing them in italics, leaving only the numbered non-finites available for discussion.

Non-Finite Citations

They *have* to [1]deal with it in the sort of way they *might find* themselves [2]having to [3]deal with [4]conflicting medical opinion in the ordinary course of their lives. [5]Suppose, for example, someone dear to them—one of their family or a relative—*was* a patient and they *called* in doctors, and [6]having [6]called in all the best doctors they *get* [7]conflicting opinions, as one *may do;* in the end they *would have* to [8]make up their mind as to which *was* the more likely to [9]be right. [212:195; reported speech]

"One of the questions to [10]be [10]considered in this case *will be:* why *were* they *given?*" [6:16]

"Thère *are* several points to [11]consider." [174:161]

"you *may think* that thère *was* nothing *left* of it, nothing substantial for the Doctor to [12]meet, and it *is* not our duty—and you *would* not *want* us to[13]—to [14]put the Doctor in the box . . . " [194:178]

If to [15]speak out *may be* relief, it *is* also an ordeal . . . [175:162]

They *will hear* that for pain to [16]accompany such a condition *is* most unusual. [5:16; reported speech]

" 'patient *awoke* [17]perspiring freely, *refused* to [18]be [18]turned over, *said* that it *hurt* her to [19]turn.' " [22:30; read from the nursing record]

"Lawrence *is going* to [20]call the Doctor and no one else." — "He *will talk* his head off!" — "Hè *must be longing* to;[21] *would* nòt you?" [72:75; conversation]

"I *would expect* a person of her age to [22]be [22]suffering to some extent from arterio-sclerosis . . . " [112:108]

"I *would have expected* her to [23]have [23]lived only for a matter of a few weeks . . . " [149:141]

the pattern of the Crown case *seemed* to [24]have [24]been [24]outlined in the Attorney-General's [24a]opening speech . . . [69:71; author's comment]

"She *seems* to [25]have [25]been [25]getting on very well . . . " [185:171]

"But, again, you *might have liked* to [26]have [26]heard his own explanation about it." [234:215; Judge charging the jury]

"I *do* not *see* a mystery here, but it *is* something one *would have liked* to [27]know about . . ." [235:216; same]

Infinitive

The above citations were selected for their abundance of non-finite verbs, especially the infinitive. I count 8038 occurrences of finite verbs in *Trial*, and 958 infinitives; the other non-finites are rarer by about seven to one.

The first word of an infinitive is always its marker *to;* that is, I refuse the title to verbs that lack that marker. The words that lack that marker but otherwise resemble infinitives are especially some that I treat as parts of finite verbs (e.g., *find* in the first cited line of print) and others that I call *presentatives,* to be cited and dealt with later. Thus *5* is a presentative and could have been cited later along with *55.*

The essential marker may be all that is spoken: *13, 21* in the citations. (The numbers from there will be given in italics here, and that is what italicized numbers will always mean.) Beyond this *to,* the infinitive most often has only one word, and at most may have three more; two more: *10, 18, 22, 23, 26;* three more: *24, 25.* This is the limit in *Trial;* in my own English there is no rule against saying 'But she was supposed *to have been being watched* by the nurses.' Again, in *Trial* the clipped infinitive is always clipped all the way to the single word *to;* but in my English the clipping can leave another word, as in 'We haven't told you all about it, and you wouldn't want us *to have,*' clipped from *to have told* as *13* is clipped from *to put.*

A parallel effect upon meaning of such clipping will be treated later, when I come to speak of finite propredicates; that discussion will apply in full, *mutatis mutandis,* to the clipped infinitives; hence I say no more about them here: it would be a waste of space. Further, the later treatment of finite-verb formations such as *would have liked,* with respect to their constitution and the associated meanings, will completely take care of the three-word constitution of *23 to have lived* and how that affects the meaning of this infinitive. In the treatment of the finite verb, those matters will be spread out, of necessity, through three chapters at least.

Here, therefore, the discussion will treat all infinitives alike, whether complex or simple or clipped; and this will be safe because such things have no effect on the topic here, which is the employments of infinitives and their categorical meaning. Early in this chapter the categorical meaning of the finite verb was named 'assertion,' and that is not hard to understand; for example, it is easy to see that an assertion has a truth-value, as logicians say: the sentence 'It *is raining*' is in principle either true or false, a fact that is not impaired by any difficulty in making up one's mind whether it is true. Many other equally transparent and useful things can be said about assertion, the function of finite verbs or in other words their categorical meaning. The categorical meaning of the infinitive is vastly more difficult to deal with, and the reason for that is that it is too simple to be described clearly; in one word, it is axiomatic.

It is easy enough to see that the infinitive can serve simply as a sort of name: *14 to put* is one English way to name the act of putting. Names in English are usually nouns, grammatically, and 'To put the Doctor in the box is our duty' is grammatically parallel to 'Patriotism is our duty,' where *patriotism* is of course a noun; in the longer sentence the parallel noun is not *Doctor* nor *box*, but *to put* (*the Doctor in the box*), and similarly *to think* in 'To think is our duty.' Hence the infinitives *to put* and *to think* can safely be called nouns, in such sentences at least, and this choice is not impaired by the fact that one of them needs a complement such as *the Doctor in the box* while the other does not.

The infinitives used as nouns in the citations above are *1, 3, 8, 13, 14, 15, 16, 18, 19, 26, 27* at least. We can say this because *1, 3, 8, 13, 18, 26, 27* appear as objects of transitive verbs: *1* as in 'They have a duty,' *13* as in 'You would not want whiskey,' *27* as in 'One would have liked the experience.' And *14, 15, 16, 19* are nouns because *15 to speak out* is parallel to *confession*, a notorious noun, in 'If confession may be relief, it is also an ordeal.'

This is in principle not altered by the fact that the infinitive is usually postponed to a late position in the sentence, the early position appropriate to the subject of the sentence being filled by the infinitive's temporary substitute *it* as in *14, 19;* the second of these is equivalent to 'She said that any new position hurt her,' and the first similarly equivalent to 'To put the Doctor in the box is not our duty.' This rearrangement now has put the infinitive in the standard position for the subject of a sentence; if an infinitive in this position has its own subject, that is preceded by *for*, evidently not a preposition but simply a marker saying 'an infinitive's subject comes next,' as in *16*.

Now the infinitive can also be the complement of a verb that refuses to have any other sort of object: an 'intransitive' verb, as in *20, 21, 24, 25*. There would be no point in arguing whether the infinitive is then the verb's object and is therefore a noun, or is instead an adverbial complement; it is enough to know that the infinitive can occupy this complement position, and this means that *22* and *23* need no further explanation.

The other four infinitives (*9, 10, 11, 12*) are not similarly placed with respect to any finite verb—not, that is, functioning as subject or object or complement of any other verb, finite or not. Clearly *10 to be considered* and *11 to consider* are clusters, groups of words, each modifying the noun that comes before it. Each can be called a 'group-modifier'; and in English the group-modifiers, such infinitives or other group-modifiers (clauses and prepositional phrases), follow what they modify. These infinitives can in fact be transformed into the other two types of group-modifiers: 'which are to be considered' and 'for consideration,' with substantially the same meanings.

Then *9 to be right* is of the right constitution and is in the right place to be a group-modifier of the preceding adjective *likely*, so we can call this *to be (right)* an infinitive used as an adverb. And *12 to meet*, together with its subject *the Doctor* (with the marker *for* used to indicate that it is the subject of some infinitive or other), constitutes a group-modifier of: what? If we say it modifies only *substantial*, we are saying that it is an adverb; if we say it modifies *nothing*, we are calling it an adjective. Then *nothing* is separately modified by *substantial*, following it as usual; *nothing, anything,* and *something* have the special peculiarity that their modifiers always follow them anyhow even when they are single words, as in 'Something old, something new, something borrowed, and something blue' or 'anything else to wear?'

Either interpretation of the whole sentence will work, but calling *to meet* an adjective seems easiest. It would, however, be an adverb in 'I'm pleased to meet you.' Yet this is rather like 'He will be the right man to meet you,' and this is in turn similar to 'He is the man to meet.' Altogether, such discussions of whether an infinitive is an adjective or an adverb seem profitless; it is enough to see that infinitives can restrict meanings the way adverbs and adjectives do, as well as serving noun functions.

With respect to meaning, then, the English infinitive is a sort of name of the same events that can be narrated by finite verbs, and it can serve to restrict the meanings of nouns and adjectives and adverbs as adjectives and adverbs do; and that seems to be all that can be said both safely and profitably.

From *10* and *11* we learn that the difference in form between 'active' and 'passive' infinitive may matter not at all. And from *26* and *27* we learn that the difference in form between a 'perfect' and a 'current' infinitive often doesn't matter either. This sort of thing will become clearer when the same differences are discussed later with respect to the finite verb, respectively in Chapter IV and Chapter V. On the other hand, the difference between *22 to be suffering* and a possible *to suffer* is more constant and important; this will also be discussed in Chapter V under the heading *Aspect*.

Above there has been mention of the 'subject' of an infinitive, though not when it was the object or complement of a verb; now it may be remarked that other grammarians deny that the *us* of *13 want us to* is the subject of the clipped infinitive *to*, saying instead that it is another object of the verb *want*. Fortunately this choice of terminology will not upset anything important in this treatise. Other instances are *12, 16, 22, 23* at most. It is when the infinitive is not object or complement of a verb, we see, that its subject is marked by a preceding *for*.

Quasi-Auxiliaries

In just half of its occurrences in *Trial*, the infinitive is the object
or complement of a verb, either finite or non-finite, as in 'Are
you going *to invite* the jury *to say* that these two . . . injections
. . . were given . . . ?' [65:68], where the finite *are going* has
the object *to invite*, and the non-finite *invite* in turn has the object *to say*. Now *are going* is typical of the verbs that very
often have such infinitive objects or complements; and certain of
these are more or less interesting in their own right, especially the
more frequently used ones.

In *Trial*, 75 different verb-bases (like this GO and this INVITE)*
are used with following infinitives. Only 24 of the 75 bases occur
just once each in this use, the other 51 each more than once. Then
the laws of vocabulary statistics suggest that perhaps a few
hundred different verb-bases are freely used in this way, but certainly not over a thousand, from among the dozens of thousands of
English verb-bases. Twelve of them appear in *Trial* 10 times or
more in this pattern; here is the list, with the number of times each
occurs: APPEAR 10, ASK 15, BE 25, BEGIN 12, EXPECT 19, GO 28,
HAVE and HAVE GOT together 77, LIKE 16, SEEM 13, TRY 37, WANT 49,
WISH 10; to this list it is expedient to annex two BE phrases: BE
ABLE 10, BE ABOUT 7. And for contrast, here are a few of those 24
which are thus used only once each in *Trial:*

he could AFFORD *to try*   [176:163]

". . . she had FORGOTTEN *to do* this . . ."   [78:80]

"Must be LONGing *to;* wouldn't you?"   [72:75]

The Doctor is MADE *to disappear* into his waiting cell   [237:218]

"If that is so, you don't really NEED *to bother* about these two injections
of paraldehyde."   [222:204]

---

* Verb-bases are bread and butter to us. Whenever I mention them as such, I
mean to print them in small capitals. Occasionally it is expedient to do the same
with an inflection form, to call attention to the base hidden in it, for example,
FORGOTTEN a little later on here: this calls attention to the base FORGET.

Now taking the 19 together and observing their meanings and frequencies, we see a gradation—not precise, but still very clear—from one extreme of pregnant meaning and rare use to the other extreme of banal meaning and frequent use. The latter extreme reminds us of the fact that certain languages provide for such banal significances in the inflectional systems of their verbs, so that in such a language a typical verb—almost any of all the thousands of verbs in the vocabulary—can be inflected, e.g., into a conative form meaning 'tries to' do what the verb basically means, or into a desiderative form meaning 'wishes to' do the same.

These can be roughly translated into English as just shown, but that does not mean that *English* has conative and desiderative inflections. Similarly, the sentence 'There is a measure of curiosity as to how this is going to be met' [47:52] can be crudely translated into ' . . . how this will be met'; but that doesn't mean that BE GOING TO and WILL occupy similar offices in the system of English grammar. This WILL is an auxiliary (specifically, a modal auxiliary, 'modal' for short), and every occurrence of it will be described as part of a finite verb: Chapter VI. There are compelling reasons for that treatment, of many kinds; there is only a single reason for calling BE GOING TO the same sort of thing, namely a part of its meaning (not all of it); and there is a compelling reason for not doing that, namely that if we start along that road there will be no place to stop and the whole system of English will become incomprehensible. Chapter VI will demonstrate the truth of this statement; here there is room only to list the two leading criteria: (1) modals and quasi-auxiliaries have totally different grammars; (2) they have essentially different kinds of meanings: modals have purely privative meanings, quasi-auxiliaries are additive too.

Accordingly, when I now discuss a short list of quasi-auxiliaries, roughly the same list that other grammarians have taken seriously in similar connections, it must be understood that the list, however carefully selected, is arbitrary. Its members have been chosen for temporary convenience, without any implication that they differ essentially from any that have not been included.

BE TO seems to mean *a practical determining of subsequent events.*
The determining agent appears to be a single compelling factor:
fate, an authority, or a decisive circumstance.

Form B has to be filled in by the doctor who attended the patient whose
body *is to* be cremated. [42:47]

And now begin those relentless readings from the nursing books . . . that
were to become as the days went on a kind of merciless obbligato to the
case. [24:32]

Mr. Lawrence [not letting up] . . . [Lashing out] "Whát was it she told
you not to say? . . . And WHAT WAS IT you *were* not *to* say?" [34:40]

How refreshing it would be if he *were to* lift his voice . . .   [136:129]

Note that here we have contemporary reality [42:47], past
reality [24:32, 34:40], and contemporary unreality [136:129], all
neatly sorted out; this is impossible to accomplish within the system
of the finite verb itself, including the modals. Thus there may be
this advantage among others in having such additional means of
expressing more or less the sort of differences in meaning that the
finite verb is competent to do but does in more strictly organized
and therefore occasionally more hampered ways.

BE GOING TO differs from the preceding mostly in one way. Here
the future event is *assumed rather than determined;* it is taken
for granted as a proper part of future reality without any suggestion that there had to be a cause to make it so. For an exact
technical definition, see the footnote on page 141.

"You now understand . . . that you must not discuss with anybody at
all the evidence you have given or *are going to* give . . ." [49:54]

"I had no reason to suppose that any police evidence *was going to* be
reached at all to-day. . . . This is my real difficulty. With the complexity
of the medical position, I was under the impression that *was going to* be
dealt with first." [75:77]

"I know she *was going to* leave it to me and her . . . car." [82:84]

"Judge *is going to* throw out the case. You wait—he's got to."
[105:102]

"In a case where one *is* only *going to* see the patient for a few days one
would not change the treatment that had been instructed." [108:105]

Here there is no emotion, desire, intention, resolution, compulsion, or the like. That is to say, this is a completely colorless 'future tense' way of speaking. Indeed this seems to be the only uncolored future that English has; and we note that it is equally usable as a real future relative to a real past epoch [75:77, 82:84], something that is hard to accomplish neatly in a good many languages.

In most standard English, it is always BE GOING TO, never simply GO TO. Regionally, however, the short form occurs too: 'I *went to* open my eyes' and 'Now when you *go to* turn the hem, make sure . . . ' from a native speaker from a Wisconsin area settled by Welsh and Cornish mining folk who presumably brought the formula with them from Britain in the early nineteenth century. Novelists use it to represent vulgar speech: 'I didn't go to do it' and 'Who would go to do such a 'orrible thing?'

BE ABOUT TO also takes the subsequent event for granted; but in addition *represents it as imminent and perhaps even threatened, and furthermore it allows that the event may be forestalled.* The first two examples adequately contrast this to the meaning of BE GOING TO:

Did the inspector have any idea that he *was going to* be sent out of the room during the search? The inspector says he definitely did not. What was his impression of the Doctor when he *was about to* be arrested? He was stunned. [95:95; reported speech; note that the inspector was going to be sent out by a fellow officer: not a threat!]

Mr. Lawrence [wholly second violin] "Looking at the nursing notes up to the spring of 1950, what do you say is a fair summary of the position?" — Dr. Harman [trenchant and urbane] "I should say she had recovered from her stroke as far as she *is* ever *going to;* that she's reached a stage at which one might describe her as being partially crippled, but there are no signs of anything further *about to* happen." [172:160]

What Mr. Lawrence is saying here is in effect, "A. whips out a revolver, aims it at B. and *is about to* pull the trigger when the ceiling comes down and kills B." [168:156]

Mr. Lawrence looks as though he *might be about to* say, Thank you, Dr. Harman. Then everything goes on. [178:164]

This BE ABOUT TO is never negated in *Trial;* and indeed it is hard to say what the meaning of *not be about to* would be good for in real life if that meaning were a simple reversal such as NOT usually accomplishes. However, in some kinds of English the negated formula is in use with a very special meaning that could hardly have been predicted from the above. It signifies that the actor is not the sort of person from whom such a deed can be expected, particularly in the actual circumstances and actual company. Thus the following italicized expressions:

"It is no good, I cannot remember the details, and I *am not going to* discuss it." [97:96; Mr. Lawrence suggesting that this is what the Doctor once said to the police, contrary to their report that he was loquacious]

The Judge . . . [Showing no expression] "It is very important to see how far you go . . . It would be quite easy for a medical man in your position to say, 'I am saying no more about this treatment by the Doctor than that I think it was wrong and dangerous, and I think it caused death; but whether it was administered through error, ignorance or incompetence or intent to kill is not for me to say and I *am not going to* say it.' " [148:140]

are sure to become 'I'm not about to discuss it' and 'I'm not about to say it' if spoken defensively (in my observation always with some extra adrenalin in the blood) in the kind of English that has this formula available. I believe this to be native to what we call Southern American, and I think its spread beyond the confines of our southeastern states is rather recent: since 1945 I have heard it sporadically from people of the right age to have consorted with Southerners in uniform during that war. It gets into print now too:

Military men admit that in an all-out war the canal would go. A single Soviet Polaris-type missile would knock it out. It won't take the biggest aircraft carriers. But short of all-out war it remains a crucial element in our commercial and defense dispositions. We *are not about to* give it up. [*Life,* 24 January 1964, p. 4; editorial]

These congressional grandees are acutely jealous of congressional prerogatives, and they *are not about to* let any executive agency, in Senator [Eugene] McCarthy's words, "[decide] for itself just how much or how little Congress ought to know." [*Saturday Evening Post,* 15 February 1964; article by Stewart Alsop]

It is somehow comforting to know that the grandees can be true Southerners: Senators Russell and Hayden, Representatives Vinson and Cannon.

HAVE TO, and so of course also HAVE GOT TO (without detectable difference either in denotation or in connotation) are the most frequently used of the quasi-auxiliaries: 77 occurrences in *Trial*. The meaning is *compulsion from force of circumstances;* in fact, the familiar phrase *force of circumstances* seems made to order to explicate the formula. In Chapter VI the essentially different meaning of MUST will be explained.

At certain assertions his mouth compressed slowly and hard, and he shook his head to and fro . . . as if prompted by an inner vision that did not correspond to what he *had to* hear. [6:16]

"But one always *had to* remember that she had a stroke and couldn't get out of bed and *had to* be lifted into her wheel-chair?" [30:37]

"And now let us look at one of your entries for December. You see what you *had to* encounter on that day. 'Patient very disturbed this afternoon . . . hysterical. . . . Another outburst in the evening.' That was the sort of temper poor Mrs. Morell displayed from time to time?" — "It was." [31:38]

"You mean to say she *had to* have every blanket in the house brought to her room?" — "That's right." [36:42]

"Obviously she was in a bad state of restlessness. Dr. Harris *had to* deal with it because the Doctor was away, and he does so by increasing the morphia . . ." [54:58]

Once tolerance is acquired the drug has less and less effect and lasts a shorter time; larger doses *have to* be given to secure any effect at all. [114:110; reported speech]

Dr. Douthwaite [dryly] "The first object would be to restore her health." — "That of course is the highest level. But no doctor in his senses would think that short of a miracle he could restore a woman of seventy-nine or eighty to her pre-stroke health?" — "Oh, no, I agree with that." — [Co-operative tone] "So what he *hàs got to* do is his reasonable best for what is left of her life?" — "Oh, yes." — . . . "Now if you are dealing with a case where you are giving morphia either to deal with pain or some physically degenerated condition, the time will come when you won't *be able to* deal with what you are trying to deal with by means of a level dosage?" — "I agree." — "And you are at the point where you find that you *have to* adopt one of two courses? . . . And as the irritation of this later stage was getting worse, her doctor would be faced with this dilemma of either *having to* stop the drugs and thus risk collapse, or giving increased doses of it? . . . Is it fairly obvious that there is no perfect drug that has nôt got some disadvantage?" — "No, I agree." — "If a general practitioner decides that he *has to* make use of some sort of drug he *has got to* balance up the advantages and disadvantages in his choice?" — "Certainly." [122:117]

"If the case of the Crown is right, then one or more of these acts was attempted murder, and I should like to *be able to* assist the jury by pointing out to them precisely what in relation to each act it is that *forces* you to postulate murder was being committed or attempted." — Dr. Douthwaite: "I *may have to* postulate it in relation to the doses that had gone before, or, more exactly, in relation to the doses that were nôt given." [133:126]

It *must* be hampering to *have to* thrash this out in front of an audience of eighty avid pressmen. [187:173; author's comment]

In the last three citations certain other words have been italicized to call attention to the kind of evidence we use all along in learning about meaning: *forces* throws light on *have to*, and the added *may* shows Dr. Douthwaite carefully adjusting the relation between them. And each *be able to* can be a citation for the next paragraph.

BE ABLE TO superficially seems to be a substitute for CAN, furnishing, by means of its own elaborate inflection, ways of distinguishing meanings which CAN is not fitted to cope with. There is a modicum of truth in this notion.

A slight pause; then before the court *has been able to* take stock: "The case for the prosecution does not rest here." [10:19]

"Just tell me a little about Mrs. Morell so far as you *were able to* know about her case at the time you were there." [18:27]

"Within a few days, as soon as one *is able to* obtain co-operation of the patient, one should at once try to mobilise the patient and encourage movement . . ." [110:107]

Ten minutes pass. — Mr. Lawrence makes a movement. The prosecution has one or two more questions. At a quarter to eleven Mr. Lawrence *is able to* go over the top. [118:113]

"Now if you are dealing with a case where you are giving morphia either to deal with pain or some physically degenerated condition, the time will come when you *won't be able to* deal with what you are trying to deal with by means of a level dosage?" [123:118]

". . . like to *be able to* assist . . ." [133:126]

"You have experienced many such cases?" Dr. Harman has. "You are familiar with the problems arising in the treatment?" Dr. Harman is. "*Are* you *able to* deduce the nature and degree of Mrs. Morell's illness at that time?" [171:159]

"Let us get on to November. *Are* you *able to* take the view similar to the other doctors that she was clearly a dying woman by then?" [176:163]

When a doctor gives medical evidence at a trial, the eyes of the profession are upon him; and, although God knows that the profession does not appear united in their views, an expert witness *is* hardly *able to* postulate something entirely wild. [189:174]

"The fact that I held that it was a matter for you to determine and not for me, does not mean he *was* not *in a position to* make a strong submission. On the evidence of Dr. Ashby, he clearly was; and he *has* now *been able to* fortify it by the evidence of Dr. Harman." [231:213; Judge charging the jury]

These ten are all the occurrences in *Trial* of BE ABLE TO. Now there is something quite remarkable here. More often than not, there is a carefully chosen indication of the time measured by clock or calendar: *before* [10:19], *at the time* [18:27], *as soon as* [110:107], *at a quarter to eleven* [118:113], *the time will come when* [123:118], [171:159; rather diffuse expression of the fact that the speaker is arriving at the present time], [176:163; similar to the last example], *when* [189:174], *now* [231:213]; in from seven to nine of these ten instances the exact time is prominent. It is only once [133:126] that we find a formula, *I should like to be able to assist,* in which the grammatical versatility of BE ABLE TO is the adequate motive for using BE ABLE TO instead of *can* or *could.* The latter is, then, an occasional value of BE ABLE TO; its principal value is *time-focussed freedom, time-limited freedom.* With more diffuse focussing on time, we instead find BE IN A POSITION TO, a far rarer formula, in one citation [231:213]. And when clock-and-calendar time is irrelevant, we find *can* or *could*, the former for everything but remote tense: see later in Chapter VI. It is only when *can* and *could* are grammatically *impossible* [133:126] that grammar becomes a motive for using BE ABLE TO. This is the correction we are now able to make to the traditional view that grammatical *convenience* is the reason, and this correction improves the statistics by a factor of ten according to the *Trial* data.

BE SUPPOSED TO represents *a mild compulsion based on the arrangements* for this occasion and perhaps similar ones. It differs from *should* at least in that it allows for mutability both in the arrangements and in the sanctions for violation, implying that failure to act accordingly is excusable and can be compensated for, while *should* treats mutability and adjustments as irrelevant. It differs from *ought to* at least in that those arrangements can be different from arrangements for other occasions, while *ought to* treats the rule as stable, part of the mores of the community. All this will be treated later in Chapter VI; it is brought up here to call attention to the essential differences, and that is needed as background for the common experience that any of the three may on occasion serve the identical practical purpose. All three are italicized below for comparison; but *should* appears once in small capitals, substituting for original italics.

A trial *is supposed to* start from scratch, *ab ovo*. A tale is unfolded, step by step . . . The members of the jury listen. They hear the tale corroborated, and they hear it denied; . . . they all but hear it backward again through a fine toothcomb. BUT THEY SHOULD NEVER HAVE HEARD IT BEFORE. . . . And this, one is conscious from the first, cannot be so in the present case. [4:14; author's comment]

"When did you leave the house on the morning after Mrs. Morell's death?" — "At ten o'clock." — "You did not wait for the Doctor? And your patient was dead?" — "Yes, passed away." — "AND YOU DID NOT WAIT?" — "I *was supposed to* get off at nine." [63:66]

"We *àre supposed to* get cracking to-day." There is always someone who has heard, goodness knows from where. . . . — "Thère ìs the other indictment. It hås been kept very dark, the jury *is* nòt *supposed to* know." [72:75]

"Thère *is* nôt *supposed to* have been anything wrong yet, at the time he was around . . ." [104:102]

The Attorney-General: "At what intervals *is* this maximum dose *supposed to* be given?" — Dr. Douthwaite [nonchalant assurance] "To people in pain it could be given perhaps every four hours. If there were really agonising pain, it might be given every hour." . . . — "In your opinion, *should* heroin be given to old people?" . . . — Dr. Douthwaite: "It is axiomatic that people over seventy *should* not have heroin unless . . ." [113:109]

"It has been suggested that because of the after-effects of morphia and heroin they *ought* only *to* be used in cases of severe pain?" — "That is the usual indication . . ." [107:105]

The curious episode in the surgery when the Doctor *is supposed to* have stated that he gave nearly all the drugs . . . [199:183; reported speech: casting doubt on testimony]

"One of them lied . . . one of the others . . . lied about the conversation in the train in which Nurse Randall *is supposed to* have said, 'Don't you say that or you will get me into trouble'; either she said that or she did not, they could not both have been telling the truth . . ." [224:206; Judge charging the jury]

When BE SUPPOSED goes with a perfect infinitive the meaning is closer to the presumable original meaning of SUPPOSE 'hypothesize.' With more data we could perhaps find a gradation from that meaning to the 'arrangements' meaning first pointed out.

USED TO is always 'past' in modern English; there is no longer any *uses to;* and *had used to* is rare. Its categorical meaning is *characterizing the real past era as a whole by specifying events proper to the era and perhaps even peculiar to it.* Then the character of the era may be reflected back upon the actor, implying that 'he was wont to' act thus; that was presumably the original meaning of USED TO, but today it seems to be instead only an occasional implication.

She told his learned friend . . . that she *used to* give Mrs. Morell an injection of a quarter-grain of morphia? Yes, she did say so. . . . And she never gave anything else by way of an injection? She did not. [19:28; reported speech]

He *used to* be a medical referee at Brighton Crematorium, and it was he who had dealt with Mrs. Morell's cremation form. [42:47; reported speech? author's comment?]

Victorian juries *used to* grow quite restive. [73:76; author's comment]

The chauffeur . . . tells about his mistress's illness. — "She was stricken while staying with her family in Cheshire, sir. . . . I *used to* lift her into her wheel-chair and push her about the garden." [74:76]

Infinitive: Conclusion

After the preceding survey of the seven strongest candidates for inclusion among the notional group of auxiliaries, I feel safe in leaving them where I found them among the hundreds of verbs that govern infinitives. The true auxiliaries are treated later, beginning with the next chapter; and there it will become clear that they all fit together to make a perspicuous system which would become distorted and unclear if any of the quasi-auxiliaries were included among them.

And, as remarked before, if any is included there remains no way to exclude others, through the whole indefinitely long list (presumably hundreds) of verbs that govern infinitives. I exclude them from that system by the simple test that they can be used along with modal auxiliaries: 'he *might be about to* say' [178:164], 'I *may have to* postulate' [133:126], 'you *won't be able to* deal' [123:118], and similarly with the others that I have not presented as among the quasi-auxiliaries but listed in the introduction to that section. All those others are excluded also by another test: the rule for negation. Thus the last of them mentioned is negated in the citation there: 'you *don't* really *need to* bother,' with the usual DO that will be explained later; but the auxiliary NEED, which I consider a different though ultimately related word, is negated like the other modals: 'but this *need not* necessarily *be* the case with heroin' [150:141], and gets along without *to*. The quasi-auxiliary USED TO used to be negated like a modal auxiliary (*usen't to*); the abandonment of this form has removed an irregularity.

There is not one split infinitive in *Trial*. It may be that the schools of England have indiscriminately purged well-behaved

English of all uses of the split infinitive since the time when Fowler discriminated between useful and foolish splitting and unsplitting.* Anyhow, *Trial* is also free of any noticeable tendency to seriously distort an otherwise graceful sentence by violently unsplitting an infinitive and heedlessly placing its adverb before it: "I am not in the least impressed by this circumstance, which seems so greatly to please our professors of linguistics" [Clifton Fadiman, *Any Number Can Play*, Avon No. S 105 3A, p. 213].

Presentative

The essential difference in form between an infinitive and a presentative is that the infinitive always has the marker *to* and the presentative has none; the other difference in form is, however, more striking: an infinitive freely extends to as many as four words (*24 to have been outlined, 25 to have been getting*), but in modern English the norm of the presentative is a single word—the verbbase alone, which becomes two words, apparently, only in the negative passive imperative use: '*Don't be seen!*' and in the temporary imperative use: '*Be working* busily when the boss comes in.' No such use occurs in *Trial*. Of course we pay no attention to the traditional formulas *Be gone!* and *Have done!* which are today archaisms, deliberate ones, if they still occur at all; they are absent from *Trial*.

For the treatment of imperatives as presentatives, see next after these citations. With regard to meaning, the crucial difference between the infinitive and the presentative is that an infinitive is always related to another member of the sentence, either by modi-

* H. W. Fowler, *A Dictionary of Modern English Usage*, Oxford University Press, 1926; article: *Split infinitive.*

Charles Carpenter Fries, *American English Grammar* (New York: Appleton-Century, 1940), describing thousands of letters written by Americans shortly after the First World War, shows that the split infinitive is at home especially in well-knit writing, and that infinitives were split fairly often by well-educated men but more rarely (by a ratio of ten to one) by men of minimum education. For an earlier and more detailed comment see my review of Fries in *Language*, 17.274 (1941). It is a pity that we have, so far as I am aware, no British counterpart of the Fries survey.

fying it or by being equated to it with the copula, while a presentative may be used without any such relation—and that not only in imperative use. In the citations, both the finite verbs and the infinitives are printed in italics for contrast to the presentatives, the latter all numbered for reference from the following discussion.

Presentative Citations

"Good old days: ²⁸lock up the jury, ²⁹lock up the witnesses, no drink, no food, no light, no fire." [40:46; conversation]

Yet this curiosity, as we *call* it, *is* it not one of man's oldest, deepest longings? . . . the need for pattern and design: only ³⁰connect. [175:162; author's comment]

" 'I *refused to look* after her and *did* nothing but ³¹sit down while I *was* on duty.' " [36:42; read from the nursing record]

Thère *is* no doctor on this jury (doctors *are* generally *excused*), and surely they *do* not *do* such things as ³²ring up their medical friends in the evening. [59:63; author's comment]

And what *could* the Doctor *do?* ³³Make her life as bearable as possible, ³⁴give her sleep at night and ³⁵make her co-operative with the nurses . . . [195:179; reported speech]

It *may* well *be*, this elected silence, a move from strength, counsel inspired, imposed. Economy. Why ³⁶do more, ³⁷expose more, ³⁸explain more, than you *must?* . . . Why not ³⁹leave well alone . . . why ⁴⁰take a risk? Why not ⁴¹stand back? [175:162; author's comment]

"If you *have* one doctor ⁴²say one thing and another doctor on the same side ⁴³say another, it *shows* that . . ." [168:156]

"*Could* nòt he *finish* up to-day and *have* the jury ⁴⁴come back and ⁴⁴do their stuff to-morrow?" [214:197; conversation]

This *is* not quite enough *to make* the evening-paper men ⁴⁵bolt for the telephone, but it *makes* everyone ⁴⁶sit up. [53:57; author's comment]

The Attorney-General *lets* this ⁴⁷sink in. [51:56]

"*Did* you *see* the Doctor ⁴⁸give them?" [16:25]

It *is* the first time that we *hear* him ⁴⁹speak . . . [12:21]

it *is* like hearing a man ⁵⁰call, *Banco*. [166:154; author's comment]

"I *hâve known* a murderer ⁵¹sleep in two beds and ⁵¹eat two breakfasts in order *to lend* verisimilitude to an otherwise unconvincing narrative."

[Dorothy Sayers, *Busman's Honeymoon*, London: Gollancz, 1957, page 114]

"And by the way . . . thère *is* a new copy-writer *coming* in to-day." — "Oh, yes, Mr. Hankin?" — "His name *is* Bredon. I *can't tell* you much about him; Mr. Pym *engaged* him himself; but you ⁵²*will see* that he *is looked* after." [Dorothy Sayers, *Murder Must Advertise*, the opening sentences]

"But if the doctor *sees* an old woman in the last days of her life, restless, wakeful, distressed, miserable, *is* he *to say*, 'Oh, no, you ⁵³lie there; . . . I *am* not *going to help* you'?" [196:180; defense counsel to the jury]

". . . *comes* each morning and *says*, 'Good heavens, she *is* nôt dead yet, ⁵⁴give her another one,' *do* you *think* for a moment that a man like that *would have taken* the trouble . . . ?" [196:180; same]

⁵⁵"Suppose you *are going to come* to the conclusion . . . that the Doctor *was engaged* in a sinister scheme. How *does* it *help?*" [221:203; Judge charging the jury]

"If you *are* of that view, then ⁵⁶pass to the alternative acts." [227:209; same]

"So great *is* our horror at the idea that a man *might be questioned, forced to speak* and perhaps *to condemn* himself out of his own mouth, [for the first time without detachment] that we *afford* to everyone suspected or accused of a crime, at every stage, and to the very end, the right *to say:* ⁵⁷"Ask me no questions, I *shall answer* none. ⁵⁸Prove your case.' " [236:217; same]

⁵⁹"Pléase ⁶⁰answer my questions." [91:91]

⁶¹"Let it not ⁶²be a memory that *will haunt* . . . If you *think*, as I *submit*, thère *should be* no conviction, ⁶³be steadfast in that belief to the end, ⁶³ᵃbe steadfast and so ⁶⁴reach a true verdict." [200:183; defense counsel to the jury]

"If the superintendent *cannot answer* my question without his notes, by all means ⁶⁵let him ⁶⁶have them." — Detective-superintendent [rapping out] "That *is* quite improper. I *want to be* accurate." — The Judge [cold and final] ⁶⁷"Do not ⁶⁷intervene ⁶⁸please when counsel *is addressing* me." [90:90]

Mr. Lawrence . . . [Very slow] *"Did* one or the other of you *say* something to this effect, ⁶⁹"Don't you ⁶⁹say that or you *will get* me into trouble'?" [33:39]

Mr. Lawrence: "Sister Mason-Ellis *told* us that . . . it *was* you who *said* to Sister Mason-Ellis . . . ⁷⁰"Don't ⁷⁰say that or you *will get* me into trouble.' " [63:66]

[71]"Let me [72]tell you that it *would be* . . . [73]Let me [74]illustrate this . . ."
[213:196; Judge charging the jury]

"Now [75]let ûs [76]go through your entries." [22:30]

here *was* a man clear-minded enough, conscientious enough, [77]come *to think* of it: brave enough, *to refrain* from tidying up the ambiguities of fact. [164:153; author's comment]

Mr. Lawrence [neutral, prompting] "If it [78]be [78]suggested that cases of that sort *are* freak cases, [79]let me [80]ask you if the doses recorded in the nurses' books *are* of the freak kind or not?" [179:166]

All these numbered verb-forms (except *52 will see*) are uniform in their shape, so that the burden of proof falls on anyone who tries to subdivide according to form and meaning and parcel out various names: I call them all presentatives; and as I run through their various uses I will remind the reader of the names that have traditionally been given to those uses, but that is as far as I can go on the evidence. In a way this is a confession of helplessness; but after all it is nothing but obedience to the maxim known as Occam's Razor: *Entia non sunt multiplicanda praeter necessitatem.*

What we first find the presentative doing, starting from the first citation given, is something that can be called 'positing.' The presentative simply presents the specified deed or event for any consideration that the listener or reader may choose to give it, and presents it without asserting it: *28, 29, 30;* and in *31* and *32* we find *nothing but* and *such things as* to specify that this is something comparable to others—no alteration yet from the simple positing—and *33, 34, 35* are more of the same: deeds presented as comparable to other deeds, posited without assertion. With *why?* and *why not?* we find positing with a warning that the contrary is very likely preferable: deeds to do and to leave undone presented as comparable to their contraries, specifically each as very likely inferior to the other: *36, 37, 38, 39, 40, 41.*

In *Trial*, as we must expect from a printed book representing English on its good behavior, there are no examples of the presentative simply furnished with its own subject, as in this example of normal and by no means vulgar English: 'What we can do is *John leave* it there and *me pick* it up.' In other print we occasionally find this, as in "Me fly?" [airline advertisement] and "What, me worry?" [motto of *Mad* magazine's mythical mascot]. Some call 'Him fly his own plane?' an 'elementless' sentence, meaning that it has no subject or predicate; others have called it a non-sentence. I find it more convenient to say that a presentative, if it has a subject, takes its subject from the list that includes *me, us, him, her, them,* contrary to the rule for finite verbs. And this means that we can say, if we choose, that *42, 43, 44, 45, 46, 47, 48, 49, 50, 51* have presentatives with their own subjects, and that the whole combination of subject and presentative is the object or complement of the preceding verb, in which respect the presentative appears similar to the infinitive. There is no need to insist on this choice: no substantial harm is done to the over-all description of English if we follow tradition and say that the preceding verb has two objects. But it does seem a pity to throw away the parallelism to other presentatives with subjects.

There are not a great many verbs that can govern a presentative as the cited ones do: HAVE, MAKE, LET, SEE, HEAR, HAVE KNOWN, and perhaps a few others. When any such verb is passive, it instead governs the infinitive: 'The Doctor is made to disappear into his waiting cell below-stairs' [237:218]. In American English HAVE KNOWN, like the simple KNOW and the passive BE KNOWN, requires the infinitive.

An easy consequence of all this is that the presentative is available for use with imperative meaning, both with *you* as its subject and also without subject as the more usual thing. I say it in this way, instead of saying something like 'I class the English imperative as a presentative,' because the evidence is such as to show that English has no imperative as a separate *grammatical* category, that is to say, no verb-use which is necessarily imperative in meaning. Instead, certain dramatic occasions permit and encourage the acceptance of a suitable verb-form as an imperative. Even *28, 29, 30* could be taken as imperatives if the stage were set for that, and our WILL verbs are notoriously ready for that: *52.*

It may very well be true that a speaker can force his addressee
to accept a presentative as an imperative, but that doesn't mean
that English grammar has done it. When we are the least bit uncertain about the dramatic situation, we discover that we have no
way to prove the imperative meaning: *53, 54, 55, 56, 61, 65, 71, 73,
75, 79.* And then there is the traditional formula *Feed a cold and
starve a fever* with the well-attested interpretation 'If you feed a
cold, you will have a fever to starve.' No doubt all such evidence
could be explained away by starting out from imperative-as-
command and adding successive footnotes on the various displace-
ments and attenuations of that meaning; it just seems simpler, at
least to me, to set up a compact description that leaves nothing to
explain away.

It is now easy to understand the use of LET for first-person and
third-person counterparts of imperative meaning. We already know
that LET can govern a presentative (*47*), and we know that a verb
can equally well govern a presentative no matter what its own
form is: *45 to make, 46 makes.* Then we are not surprised to find
presentative LET governing other presentatives: *61, 62; 65, 66;
71, 72; 73, 74; 75, 76; 79, 80.* We note that the practical effects do
not depend on any theory that the defense counsel (*61, 65*) or the
Judge (*71, 73*) has to ask permission or to command, in order to
make the desired impression; the very first description I gave for
presentative meaning is still adequate: presenting the specified
deed (without asserting it) for any consideration that the reader or
listener may give it, and presentative LET is in this regard no different from 'Suppose . . . ' (*55*), and this in turn has the same effect
as 'Supposing . . . ' (see p. 184).

In 'May it please your Lordship' [4:14], the archaic use of inverted subject-position for imperative use need not detain us here;
the sentence is useful rather for showing PLEASE as an ordinary
verb-base, as also in 'This may please you.' Now *please*, in uses like
59 and *68*, is nowadays widely regarded as an adverb. The theory
seems to be that *please* necessarily remains what it once was:
an abbreviation, by mere ellipsis, of the adverbial clause 'an'

it please you' or 'if it please you' or 'if [it] you please' which had a third-person-singular present verb *please* marked as subjunctive by its lack of the ending on indicative *pleases*. That theory would make it an adverb because such a clause was one. But there is a difficulty here that has apparently been overlooked: the rhythm (unfortunately not customarily represented in print) which is different from the rhythm with an adverb such as *kindly*. *Please* is rhythmically treated as a separate one-word clause, not as an adverb belonging to the same clause as its neighboring words. And as a one-word clause it is of course a presentative if it is a verb at all, which I needn't insist on; but it differs from *let* by neither governing another presentative nor being governed by one, so that it can either precede a presentative (*59*) or come later (*68*), and it further differs from *let* by never being negated.

In *77 come to think of it*, the *come*, whatever its ultimate origin (and no doubt its history was influenced by the identity between its old subjunctive and its perfect participle) today falls neatly into the presentative category.

Besides *78 if it be suggested*, *Trial* has one parallel example: 'people can rest stolid in their trust that *if a man be accused* of poisoning or stabbing it must be shown where the poison or a knife came from' [12:22].

The meaning is uniform; it can be paraphrased 'in case it is suggested, in case a man is accused' or with another placement of the presentative '*suppose* it is suggested, *suppose* a man is accused.' None of these three formulas expresses a 'condition' properly so called, a premise or presupposition; each such sentence is *provisional*, looking ahead into an indeterminate future and making provision for a possible 'case' by *positing* the case and indicating what is to take care of it: It has not yet been suggested in open court that cases of that kind are freak cases, but let me ask you (*79, 80*) something so that I'll have your answer ready; this man has in fact been accused of poisoning, but not of stabbing, and anyhow what we are interested in is the provision made in English law for all such cases.

This use of presentative BE is rare and always formal, and nearly every time it is in passive voice nowadays; with other verb-bases it is still more rare and hardly valid as present-day English. Its two equivalents *suppose* and *in case* pass current everywhere: 'Better take your umbrella: suppose it rains!' and 'Better take your umbrella in case it rains.' In immature usage, conditional *if* sentences may replace them in border-line instances: 'if a man is accused' but hardly 'If it is suggested [though it hasn't been], let me ask you ...'

Citations for Other Non-Finites

Now that the infinitives and the presentatives have been described, we need citations exemplifying the other non-finites. In these, the finites, infinitives, and presentatives will all be printed in italics; the other non-finites will be numbered. We begin with a few left over from the two preceding blocks of citations.

They *have to deal* with it in the sort of way they *might find* themselves [2]having *to deal* with [4]conflicting medical opinion in the ordinary course of their lives. *Suppose*, for example, someone dear to them ... *was* a patient and they *called* in doctors, and [6]having [6]called in all the best doctors they *get* [7]conflicting opinions, as one *may do;* in the end they *would have to make* up their mind ... [212:195; reported speech]

" 'patient awoke [17]perspiring freely' " [22:30; from nursing record]

It *may* well *be*, this [81]elected silence, a move from strength, counsel [82]inspired, [83]imposed. [175:162; author's comment]

it *is* like [84]hearing a man call, *Banco.* [166:154; author's comment]

"we *afford* to everyone [85]suspected or [86]accused of a crime ... the right *to say* ..." [236:217; Judge charging the jury]

brave enough (,) *to refrain* from [87]tidying up the ambiguities of fact. [164:153; author's comment]

Mr. Lawrence [neutral, [88]prompting] "If it *be suggested* that cases of that sort *are* freak cases, *let* me *ask* you if the doses [89]recorded in the nurses' books *are* of the freak kind or not?" [179:166]

"in the middle of [90]giving your evidence" [34:40]

"within an hour of [91]being [91]given that injection" [62:65]

"recollection ... of [92]having [92]said anything" [94:94]

a cast of features suggestive of [93]having [93]been [93]reared perhaps under another law. [3:14; author's comment]

[94]" 'Having [94]attended [95]deceased before death and [96]having [96]seen and [96]identified the body after death, I *give* the [97]following answers to the questions [98]set out below.' " [42:48; read from a printed form]

"What usually *happens is* that one officer [99]having [99]written up his notebook, the other officer *copies* down the same thing." [219:202; Judge charging the jury]

[100]"Looking back now, [101]supposing you *had been told* it *was* paraldehyde, *do* you *think* you *would have noticed* the absence of smell, or not?" [66:69]

Mr. Lawrence *hurries* on as if [102]forestalling interruption. [167:155]

For what the Doctor *is undergoing* now, . . . *is* thère ([103]assuming him *to be* innocent, [104]assuming him about *to be acquitted*) reparation? [238:219; author's comment]

The Judge *came* on swiftly. Out of the side-door, an [105]ermined puppet [106]progressing weightless along the bench, head [107]held at an angle, an arm [108]swinging, the other [109]cróokèd under cloth and gloves, [110]trailing a wake of subtlety, of secret powers, age: an Elizabethan shadow [111]gliding across the arras. — The [112]high-backed chair *has been pulled, helped* forward, the figure *is seated, has bowed,* and the hundred or so people who *had gathered* themselves at [113]split notice to their feet *rustle* and *subside* into [114]apportioned place. And now the prisoner, the [115]accused himself *is* here—how *had* he *come,* how *had* one *missed* the instant of that other clockwork entry?—[116]standing in the front of the dock, spherical, adipose, [117]upholstered in blue serge, [118]red-faced, bald, [119]facing the Judge, [120]facing this day. And already the clerk, [121]risen from below the Judge's seat, *is addressing* him by full name. [2:13; author's narrative]

The motive, as [122]presented by the prosecution, *is* [123]bewilderingly inadequate. *Can* they *be suggesting* that a—sane?—man in the Doctor's circumstances *would commit* murder for the chance of [124]inheriting some silver and an ancient motor-car no longer [125]mentioned in the will? Unless some sense or strength *can be infused* into the motive it *must become* the [126]sagging point of this unequal web. Yet in a way the motive *has* already *drawn* sustenance from an irregular but not secret source; it *has waxed* big by headlines, by [127]printed innuendo, by items half [128]remembered from the preliminary [129]hearing. Thère *have been published* rumours of rich patients, mass [130]poisonings, of legacy on legacy in solid sterling . . . Everybody *knows* a bit too much and no one *knows* quite enough; thère *is* a most [131]disturbing element in this case, extra-mural half-knowledge that *can*not *be admitted* and *can*not *be kept* out. [14:23f; author's narrative]

Gerund

Some but not all of the numbered words ending with *-ing* are gerunds, and there are also *-ing* words in the italicized finite verbs. The other numbered *-ing* words are present participles; and the numbered words without *-ing* are either past participles (most of them resembling words which are finite verbs or parts of finite verbs) or else non-verbs cited for comparison. These various things are fairly easy to sort out if a start is made by carefully defining the gerund.

A gerund is always a noun. Its first or only word ends with *-ing*. It belongs to the verb system. In 'after bedding down the animals' *bedding* is a gerund belonging to the verb-base BED; like other verbs the gerund is modified by the usual adverbs (*carefully* bedding them down), and the gerund of a 'transitive' verb-base can have an object (*the animals*), and so on. Obviously in things like 'sent the bedding to the laundry,' the *bedding* is not a gerund but an ordinary noun of related meaning; and in 'by careful bedding down of the animals' we have no gerund but instead a still more closely related ordinary noun modified by an adjective *careful* and linked to *the animals* not directly but via the preposition *of* so that *the animals* is not the object of any verb. There is an Appendix note on such distinctions.

The gerund as a name of the deed specified by the verb-base is in competition with the infinitive, and in some uses the two are equally available. 'Tearing up a document is not an effective way of reviving gifts' [79:81] could have been any of 'To tear up a document is not an effective way of reviving gifts' and 'Tearing up a document is not an effective way to revive gifts' and 'To tear up a document is not an effective way to revive gifts' with no substantial difference in meaning but only stylistic differences. Our children freely use the gerund *tearing* for some years before their average age of finally learning how to use the infinitive *to tear* at the beginning of a sentence. But the children do learn very early to use the infinitive as a noun in such sentences where it is anticipated by its temporary substitute *it:* 'it is not our duty . . . to put the Doctor in the box' [194:178]. In this sentence-pattern, the infinitive is imitated by the gerund: 'It is no use taking one day in isolation' [141:133], and then the pattern is in competition with 'Thère is no use [in] taking one day in isolation' (either with or without *in*); statistics are not available in adequate quantity, but I have the impression that British usage either strongly prefers *it* or uses it exclusively (as in *Trial*) while American usage prefers *thère* without excluding *it*, though *it* is commoner in certain formulas: 'It's no fun swimming alone' against 'Thère's no fun in swimming alone.'

When a name of the deed is used as object or complement of a verb, the gerund is exclusively in use with a few verbs, for example RISK: 'Here some counsel might have left well alone, Mr. Lawrence risks carrying it to the limit' [158:148]. But when both are idiomatic, the infinitive is generally far more common than the gerund: 'The nurse did not like giving another large injection from this unusually large syringe' [9:19] is the sole example of a gerund after LIKE in *Trial*, while there are sixteen examples with the infinitive: 'that is not a state of affairs that you like to see' [210:194], nearly all of them with *would* or *should:* 'I would like to ask' and 'I should like to be able to assist' both spoken by the Judge [132:125]. In this connection it should be remembered that there are over ten times as many infinitives as gerunds in *Trial*. The infinitives have been counted exactly (I count 958 of them and may have missed say half a dozen), but the gerunds have not, incidentally.

What accounts for most of the gerunds in *Trial* is the fact that the gerund can be the object of a preposition while the infinitive can't, contrary to the rule in other Germanic languages: Norwegian *uten å vite* and German *ohne zu wissen* 'without knowing.' I do not count the infinitive's marker *to* as a preposition, for obvious reasons; yet when the infinitive modifies a preceding noun or adjective or adverb it has the meaning of an adjective or an adverb just as prepositional phrases do, as pointed out in detail in the preceding section of this chapter. This encourages the illusion that the infinitive's marker is a preposition.

In *this* function the gerund has the colorless preposition *of: 90, 91, 92, 93, 124;* the last of these examples (*chance of inheriting*) is strictly parallel to 'no chance to inherit,' and that is why I call this *of* 'colorless.' The point is that a preposition is a relator; the infinitive gets related without a preposition; when relating needs to be done but no specific relation (no contrast against other possible relations) needs to be specified, English uses *of* to signify the fact of relating a gerund and nothing beyond that fact. This one preposition *of* is used more times with the gerund (30 times) in *Trial* than all other prepositions together (19 times).

Now when a language like English is in comparison with languages of quite different structure, it is crucial to understand that most relations are asymmetric and that from this point of view what is being related is not the preposition's object (here, the gerund); what is being related is rather whatever sentence-element the prepositional phrase modifies, that is to say, the referent of the one and the referent of the other in the world of topics. This general truth becomes particularly evident when we paraphrase the relations specified by prepositions, other than *of*, with the gerund.

Concerning all those others, one general statement is valid: the preposition specifies a relation between one deed (or event, etc.) and others *on a scale of occasions in sequence* or something like sequence. Then the deed named by the gerund is generally in relation to *the occasion of* the other deed (rather than in relation to the other deed itself), thus:

BEFORE: The deed specified by the gerund is specified to *follow* the occasion of the other deed: 'Dr. Douthwaite says he would like to have a look at the summary *before answering* the question.' [140:133]

ON: The gerund's deed is specified to *be* the occasion of the other;
AFTER: The gerund's deed is specified to *precede* the occasion of the other: 'It is explained that *on returning* home *after finishing* her evidence . . . she recalled something' [98:97; author's narrative]

PAST: The gerund's deed is specified to *have been left behind on* the occasion of the other: 'Does Sister Mason-Ellis believe herself forgiven, or is she *past noticing?*' [35:42; author's comment]

WITHOUT: The gerund's deed is specified to *be absent from* the occasion of the other: 'You know quite well . . . that the dosage . . . was well within the experience of general practitioners in terminal stages of illness *without producing* fatality?' [140:133]

BY: The gerund's deed is specified to *be essentially present on* the occasion of the other: 'Dr. Harris had to deal with it because the Doctor was away, and he does so *by increasing* the morphia and heroin and *introducing* Omnopon at night?' [54:58]

IN: The gerund's deed is specified to *enclose* the occasion of the other: 'Is he right . . . *in thinking* that the report contains five separate entries?' [58:61; reported speech]

FOR: The gerund's deed is specified to *be a basis for the other deed* [note the altered paraphrasing here (deed rather than occasion) and the ambivalence: see next]: 'Was Mrs. Morell angry and annoyed with the Doctor *for having gone* away on holiday?' [100:99]

FOR: The gerund's deed is specified to *have a basis in the other* [see just above]: 'The Doctor may have thought she should have no further opportunity *for altering* her will!' [8:18]

TO: The gerund's deed is specified simply to *be there for the other to be related to;* the specific relation is given by the wording of the related sentence-element: 'she became breathless and rather collapsed. What did you put this down to?' — 'I put this down *to the heroin not suiting* her and I told the Doctor so.' [45:50]; 'The Attorney-General says that perhaps it might help if the prosecution had no objection *to his learned friend's reserving* his cross-examination . . . ' [75:78; author's narrative]; 'If the Doctor had withdrawn, he would only have done it with a view *to starting* again later . . . ' [173:160]

These nine prepositions exhaust the list of those used with the gerund in *Trial*, and it may be that they also exhaust the English prepositions in use for relating deeds on the scale of occasions. Since they occur only 19 times altogether, we see that this rather full, elaborate, and homogeneous equipment for specifying occasional relations among events is rather sparingly exploited. In fact, these devices have the status of rather formal or full-dress ways of expressing such relations; the everyday procedure is to use clauses related by conjunctions, as in 'Last night . . . *after you left the witness-box* you were talking to Nurse Stronach and Nurse Randall, weren't you?' [32:39].

The history of English tells us that one of those devices, the preposition *on* with the gerund, signifying that the gerund's deed is itself an occasion, was the primeval form of the modern formula in the last citation: *were on talking* weakened to *were a-talking* and then either surviving in marginal modern English or reduced ultimately to the *were talking* which now can (and in my opinion must) be described as part of the finite verb's inflectional system. History is not my proper concern in this treatise, but I cannot forbear to remark here that this looks like an example of homeostasis: the very commonest of all the occasion-relating prepositions taking its gerund away with it and leaving the normally rare ones behind in going to join the finite system. What is more apposite here is to point out that when foreigners learn English one of the principal hindrances is the common assumption that the *-ing* forms in the finite verb system are present participles, for that has an essentially misleading effect: the meanings are quite different: see Chapter V, pages 106–138.

The actor of a deed is commonly named by the grammatical subject of the verb specifying what deed. When the verb is finite, such naming is essential; see later, on the illusion of the missing subject (p. 57 and note). With non-finites the English rule is that the actor needs no second mention when he is already mentioned as the subject of the governing verb; but when the non-finite verb specifies a deed with a new actor, a new subject is requisite. In the last sentence cited on page 43, the reason why there is no subject for the gerund is that it is still the Doctor who does the starting if it is ever done; if it had been someone else, we would instead have found 'with a view to her starting again on morphia' or the like. Conversely, in the two preceding sentences, if the actor for each gerund had been the same as the actor specified just before, the result would have been 'I put this down to not suiting her' (meaning that *the nurse* didn't suit the patient) and 'if the prosecution had no objection to reserving their cross-examination' (since 'the prosecution' is treated as plural in British English).

The actor for the gerund is specified either by words from the list that includes *me, us, him, her, them,* such as *the heroin,* or else from the list that includes *my, our, his, her, their,* such as *friend's.* The fact that heroin is a thing and a friend is a person seems to have nothing to do with the question. The fact that the first speaker was a nurse and the second was a lawyer does have something to to do with it, but not very much; for the chances are that the same lawyer in more cozy situations would agree with W. Stannard Allen, *Living English Structure* [London: Longmans, Green, and Co., 1947; 3d ed., 1955], pages 186, 190:

. . . a possessive adjective. — *Examples:* I don't like *your* wearing that tie. — Do you mind *my* smoking a pipe? — Although this is grammatically logical, we more frequently meet with a pronoun instead of a possessive in spoken English . . . — *Examples:* I don't like *you* wearing that tie. . . . *Read the following, replacing the possessives by pronouns:* 1. Would you mind *my* coming too? . . .

In other words, *Get rid of those tight shoes and put on the speech of slippered ease,* as Henry Sweet called it. The Fries survey found equal numbers of *me* (etc.) and of *my* (etc.) when the subject of the gerund was a pronoun (including Allen's 'possessive'), but one example only of possessive noun. Again it is regrettable that we lack comparable data from British usage. For semi-formal British speech the picture is fairly clear: complete indifference. In *Trial* the few pronoun subjects are ambiguous (*her* and *thère*) except for the first citation here; the others show the noun subjects balanced:

"Then this is right—you knów that it has a distinctive smell, but you do nót remember *it having* a distinctive smell at the time?" [66:68]

"I regard it as the time when there was virtually no hope of *the patient's recovering* from the effects of the previous circumstances." [155:145]

"I think an anæsthetist is particularly conversant with the dangers of *a patient being* unconscious . . ." [158:148; same speaker!]

I call all these equally *subject* of the gerund because I can find no rational motive for calling them anything else and they do designate the actor.

In discussing the favorite prepositions with the gerund, I have disregarded *87 refrain from tidying up* for good and sufficient reasons. That is not a preposition with a gerund; it is a preposition with a verb, here the verb *refrain*, and the reason for that can be found by looking up *refrain* in the Oxford Dictionary.

The gerunds with prepositions in the block of citations preceding this section are *90, 91, 92, 93, 124*. The gerund in *84* has no preposition unless *like* is to be called one. Finally, *129* shows how the gerund can escape from the verb-system and become an ordinary noun, and *130* shows how it can then become plural.

Present Participle

The other verb-forms in *-ing* are either parts of finite verbs, italicized in that group of citations so that they can be disregarded, or else present participles: *88* and twenty-three others. A present participle can be used either as an adjective or as an adverb, and often it is pointless to try to decide which it is.

Coming just before a noun to modify it like any other adjective, we find *4, 7, 97, 126, 131*. From *131 disturbing* we could easily get an adverb *disturbingly*, and there is one in the citations: *123 bewilderingly*. But it seems clear that a present participle can also be an adverb without *-ly*, thus: *100, 101*. Then it can have its own subject: *99*. This is the only present participle with a subject in *Trial*, unless we include these two examples:

"Thère are two interpretations of the medical history: one, that it was the natural result, the spiral *taking* its course, the Doctor *coping* with a situation which, however it had arisen was in fact thére . . ." [229:211; Judge charging the jury]

—which can also be taken as gerunds with subjects. For lack of evidence, then, we are left wondering whether a pronoun subject with a present participle would come from the list *I, we, he, she, they* or from the list *me, us, him, her, them.**

Adverbial present participles without subjects are at least *6, 94, 96, 100, 101, 103, 104*. On the other hand *88* is so grouped with an ordinary adjective (*neutral*) that it is surely an adjective too; and *2* is an adjective by the test that it is parallel to things like 'they might find themselves wet and cold.' But *17* shows us that the decision can easily be impossible, so that the question is really an empty question: *106, 108, 110, 111, 116;* then *119* and *120* can be called adjectives because parallel to *bald*, but the ambiguity of the others is apparently part of the author's literary technique.

Past Participle

The past participles in the group of citations beginning on page 38 are at least *81 elected, 82, 83, 85, 86, 89, 95; 98 set, 113; 121 risen*. Of all these, only the last is unmistakably a past participle according to its shape: *elected* and six more look and sound exactly like 'past' finite verbs, *set* and *split* also look and sound exactly like their bases, but *risen* shows by its own shape that it could hardly be anything but a past participle. It is this one and only distinctive past-participle formation that will be taken, from now on, as the canonical form of the past participles, even though there are only about fifty more like that, against all the thousands of others.

For reasons that will become clear when the forms of finite verbs are treated, the best *abstract* representation of any verb-form is constructed by writing its suffix before it with a hyphen, so that -N RISE = *risen*. From now on, small capitals will be used for abstract representations, and such a hyphen will mean 'suffix to the next

* Grammarians call the latter erroneous. I have encountered no authentic example as far back as I can remember, of either kind, so I heave a sigh of relief and dismiss the question as moot.

item.' But now *suffix* must also be understood in an abstract sense, for some of them are not spoken or written in any way that agrees with their abstract form very well. As far as past participles go, the meaning of this mysterious statement becomes adequately clear from a mixed list of examples:

-ING SAY = *saying*	-N SAY = *said*	-N ELECT = *elected*
-ING TAKE = *taking*	-N TAKE = *taken*	-N SET = *set*
-ING LIE = *lying*	-N LIE = *lain*	-N SPLIT = *split*
-ING SIT = *sitting*	-N SIT = *sat*	-N RISE = *risen*
-ING SING = *singing*	-N SING = *sung*	-N SHOW = *shown*

All the forms in the first column are completely predictable from their abstract representations, for the spelling changes are not our concern here. The others are past participles, and this is where all the non-finite irregularities of English are concentrated: in principle, no past participle is ever predictable in English; the practical experience that surely -N TELEPHONE = *telephoned* because the word is modern, constructed from Greek components, etc., does not alter the principle.

This unpredictability does not affect any other topic in this whole book, so that I mean to dismiss it as summarily as I can. When the word *form* was chosen for the subtitle of the book, such unpredictability of shape was not meant. Instead, *form* here always means canonical form or its abstract representation: RISEN = -N RISE. The fact that -N RISE = *risen* is of no further interest to us, once we have acknowledged that such facts exist. Whole books have been devoted to such facts, books with titles including or implying the word *form*, so that there is no need for me to include here any of the details that they have already treated. For our purposes, such details can safely be relegated to those other treatises, to the dictionaries, and of course best of all to the habits of native speakers. I say "safely" because none of them have even the most trifling effect on the relations between meanings on the one hand and on the other hand the canonical or abstract forms which will serve to represent them in this and the later chapters.

Now the categorical meanings of the participles (both 'present' and 'past') deserve a preliminary statement too, before the citations are considered in detail. It has already been remarked that finite verbs always assert (whatever that means: see Chapter VI), and that no non-finite does that. And the other non-finites have been described individually as to their categorical meanings. Now what is the categorical meaning of the participles? Before attempting to answer that, I must remark that the traditional title 'present participle' is deceptive; this aspect of meaning would be better represented by some such label as 'contemporary' which fits *17* with its past-time meaning just as well as the present-future meaning of *126*. To provide the 'past' participle with equally adequate labeling, we must first split it into two varieties as to meaning: *121* is active and has the 'precedent' meaning called *perfect*, while the others have passive meaning without any necessary implication of time: *114* alludes to a precedent apportioning, while *122* demonstrably refers to a presenting which is contemporary and is indeed taking place, more and more of it, as we watch the courtroom drama and listen to the author comment on it.

This gives us these semantic subdivisions of the identical form: (1) *risen* is a 'perfect active' participle because it both necessarily refers to a precedent event *and* describes the actor; (2) *98 set* is a 'passive' participle because it describes what we may fairly call the victim of an act, and it doesn't need a two-word label because passive 'past' participles are not time-limited: *114, 122*. Yet the form (in our sense of the term) is the same: -N with the verb's base. How do native speakers know the difference, apart from the context? From their abundant experience with the base RISE and the base SET (FORTH), which has taught them a lesson which has this technical labeling: the first is *intransitive* and the second is *transitive*. Assuming that one has that experience, the rule becomes: the 'past participle' of a transitive verb has timeless passive meaning, that of an intransitive verb has perfect active meaning.

Such covert categorizing, with such powerful practical effects, is the adequate basis for a striking economy of form: the identical abstractly suffixed -N can be now active and now passive, now precedent and now contemporary or even future (*125*) without danger of confusion, and yet the form never consists of more than one word.

Conversely, the present participle in one-word form is always active in meaning, no matter whether the verb-base is transitive or intransitive: it always describes the actor and never describes the victim; further, in one-word form its time value is 'contemporary.' To cover the range of times, and the alternatives between active and passive, that the other participle covers with a single word, the present participle has to be expanded to two or three words: (1) *6 having called* has active precedent meaning, (2) *having been informed* has passive precedent meaning [no *Trial* example], and (3) *being informed* has passive meaning without time-limitation [no *Trial* example], which makes it pleonastic: plain *informed* will serve equally well.

Saying that the participles describe either the actor or the victim amounts to giving a fairly adequate statement of the categorical meaning of participles. Otherwise they do not differ radically from ordinary adjectives: they can be similarly used as adverbs, they similarly are used as predicate adjectives or precede or follow their nouns like other adjectives; the reader can make his own collection from the last block of citations to observe all this, and it will be enough if I remark that *doses recorded in the nurses' books (89)* merely follows the rule covering also *doses unusual in the circumstances.*

Accordingly, the line between participle and ordinary adjective is not always easy to draw. Thus *109 cróokĕd* is marked as a participle by its one-syllable pronunciation *crookt*, against the ordinary adjective *cróokĕd* 'not straight' in two syllables, and there are a few others like that: *agèd whiskey* against *agĕd man*. But there can be no such difference if *-ed* is preceded by certain other consonants, each of which requires *-ĕd* in both word-classes, while certain others require *-èd* in both, so that *105 erminèd* could be either a participle or an ordinary adjective.

When a person or thing is sufficiently specified by describing with a past participle, no separate noun-specification is needed and the participle behaves like a noun: *95 deceased, 115 accused.* There are rather few of these, mostly legal terms; and they can be said to be no longer participles but ordinary nouns. Here we find 'the aged' for our senior citizens, called *the agĕd* by candidate Kennedy in the 1960 television debates, but *the agêd* by candidate Nixon.

Words like *105 ermined* are often called 'participial adjectives.' A very common type has a prefixed ordinary adjective which is logically a modifier of the following noun, with *-ed* then added to the combination: *118 red-faced, 112 high-backed.* Here we have left the verb-system entirely.

Returning to the verb-system, we note an interesting use of the past participle with certain governing verbs, probably no more than half a dozen different ones:

". . . she had to *have* every blanket in the house *brought* to her room . . ." [36:42]

". . . the defence actually *had* them *fóllowed*" [40:46]

"Heroin ĩs useful— I remember a woman of seventy-three who *had* it *prescribed*." [128:122]

Advocates have to try to bring out certain answers and to *keep* others *covered* . . . [41:46; author's comment]

Is it proper treatment to *keep* a person who has had a stroke *drugged?* [185:171; reported speech]

A loquacious man, then, under evident pressure to *make* himself *heard* . . . [3:13; author's comment]

Besides HAVE, KEEP, MAKE, this is usual with ORDER; but not with DIRECT, COMMAND, and other synonyms, so that the list seems to be closed. It is of course common with GET; no *Trial* example. But the very most interesting use of this pattern is with HAVE as in 'The nurses have had their notes put to them' [194:179], where the nurses were not the person who caused it to be done. This can go as far as *He had a son killed in the war* 'Ihm ist ein Sohn im Krieg verloren gegangen'; *I had my bicycle stolen* 'On m'a volé . . . ' This, then, is a very compact English device for beginning a sentence

with the designation of the person most (unsatisfactorily) interested in the event, a placement which requires that designation to
play the role of grammatical subject although he is not the actor.

In a subordinate clause in print, this may seem identical with a
quite different sort of message:

the trunks which he hâd sênt hóme for him
the trunks which he hăd sênt hóme for him (*or* hàd *or* håd)

—but in speech, which is after all the real language, there is no
ambiguity. The first, with major stress on *had*, is the formula last
discussed; this *had* is marked as an ordinary verb by the major
stress, a form of the ordinary verb-base HAVE; and this tells us that
John caused Cook's to send some trunks home for either himself or
Charles. The second, with any minor stress on *had*, does not contain
the verb-base HAVE; instead, it has a finite verb *had sent* in which
the only base is SEND and the *had* is only an auxiliary, an entirely
different word.

The non-finite verbs have now been treated under their four
headings, *Infinitive, Presentative, Gerund, Participle*. All other verb
forms are finite. Chapter III will deal with the finite *forms* and
those of their meanings which are correlated to the choice and placement of subject and adverbs; it is accordingly another preliminary
chapter. Chapters IV, V, and VI deal with the categorical meanings
of English finite verbs.

III

The Finite Schema

Page 48 tabulates some participle forms, with explanations which should be kept in mind while beginning this chapter. There was also a promise which I am about to fulfill. First I will show what a *schema*, any schema, is good for. The gerunds cited as *90, 91, 92, 93* fit into this schema:

1XXX	-ING	HAVE -N	BE -N	SHOW

1001 showing: in the middle of *giving* your evidence
1011 being shown: within an hour of *being given* that injection
1101 having shown: recollection of *having said* anything
1111 having been shown: *having been reared* under another law

In the formula beginning each line, a 'one' means that the corresponding schema position (there are four in sequence) is filled properly, while a 'zero' means it is empty; 'x' means it *can* be either filled or empty: since the first position must be filled (with -ING) or else this wouldn't be the *gerund* schema, all formulas here begin with a 'one.' In *Trial*, all the gerunds have a verb-base, so that the specific *Trial* gerund schema would be 1XX1. In my kind of English (perhaps in the *Trial* dialect too: I just don't know) we encounter sentences like 'She wasn't paid any compliments and she didn't like not *being*.' The formula for this is 1010 -ING BE -N with a final -N that has vanished for lack of anything for it to be suffixed to; all hyphened bits will vanish in these circumstances.

The schema for English finite verbs is far more complex. It has six positions (against four in that gerund schema) and some variety in choice of fillers for the positions. Here it is temporarily simplified by neglecting the alternatives to WILL and by leaving -s and 000000 and 100000 unexplained:

XXXXXX	-D	WILL	HAVE -N	BE -ING	BE -N	SHOW

000000 And you still say so? — I *do.*

000001 I always *say* no good *comes* of these cases with no body.

000010 more is known about drugs to-day? — It *is.*

000011 both morphia and heroin *are administered* to people

000100 You are not suggesting—*are* you?—there was any

000101 *Are* you *standing* there and *saying* as a trained nurse

000111 do they feel they *are being led* into the light?

001000 You have experienced many . . . ? Dr. Harman *has.*

001001 the defence *have decided* . . . not to call the Doctor

001011 cases where this amount *has been given*

001101 You *have been* constantly *nursing* other patients

010000 Why doesn't he say so? — He *will.* It isn't his turn yet.

010001 I *will* certainly *help* you.

010011 unless he fears that questions *will be put* to him that he

100000 did the Doctor ask you for anything? — He *did.*

100001 When the Doctor *went* away, *did* he *leave* any instructions?

100010 Were you sent for again by her? — I *was.*

100011 morphia and heroin *were* commonly *used* as hypnotics

100100 The three of you were talking, *wére* nŏt yòu?

100101 the period when he *was prescribing* for her

100111 I increased the same drugs that *were being used.*

101000 had the detective-sergeant sígned . . . ? — He *had.*

101001 *Had* you *made* any inquíries before giving evidence . . . ?

101011 just as it *had been quoted* by the Attorney-General

101101 comatose for days and *had* not *been suffering* real pain

110000 He'll talk his head off! — Must be longing to; *wŏuld* nŏt yóu?

110001 If there were, I *would take* them and *destroy* them.

110011 doses *would be given* during the night

110101 he *would be saying* he held a view which he cannot

111000 it might have . . . it *would* more probably *have* not

111001 *Would* you *have expected* the doses to have . . .

111011 he would have thought morphia *would have been stopped*

111101 She *would* nŏt *have been having* much, those would . . .

The notes following these few examples may be helpful:

```
A 000111   0      0        0       BE -ING   BE -N    LEAD
                                   are        being     led
B 001001   0      0      HAVE -N     0         0       DECIDE
                         have                decided
C 001011   0      0      HAVE -N     0       BE -N     GIVE
                         has                 been        given
D 010011   0    WILL       0         0       BE -N     PUT
                will                 be                 put
E 100010  -D      0        0         0       BE -N      0
                        was                [zero]
F 100100  -D      0        0       BE -ING     0        0
                      were          [zero]
G 101101  -D      0      HAVE -N   BE -ING     0        SUFFER
                         had        been     suffering
H 111011  -D    WILL    HAVE -N     0        BE -N     STOP
                would   have                 been       stopped
K 111101  -D    WILL    HAVE -N   BE -ING     0        HAVE
                would   have       been               having
```

A hyphened bit functions as a suffix to the next item, so that when there is no next item it vanishes: E, F. Note that -D BE is *was* if the subject is singular and the meaning is either 'real past' or else 'vivid hypothesis'; otherwise it is *were*. Note that the shape *been* can be constituted in more than one way: C, G, H, K. After nothing but empty positions, items are unchanged except that BE is *are* (or *am* or *is:* see p. 72): A, B, C, D. And HAVE preceded by nothing but empty positions is *have* (or *has:* see p. 72), while -D HAVE is *had*. The combination -N BE = *been* is easy, and the -ING combinations are obvious. The other combinations in the page of examples are these:

000000 = *do* (or *does:* see p. 72)	-N DECIDE = *decided*
0 SAY = *say* (or *says:* see p. 72)	-N GIVE = *given*
0 COME = *come* (or *comes:* p. 72)	-N PUT = *put*
-D 00000 = *did* (see p. 59)	-N USE = *used*
-D GO = *went*	-N MAKE = *made*
	-N QUOTE = *quoted*
-N ADMINISTER = *administered*	-N EXPECT = *expected*
-N LEAD = *led*	-N STOP = *stopped*

It is evident that the unpredictability of -D combinations and -N combinations, beyond *do* and *did* and those presented before this last tabulation (and later a few others like them), belongs to the lexicon rather than to the message-bearing forms which are our proper concern. Accordingly, all the hundred or so others that turn up later in the citations will be passed over without comment from now on.

This schema, although it has been simplified and still awaits completion, suffices for our next topic: the relations between the finite verb and the rest of the sentence. The finite verb may consist of one word or of several; in any case, what is the relation in form and in meaning between the finite verb and a word or group of words which precedes it, interrupts it, or follows it?

Finite Subjects

The crucial difference between finite verbs and the non-finites has already been spoken of, first by way of definition and for the sake of sorting them out from each other: A finite verb requires a grammatical subject and can have one from the list *I, we, he, she, they* (while a non-finite may need none and can never take one from this list). When I say that it *requires* a subject (contrary to the rule in Latin and many other languages) I am stating a master rule of English grammar. The instances of unspoken subject are such as to confirm the rule rather than weaken it: then the verb is obviously finite to begin with, and the addressee infallibly reconstructs the subject—which he wouldn't bother to do for a non-finite without subject. This apparently happens in English in only one way: in casual style any minor-stress words can be left unspoken from the beginning of the sentence as far as the first major-stress word.*

"He'll talk his head off!" — "Must be longing to; wouldn't you?" [72:75]

"he wrote me a letter after that little affair when he fined you. 'Took ten days to think it over." [Rudyard Kipling, *The Village That Voted the Earth Was Flat*, in *A Choice of Kipling's Prose*, London: Macmillan, 1952, p. 315]

"By the way," said he, "I've assigned 'Dal all the gramophone rights of 'The Earth.' She's a born artist. Hadn't sense enough to hit me for triple-dubs the morning after." [same, p. 328]

"Just let me run through that little case of yours again," said Pallent, and picked up *The Bun* which had it set out in full. — "Any chance of 'Dal looking in on us to-night?" Ollyett began. [same, p. 334]

The first citation is given elsewhere in reconstructed form as 'Hê must be longing to'; and similarly the Kipling quotations could be cited as 'hê took ten days' and 'shê hadn't sense enough' and 'is thêre any chance.' This is not merely cooking the data to satisfy the rule that a finite verb must have a subject, for several reasons well known to professional linguists. One will suffice: as any native speaker of English knows, in consultative and in formal style the deleted words are regularly spoken, thus: 'is thêre' in consultative and 'is thère' in formal style. Conversely, such ellipsis is a distinguishing character of casual style.

With this cleared out of the way, let us consider the relation between the subject and the finite verb. Its form has been spoken of already; now its placement. The pattern is that the subject either is the last noun or pronoun before the verb that is not pre-empted to another employment, or else it immediately follows the first word of a verb consisting of two or more words.

* For 'casual style' and the unspoken words see my monograph *The Five Clocks*, Publications of the Research Center in Anthropology, Folklore and Linguistics, Indiana University, 1962, Publication 22. For 'minor' and 'major' stress see Chapter I above, heading *Stress*.

the hundred or so people who had gathered themselves at split notice to their feet *rustle* and *subside* into apportioned place. [2:13]

"*One* of the questions to be considered in this case *will be:* why were they given?" [6:16]

"*What happened* to thése nursing books?" [51:56]

"*What the Doctor did was* to go into the surgery . . . ?" [92:92]

"It was quite obvious that *your announcement* of his arrest *was* a shock?" [94:94]

"To whom *were they addressed?*" — "*They were addressed* to Miss Lawrence . . ." [95:94]

"*Did he ask* her for his warm overcoat?" [95:94]

"For what legitimate purpose *can morphia* and *heroin be* daily *administered* over a prolonged period?" [112:109]

"What conclusion *do you draw* from the dosage . . . ?" [116:112]

What was done in a nursing home in Cheshire *is* wholly irrelevant and *throws* no light on subsequent events. [201:184; reported speech]

"What impression *did the doctors make* upon you in the witness-box? *Which* of them *inspired* the most confidence?" [212:195]

What may be their reflections? [31:38; author's comment; another way to say it is 'What *may their reflections be?*']

Now 'Their feet rustle and subside' could be a complete English sentence; above, however, *feet* [2:13] is preempted to serve as object of a preposition, and when we examine still earlier nouns and pronouns we find them all preempted (*who* as subject of *had gathered*) until we come to *people.* Then either *people* or *hundred* is the subject of *rustle* and *subside,* and we have no need to decide between them but can safely take all the first five words together as the subject. And just as they now constitute the last noun or pronoun before the finite verb that is not preempted, so also *subside* comes next after the subject as effectively as *rustle* does; for our purposes, that is, for all such matters belong to other chapters in other books than the present treatise.

Four of the citations have a subject immediately following the first word of a verb consisting of two or more words [95:94, 95:94, 112:109, 116:112]. This is called 'question word-order'; but the facts are too complex to be disposed of so summarily. To begin with, a simple English question is either an information question (asking for specific information such as an identification: 'Miss Lawrence') or else a confirmation question answerable by 'yes' or 'no.' And a confirmation question does not need to use 'question word-order'; it is enough to use the wording of a statement and interrogative intonation [94:94]. Such a question is always *anaphoric*, alluding to previous discourse or at least to information shared by speaker and addressee; often it is marked by some anaphoric word such as *it* in 'All experienced nurses do it?' [20:28]. When a confirmation question can't be anaphoric because speaker and addressee lack the shared information, or when they have it but the speaker doesn't choose to appeal to it, 'question word-order' is requisite: 'Will you help me?' with the subject after the first word of two or more constituting the verb.

Meaningless DO

Then if the question is a transformation of a statement using a one-word verb, such as 'He asked her for his warm overcoat,' there is no 'first word of two or more' for the subject to follow and the rule can't be applied immediately. The English solution is to expand the one-word verb *asked* into the two-word verb *did ask* [second 95:94] with no other function than to make application of the question-word-order rule possible. That is, -D ASK = *asked* gets the completely meaningless component DO inserted to form -D DO ASK = *did ask;* this now has the same shape as -D WILL ASK = *would ask* (or for that matter the same shape as WILL ASK = *will ask:* 'Will you ask her for his warm overcoat?') and the 'question word-order' has become possible. The procedure is purely mechanical; therefore the inserted DO has no meaning whatever, contrary to the school tradition which calls it 'emphatic.'

This is a small-scale but entirely typical sample of modern linguistic argument. It would collapse, and the theory of meaningless DO would be abandoned, if a grammatically identical DO were ever found with a demonstrable meaning.

When an information question begins with questioning words (which is the normal place to put them; 'He said whát?' is unusual though equally English), the same 'question word-order' is used ('What did he say?'), and again a one-word verb has to be converted into two words to make this possible: 0 DRAW = *draw* replaced by DO DRAW = *do draw* [116:112]. However, if the questioning wording is the subject itself, it precedes the verb, and the verb can be one word: [51:56]. Both treatments of the questioning wording are exemplified in one citation: [212:195].

Just before and just after the block of citations, I spoke of how nouns and pronouns could become ineligible to serve as subject by being "preempted to another employment." Now there is one exception to that general rule: *what* and the words ending with *-ever* can still serve as subject even when already employed otherwise; the citations are [92:92, 201:184].

In the first of these, *What* has two offices. First, *the Doctor* is the subject of *did*, and *What* is the object of *did*. Second, *What* is the subject of *was*. Incidentally, *what* can be object of two verbs: 'He told me what the Doctor did' has *what* both as object of *told* (as *a lie* is its object in 'He told me a lie') and again as object of *did*. Or it can be both object of a preposition and object of a verb in the same sentence: 'He objected to what the Doctor did.'

In the second of these, *What* is equally *subject* of two different verbs, the second of them split into two verbs again by means of *and*. *What* is subject of *was done* to begin with; then it is also subject of *'is* wholly irrelevant' and of *'throws . . .'*

This is enough to indicate the possibilities. Exactly the same is true of *whatever, whichever, whoever,* and of course *whomever.*

'Question word-order' is not the only occasion for using meaningless DO in English. It could be said that 'Not only does she show her age, she even boasts about it' is the same thing; no discussion is needed here, especially because I have noticed no example in *Trial.* But there still are three uses of this DO that do call for discussion; one of them is the use in insistent clauses like the second one of this sentence.

Insistence

This use no doubt gave the impulse to call meaningless DO 'emphatic' as in some school grammars, and as a matter of fact it does seem as though the added word added the emphasis. This is, however, an illusion. What is added is not emphasis in general, nor emphasis on a certain word or its meaning; what is added is insistence on the truth-value of the whole clause. Now here is the pattern or 'rule' for accomplishing that in the most economical way possible in English: Remove the *primary stress* from wherever it belongs in the colorless clause, and place it on the *first word* of the finite verb constituted of two or more words (which in a colorless clause has minor stress automatically: indeed, that is what we must mean by 'colorless').

Note that this is not any addition of stress; it is simply a relocating of the primary stress that has to be somewhere in that clause anyhow. It is true that many speakers have the habit of also raising the pitch of the voice at the relocated primary stress, or otherwise adding extra expressive coloration there, in nearly all their insistent clauses. But that is irrelevant and can with most speakers be obviated on occasion. Thus what I wrote not far above would have been in colorless form 'that câll for discússion' and 'it séems as though'; in such dispassionate discourse the expressive colorations naturally do not come into play in the insistent forms actually written, and they are necessarily spoken 'that dó câll for discûssion' and 'it dóes sêem as though' with mere relocating of the primary stress—unless the reader chooses to ham them up, a choice for which English grammar can't be held responsible. Perhaps the speaker was thus dispassionate in 'I cannôt remémber. I díd knôw, but I cannot remémber' [28:36].

Of course when the colorless clause already has a verb of more than one word, nothing gets inserted: 'I wăs wáiting' becomes 'I wás wâiting' with unaltered wording to add the message 'and please don't imagine that I was not waiting!' Presumably no language on earth can surpass this for economy.

Negation

The remaining two employments of meaningless DO are in negation and in the British extended propredicates. For negation, we
begin by noting that although a verb of two or more words can be
interrupted after its first word by having the subject there, it can
be interrupted anywhere by inserting an adverb—simple or complex, even a long adverbial phrase or clause. It cannot be interrupted
by inserting anything but an adverb, or else the subject after its
first word: not, for example, by inserting a noun or pronoun that
is not the subject (as is done routinely in German) nor by inserting
one later than just after its first word. Examples are, from the
citations so far in this chapter:

"You *have been* constantly *nursing* other patients" [18:27]

"I *will* certainly *help you*." [89:89]

"morphia and heroin *were* commonly *used*" [124:119]

"it *would* more probably *have* not." [190:175]

"*can* morphia and heroin *be* daily *administered*" [112:109]

Now in four of these five it is obvious that the inserted adverb
affects the meaning of ('modifies') that part of the verb which
follows it more than it affects anything else, while in the remaining
instance [89:89] it affects the whole verb *will help*. Exactly the same
scope of modification—modifying just what follows it—is characteristic also of the negative adverb NOT, once we have repaired the
customary mutilations of court transcripts and of special styles and
have also recognized a special grammatical rule valid for NOT and
for no other word. First the exact quotations from *Trial:*

"And you still *say* so?" [19:28]

"You *are* not *suggesting*—are you?—there was any . . ." [126:120]

"The three of you were talking . . . *were*n't you?" [32:39]

"comatose for days and *had* not *been suffering* real pain." [11:20]

"Must be longing to; *would*n't you?" [72:75]

"She *would*n't *have been having* much, . . ." [27:34]

Even in these few citations there is more than one sort of inconsistency, plus an apparent contradiction of the established rule that the subject, if not before the finite verb, comes *immediately* after its first word: here we twice find *n't* coming between. Let me immediately state a linguist's solution to this sort of mess. It is an essentially simple solution, though it will take a good many words to state it clearly enough for every sort of reader.

Like the adverb *still* in the first citation, the special negative adverb nôt modifies just what follows it; and when it is to negate the whole verb by preceding it all, it has the form ^-*nt* and requires the verb to consist of at least two words unless clipped. Once again, more slowly. The negator not regularly imports a secondary stress along with it when inserted into a sentence; so far, it agrees with *still* and other adverbs generally, and like the others it modifies just what follows it. But when it is to negate the whole clause by negating all the finite verb, and is for that purpose placed before the whole verb, it becomes a 'hyphened bit' like all the others (-d, -ing, -n) and is spoken as a suffix to the next word and imposes its secondary stress on that word—the first word of the verb but never a word containing or consisting of the verb-base (bases reject this particular suffix), so that it must be suffixed to an auxiliary. If the verb in affirmative form contains no auxiliary, meaningless do comes in, simply to make normal negation possible. This is an exact parallel to the question-word-order and insistence rules. The normal results then are: nôt shów = nôt do shów = *dôn't shów*; not shows = not -s show = not -s do show = *doesn't show; didn't show*.

The combination then is spoken in one or in two syllables depending on the final sound (vowel or consonant, roughly speaking) of that first word: nôt -d be = nôt *were = wêren't* in one syllable in most English, nôt -d will = nôt *would = wôuldn't* in two syllables by speaking a weak vowel before the *n* as in the two-syllable *wêrĕn't* of some English. In all English, nôt can = *cân't* in one syllable, nôt will = *wôn't*, etc.

If that were all, life would be simple. But in formal English speech there is the extra device of marking the formality by promoting the non-syllabic *n't* = *nŏt* of *won't*, *can't*, etc., and the weak second syllable of *wouldn't*, *wasn't*, etc., to tertiary stress: *won't* becomes *will nòt*, *can't* becomes *cannòt*, and yet the meaning is the same as before: NOT is still effectively before the whole verb, and the adequate signal for that placement is the minor stress on *nòt* which is impossible when NOT truly follows and therefore has normal adverb stress: NÔT.

So far, no harm done; when normal (admitting that it is hard for most people both to speak normally and to use formal style) the speech is still responsible, still faithful to English grammar. But there are also characteristically irresponsible styles—before a microphone, women almost invariably slip into them, and so do the lower-paid men who work in American radio—notably the reading-aloud and the oratorical style. In such styles, the postponed *nòt* gets promoted to major stress again and becomes *nôt*, wiping out an essential difference in meaning which the grammar had provided for. In conscientious formal English we find:

you are nòt suggésting 'it is false that you are suggesting'
you are nôt suggésting 'you are omitting to suggest'

the first of which can profitably use the reverse question 'áre you?' that would be illogical with the second. Now in the citation [126:120] near the bottom of page 62, Mr. Lawrence slipped into oratorical style (this is not the only time he made such a slip and got into trouble) and heard himself say 'are nôt' when he meant 'aren't' and could safely have said 'are nòt'; then to repair the damage he departed from the simple comma-pauses of the intended message 'You âren't suggésting, áre you, there was any . . . ' and put pregnant pauses (printed as dashes) around the reverse question as if to say 'I really meant the only message that can be filled out with "áre you?" after all' and gave us 'You are nôt suggésting—áre you?—there was any . . . ' He could have done a better repair job by saying 'or are you?' and perhaps that is what he actually did; in that case the court reporter crossed him up, as they so often do.

The other formal or perhaps oratorical example [11:20] in that block of citations must be left without discussion for lack of cogent evidence. The examples with *weren't* and *wouldn't* followed by the subject are normal: the effective sequence is NOT -D BE YOU and NOT -D WILL YOU, so that the subject immediately follows the verb and the rule for subject placement has not been broken as it would be broken in *were not you* and *would not you.* The latter are reading-aloud patterns, and from there they sneak into formal speech occasionally—far more rarely, apparently, in British than in American English.

In pedantic school-teaching the rule seems to be 'Do not use contractions!' (Not in normal English, which would be 'Don't . . . ') American textbooks then get edited to satisfy that kind of teaching and the result is tantamount to a conspiracy to conceal a large part of English grammar from learners of reading and writing. For example, the real reason why Johnny writes 'I would of shown it to her' is that he has not been allowed to see, printed or written, the normal spelling of both *hăve* and *hâve,* namely *'ve.* The normal pronunciation of *of* is identical to that of *hăve;* what he wrote is not in the least false grammar but purely and simply makeshift spelling. More on this in the Appendix.

Propredicates

Further consideration of negation will be requisite at the end of Chapter VI where the modals are discussed. Here I must turn to those samples on the second page of the present chapter whose formulas end with 'zero' to signify that the verb-base position of the schema is empty. I postpone formulas 000000 and 100000, and I begin the others with 110000. On that page the abbreviated citation was adequate for the temporary purpose; but now the full context is needed: 'He'll talk his head off!' — 'Hê must be longing to; wouldn't you?' [72:75]. The first half of the answering utterance ends with a clipped infinitive whose full form no doubt would have been 'to talk his head off'; so far, everything is clear, to native speakers of English at least.

The case of the clipped finite *would* is different. Its full form could be anything among 'wouldn't you long to talk your head off?' and 'wouldn't you be longing to talk your head off?' and 'wouldn't you talk your head off?'

One thing that is certainly excluded is 'wouldn't you talk?' and others are 'wouldn't you long?' and 'wouldn't you be longing?' Each of these ends with a verb-base and then sentence-final speech-cadence (faithfully represented in print by '?'), and the effect of both together is to close the message, to certify that nothing has been left unsaid. What was actually said has the auxiliary *would* (which is not a verb-base!) as its last verbal component, and now the conventions of English communication deliver another effect.

A visitor from Mars might have predicted that omitting the verb-base would obliterate its meaning; what actually happens is the reverse: the omission not only preserves the meaning of the base but continues (farther than in 'wouldn't you talk?'!) to retrieve the meaning of all the rest of the predicate 'your head off.' Or, taking it from its other end, if from the sentence 'Wouldn't you talk your head off?' we omit 'your head off' we have lost its meaning; but if we further omit 'talk' the meaning of 'talk' comes back in and along with it the meaning of 'your head off' in addition. The shorter sentence has the longer list of referential meanings, and that is the invariable effect of clipping a sentence from its end but keeping the auxiliary.

With respect to form, the *would* in the citation is only *would talk* minus *talk;* but with respect to meaning the residue is not adequately labeled if it is called a 'clipped finite verb.' Instead I call it a *propredicate* to call attention to its function: it stands for a whole predicate, not only the verb but all the rest of the predicate right to the end of the clause.

What the content of that predicate is is the addressee's affair. In the example, he could choose between LONG and TALK as his supposed verb-base, and that choice is crucial; further, there is the choice between *long* and *be longing*, making three choices in all. The speaker has left all three equally available to the addressee.

He could have limited the addressee's choice to the last of the three (though he could not by any means have limited it to either of the other two) by saying 'wouldn't you be?' Now it must not be imagined that this maximum coverage is excluded by the actual shortest possible propredicate in 'wouldn't you?' Supposing that this maximum coverage was actually meant by that speaker, it follows that the speaker has made his propredicate as short as possible.

And that seems to be the British habit, while Americans tend to limit their addressee's choices by using longer propredicates. When a British propredicate is more than one word, there is regularly some special reason; that page of citations has one example, while other examples have their other special reasons. There [190:175] the speaker could have said in full: 'I should say that it more probably would not have accelerated death' or the equivalent with a propredicate: 'I should say that it more probably would not.' (Here an American would more likely have said: 'that it more probably wòuld nót hàve.') What he instead had in mind certainly was: 'I should say that it would more probably have not accelerated death'; the propredicate equivalent is what he actually spoke: 'I should say that it would more probably have not.' He could not have shortened this sentence to leave a one-word propredicate because now the adverbial *more probably* and the negative *not* would have vanished. As it is, only ACCELERATE is negated. This is eventual negation: see page 199.

Occasionally we do find a longer-than-minimum propredicate in *Trial*, just as if it had been American: 'you would have discovered it sooner or later?' — 'We wòuld hàve; but usually . . . ' [41:47]. More usually we find either of two other devices, both serving to mark the propredicate as insistent (as the above was surely intended to be) without danger of confusion between insistence and contrast: *would* against *could*, etc., is contrast, and the same stressing would equally mark contrast. One of them: 'And would he be embarking then on a course that in fact took thirteen days to bring about her death?' — 'He mìght wéll hàve.' [149:141].

Extended Propredicates

The other device uses the ambiguous routine stress-location method of indicating insistence (primary stress on the first word of a finite verb or propredicate instead of elsewhere), but conventionally protects it from being misunderstood by a device peculiar to recent British usage as far as the documentation goes— though it may very well have been at least marginal British English for centuries before. This device consists of extending an insistent propredicate by adding DÒ (always tertiary stress); the propredicate then must include either a modal (WILL, etc.) or HAVE -N, and most often includes both, while BE -ING and BE -N are each excluded. Example: 'Would you have expected these doses to do her any good?' — [Cocky] 'They mǐght hǎve dòne.' [183:169].

This is another use of 'meaningless DO' which I promised to display eventually; but this time 'meaningless' is perhaps misleading, since this DÒ may be said to accomplish the limiting to insistence by virtue of a sort of 'doing' meaning which itself excludes interpreting *might* as contrastive. That question can safely be left unanswered, since when I display the complete finite schema this DÒ will appear in a different place from meaningless DO.

For non-British readers I must add that the meaning above is simply insistent 'They mǐght hàve.' And I must add it because of the American habit of misinterpreting the formula. Where we say 'I cán' as a complete two-word sentence, this British formula produces 'I cán dò'; and from this the casual-style omission of the first word gives 'Cán dò.' But two decades ago when this became the motto of the newly created Construction Battalions, its American pronunciation was standardized as 'Càn dó!'

British 'Cán dò' and its congeners may have evolved by stress-reduction from supplementary clauses with the verb-base DO:

"Doth he not mend?" — "Yes, and shǎll dò till the pangs of death shake him." [*Twelfth Night*, I, v, 81]

"writes himself Armigero . . ." — "Ay, thât I dó, and hǎve dône any time these three hundred years." [*Merry Wives of Windsor*, I, i, 12] he did not consider his authority had received the support it óught to have dône {*or* dòne?} [Cecily Wyndham-Smith, *The Reason Why*, Time ed., 1962, p. 59; quoting Captain Harvey Tuckett in the 1830's]

Even the last of these is not quite the modern formula, since it is not an insistent propredicate: it is in a subordinate clause. I first heard insistent propredicates extended with DÒ from Professor Barker Fairley (who had come from England not many years before) in Toronto in 1939, and I cite him from memory in the first line below; the second citation is the earliest printed example that has come to my notice; my stress-marking of the citations from print is based on hundreds of hours of listening to British speech:

"Well, I cán dò. Is it important? Then I wíll dò."

"He was not—forgive me this very painful question—the sort of man who would have been likely to lay violent hands on himself?" — "Oh, I never thought—well, I don't know—I suppose he míght have dòne. That would explain it, wouldn't it?" [Dorothy Sayers, *Clouds of Witness* (p. 23 in the Gollancz edition), first published in 1926; supposed speaker is Lady Mary Wimsey, born in 1895, who did nursing and social work during the war and was rather taken up with new schemes for putting the world to rights; Dorothy Sayers was superb at representing speech]

"Did Frank love nature or fair play?" — "Why, he múst hăve dòne. Great figure in letters and all that; honoured by the King." [Evelyn Waugh, *The Loved One*, Penguin No. 823, 1951, pp. 51f]

"Oh, yes, Gerrie, you díd. Or if you dídn't you shóuld hăve dòne." [Angus Wilson, *Anglo-Saxon Attitudes*, Signet No. CT151, 1963, p. 149]

"Have you seen her since . . . ?" — "No, . . . How cóuld I have dòne?" [same, p. 173]

Neither of them felt any embarrassment, . . . though Larrie míght have dòne had a third party been present. [same, p. 262]

"I hope it had everything you wanted." — "It mây vèry wéll hăve dòne." [C. P. Snow, *The Masters*, Anchor No. A162, 1959, p. 18; supposed speaker is a mature academic man; note the combination of two devices]

Suspicion and envy lived in him. They always wóuld have dòne, . . . they were a part of his nature. [same, p. 44; author's comment]

"I should have expected you to discuss it with me." — "If you'd been here, I shóuld hăve dòne." [same, p. 72]

"It's worse for them both now than if she had told him that first night. I'm sure she shóuld hǎve dòne." [same, p. 106; supposed speaker is an academic man's twenty-year-old daughter]

"I hoped I could make her happy, and I háven't dòne." [same, p. 323]

"Ever seen an old man just sitting in the sun, taking it easy? It doesn't have to mean he's senile. It máy dò, but very likely he can snap out of it." [John Wyndham, *The Seeds of Time*, Penguin No. 1385, 1959, p. 172]

"All experienced nurses do it?" — "They shóuld dò." — "That is what yóu did?" — "Indeed we did." [20:28; Nurse Stronach]

Nurse Stronach: "I believed that was true." — [Very bland] "What this entry shows is that your memory was playing you a trick, does it not?"— "Apparently so." — "Óbviously so." — "It múst hǎve dòne. I cannót remember. It is a long time to remember these things." [34:32; Mr. Lawrence, betrayed by elegance, made a slip in saying 'does it not?' instead of deriving 'wasn't it?' from 'was playing.' Nurse Stronach took it as meant. My wife, a member of the same profession, would have said, 'It múst hǎve bèen.' But BE -ING is excluded from the British extended propredicates.]

Mr. Lawrence: "If you were interested in finding out his state of mind . . . you could have asked him . . ." — [Scornful] "Hís state of mind—? Of course I cóuld hǎve dòne." [91:91]

The Attorney-General: "Would you have expected these doses to do her any good?" — [Cocky] "They míght hǎve dòne." [183:169]

and having called in all the best doctors they get conflicting opinions, as one máy dò [212:195; reported speech; was this *mày dó?* In that case it doesn't belong here.]

In *Trial,* just over 3 percent of all the finites are propredicates. Of these, about 2 percent are extended by DÒ; the five examples end the series of citations above. Or perhaps there are only four: the last is dubious. These citations are assembled here by way of convincing American readers that all this is standard British English, and that it is like nothing we do with DO in American English.

This DÒ has been explained away by Canadians discussing it with me; they call it a vulgar blunder for 'do so.' My British acquaintances understand it better than that, and will need no citations, so that I can cite Englishmen in American editions.

Apart from *Trial,* my printed sources all exhibit the new freedom in British letters since the First World War; but that freedom has extended rather far: Ivor Brown, *Shakespeare:* "Hardly any of this emerges in Shakespeare's plays; it might have done had he set his comedies at home instead of . . . in Italy, Greece . . . " [Garden City, N. Y.: Doubleday, 1949, p. 281].

Finite Predication

In general, a propredicate cannot be simply nothing; yet that is what would result from the literal application of the rules so far stated, if the verb consisted of only one word. Then a meaningless DO comes in: 'And you stíll say so?' — 'I dó.' [19:28]. If the missing verb-base had -D with it, the propredicate is -D DO: 'ask you for anything?' — 'He díd.' [44:50]. Note that both these have the primary stress on the meaningless word. The reason is that truth-value is the message, as also in 'The three of you were talking . . . wéren't you?' But sometimes the message is instead the identification of the subject, as it was in 'He'll talk his head off!' — 'Must be longing to; wouldn't yóu?' Then the speaker has a free choice; either he can use DO or an auxiliary, or he can do without it. If he does without it, there is no verb, not even a propredicate, and consequently there can be no subject; the identifying of the actor is done with a non-subject pronoun (or of course a noun on occasion). Both these things can be done by the same speaker: 'I asked who administered the drugs, and the accused replied, "Í did, nearly all. Perhaps the nurses gave some, but mostly mé." ' [85:86—the Detective-superintendent in the witness-box with his notebook open before him]. In some marginal usage, however, a subject-form occurs after *as* or *than:* 'She drives faster than I.' There is no example in *Trial;* and indeed it could hardly be expected to occur in unedited English—admitting that some speakers edit while speaking—so that I have no duty to explain or defend it. The Appendix continues this with examples of journalistic inversion.

When the designation of the actor has gender—is *he, she, it, then, there,* or something that can be replaced by one of these—and the finite schema is not occupied by any of WILL, SHALL, CAN, etc., or by -D, then -s is used as if it were an occupant of the first or second position in the schema: 'I always *say* no good *comes* of these cases with no body' and 'more *is known* about drugs to-day' and 'cases where this amount *has been given*.' The unpredictable combinations are few: -s DO = *does*, -s HAVE = *has*, -s BE = *is*, -s SAY = *says* [sez]. The reason why I do not say that the verb is then 'third person singular' is (*a*) the subject may still be third-person-singular in fact without having gender: the genderless pronoun *they* is then used to signify that the gender is unknown or inconsequential: 'If anybody leaves their book at home they borrow one.' [No example in *Trial*.] (*b*) the subject may have gender by custom without being in fact singular: 'Who is there?' is what we often ask even when we are absolutely certain that the answer will be plural. [No example in *Trial*.] (*c*) I know of no cogent evidence that 'third person singular' is an English category, while gender certainly is one.

Summary

In certain languages, notably Latin, a finite verb can assert all by itself, without a subject either spoken or infallibly reconstructed by the addressee. In English, the function of asserting is a monopoly, not of the finite verb alone, but of the partnership of finite with subject; and conversely the only function of that partnership is assertion—under which I subsume the transformations of assertion into a question. The meaning of that partnership is *assertion*, or in other words *finite predication;* this is a definition.

The form of the partnership is this. Enough (perhaps nothing but the zero called meaningless DO) is used from among the possible occupants of positions in the finite schema, and used strictly in the schema sequence, to constitute a finite verb or propredicate; and this is spoken together with some word or words eligible to constitute the subject of a finite, and spoken together strictly according to the rules for relative sequence of finite and subject. To be eligible to serve as subject of a finite, the subject must belong to the list *I, we, he, she, they,* or be a noun or pronoun that is not marked for another employment; such marking may be (and I hope that this list is essentially complete, but that doesn't really matter for our present purposes) membership in the list *whom, me, us, him, her, them, my, our, his, her, their, its,* or equivalence to one of these or to *John's,* or the role of object of a verb or of a preposition, except that *what* and the *wh...ever* words can fill two roles at once; and conversely *I, we, he, she,* or *they,* is necessarily the subject of a finite, except that in certain marginal usages they can follow *as, than,* or BE: 'This is she.' If this is hard to read, that is because it is a condensation of a dozen preceding pages.

Complete Schema

The data we have accumulated call for a revised and completed schema, accommodating -s, DO, DÒ, and the seven alternatives to WILL. Here the first three items have no 'meaning' beyond the mere fact that they are at home in the English pattern for finite predication; the complete schema will therefore assign marginal statuses to them. But all the alternatives to WILL are on an equal footing with it, as meaningful items, in the sense that 'they show' conveys an essentially different message from 'they will show' and 'they can show' and these two from each other. Still, with respect to form (with implications for meaning too) there is the fact that -D combines with WILL and with three of its alternatives, but not with its other four alternatives. This state of affairs calls for something more sophisticated than the binary-arithmetic formulas on the second page of this chapter; yet the advantages of binary arithmetic are too strong to be discarded entirely, and I will save them all in the disguising form of decimal arithmetic.

Because of their meaninglessness for all our further purposes (interesting as they may have been when presented above), I assign 'zero' arithmetical value to each of -s, DO, DÒ. Then to each meaningfully different occupant of a schema position (in our newer and more severe sense of *meaningful*) I assign its own number, all different, choosing those numbers in such a way that they can be added to make sums which correspond to the various forms of

finite verbs and propredicates one-to-one. These sum numbers become identifiers for the forms; they can be used as *serial* numbers
because they run from 0 to 223 without a gap: there are exactly
224 grammatically possible finites that are significantly different,
for each verb-base that is as versatile as SHOW is. (Because they
are not significantly different, those with DO or DÒ have the same
numbers as those without; they are the sole possibilities for numbers 0 and 16. The same is true of the use of -s.) This makes English
a strong competitor to classical Greek in the subtlety and elaborate-
ness of its verb-system. The subtlety is explicated in Chapters IV
to VI. The complete schema appears two pages after this one.

This numbering is for our temporary convenience; it will not be
used after the end of this chapter. Its first employment is to help
us make sure that the schema, even without numbers, fits the
English finites exactly, and conversely. First, every finite verb or
propredicate in *Trial* fits this schema. Each can be checked into
the schema by placing its verb-base in the extreme right-hand
position, removing any suffix from that word and placing it together with the preceding word of the verb in the position where
it already appears in the schema chart, and so on until the verb
or propredicate is used up. Second and conversely, any number less
than 224 can be converted into a verb or propredicate by this
arithmetical routine: Subtract from the given number the largest
number that appears in the chart, and note the printed marker to
which that number was attached; repeat this step until nothing is
left of the given number. If the given number was an odd number,
the last marker is a base chosen from the lexicon, the dictionary-
list of verb-bases. But there are some limitations resulting from
meanings and usage restrictions.

First, if one of the steps (last or second-last) consisted of subtracting 'two,' the meaning has to be 'transitive' like the meaning
of SHOW, not 'intransitive' like the meaning of SEEM; then if 'one'
remains to be subtracted, all intransitive verb-bases are ineligible.
These are very few in English, so that it would not be worth the
trouble to set up a shortened (five-position) schema for them. Then

if one of them turns up in a marginal sentence such as 'A pleasant time was had by all,' we have a measure for its marginal status. One could go beyond this measure and say things like 'only used jocularly or in ignorance of standard usage,' but a schema can't be expected to formulate such remarks for us.

Second, certain gaps in the *Trial* data indicate that there is a euphonic limitation which can be stated in ordinary spelling thus: the sequence *be... being* is illicit, that is to say neither *be being* (as in *might be being shown*) nor *been being* (as in *has been being shown*) is in use in that kind of English. The resulting gaps are clearly visible in the column of formulas on the second page of this chapter. There are certainly a great many educated native speakers of English who would never fill such a gap, as these citations do:

"All I can say is, if I had to depend on you people to save me from being murdered with arsenic . . . I *might be being cut* up and analysed by Dr. Spilsbury now." [Dorothy Sayers, *Clouds of Witness*, Gollancz edition, p. 90; fiction—Lord Peter Wimsey quoting his talkative mother]

Nevertheless, I think it is abundantly clear that Paul was on the right track, and he *should have been being read* constantly ever since he wrote his book. [Murray Fowler, February 1964; professor's handout to his class of graduate students]

The italics are of course mine. These things seldom get into print. The complete schema predicts them and to that extent can be said to have justified them; or in other words they are certainly latent in the system of the English verb; but it is easy to see why many people, apparently most people (for that has been my experience), would reject them as normal English, though Professor Fowler, having written the second and having later noticed what he had done, says he finds no reason to disavow it.

Third, the British habit of preferring very short propredicates calls for a considerably reduced total number of possibilities, though still far above one hundred for versatile bases such as SHOW. Finally, there may well be stylistic limitations which I have overlooked; these can be neglected here, since they clearly have nothing to do with the task in hand.

-S	DO			
16 -D	8 HAVE -N	4 BE -ING	2 BE -N	I SHOW
32 WILL				I *etc.*
64 SHALL		DÒ		
96 CAN				
128 MAY				
160 MUST				
176 OUGHT TO				
192 DARE				
208 NEED				

COMPLETE FINITE SCHEMA

To derive an English verb or propredicate from the complete schema, pick up its components from the chart by this routine: Enter from the left at any level, go always to the right, never cross a line but go up or down through the gaps freely. Special rule: Don't pick up DÒ unless you already have at least one of HAVE -N or WILL or the alternatives below WILL. Special rule for most speakers: Don't exit without having picked up anything more substantial than -s and -d. (Other speakers can do that when the subject is preceded by *as* or *than*.)

Now take out the numbers and add them all together to make a label for the whole string. Then combine each hyphened bit with what follows it, according to the rules presented at the beginning of this chapter plus this rule: 0 BE = *am* if the subject is *I*. (There is no need for me to recite here what happens to the sequence *I am nȏt* or *am nȏt I*.) If nothing has been picked up after a hyphened bit (-s, -d, -n, -ing) it then vanishes as explained before.

Examples of all the resultant forms in *Trial* follow below. The number at the right margin is the number of times that form occurs there, to a total of 8038 occurrences in all.

o And you still say so? — I *do*. [19:28]........................ 83
1 I always *say* no good *comes* of these cases with no body. [159:149]..2853
2 more is known about drugs to-day than it was? — It *is*. [124:119].. 3
3 both morphia and heroin *are administered* to people [125:119]..... 249
4 You are not suggesting—*are* you?—there was any ...? [126:120] 6
5 *are* you *standing* there and *saying* as a trained nurse ...? [59:62].. 175
7 do they feel they *are being led* into the light ...? [51:55]........ 3
8 'You have experienced many such cases?' Dr. Harman *has*. [171:159] 15
9 the defence *have decided* ... not to call the Doctor. [171:159].... 319
11 cases where this amount *has been given?* [178:165].............. 63
13 You *have been* constantly *nursing* other patients ...? [18:27]..... 17
16 did the Doctor ask you for anything? — He *did*. [44:50]........ 80
17 When the Doctor *went* away, *did* he *leave* any ...? [100:99]....2143
18 Were you sent for again by her? — I *was*. [79:81].............. 11
19 morphia and heroin *were* commonly *used* as hypnotics? [124:119] 292
20 The three of you were talking in the hall ... *were* nôt you? [32:39] 6
21 the period when he *was prescribing* for her [7:17].............. 177
23 I increased the same drugs that *were being used*. [102:101]....... 5
24 had the detective-sergeant sígned ...? — He *had*. [97:97]...... 8
25 *Had* you *made* any inquíries before giving evidence ...? [119:114] 164
27 just as it *had been quoted* by the Attorney-General [83:84]....... 25
29 comatose for days and *had* not *been suffering* real pain. [11:20].... 10
32 Why doesn't he say so? — He *will*. It isn't his turn yet. [64:67]... 2
33 I *will* certainly *help* you. [89:89]........................... 115
35 unless he fears that questions *will be put* to him [213:196]....... 4
48 talk his head off! — Must be longing to; *would* nôt you? [72:75] 18
49 If there were, I *would take* them and *destroy* them. [86:86]...... 219
51 doses *would be given* during the night [135:128]............... 11
53 he *would be saying* he held a view which he cannot [148:140].... 4
56 it might have ... it *would* more probably *have* not. [190:175].... 3
57 *Would* you *have expected* the doses to have a fatal result? [179:165] 77
59 he would have thought morphia *would have been stopped* [150:141] 5
61 She *would* nôt *have been having* much [27:34].................. 1
65 I *shall elaborate* on that at the end because it is so ... [213:196] 11
80 All experienced nurses do it? — They *shôuld dô*. [20:28]........ 3

81 He told me I *should prepare* a codicil [78:80]................. 59
82 should not be heard. The A.-G. submits that it *should.* [76:78]... 1
83 In your opinion, *should* heroin *be given* to old people? [113:109].. 24
89 but dearly though one *should have liked* to hear them [44:49].... 11
91 I *should* nòt *have been surprised* if she had. [189:174].......... 1
96 I want to help you all I *can.* [94:94]........................ 14
97 the answers sound as colourless as one *can make* them [100:99].... 208
99 the only way in which justice *can be done* is by judging [193:178].. 32
101 *Can* they *be suggesting* that a—sane?—man ... would [14:24].. 1
104 it was like this or it *cannot have been;* ... [14:23]........... 1
105 Nurse Randall *can* hardly *have said* those words [34:40]........ 5
112 word you used—in the best way you *could*—to describe [58:62]... 9
113 I did not think you *could prove* murder. [88:88].............. 56
115 He wonders whether ... something else *could* not *be done?* [75:77] 20
120 They could go ... and ask ... ? — They *cóuld hàve.* [43:48]... 2
121 You *could have asked* this very helpful question [91:91]........ 27
123 others that *could have been given* with safety. [129:123]......... 7
125 they *could* not both *have been telling* the truth [224:206]........ 2
128 The prosecution cannot comment ... ; a judge *may;* [174:162] 3
129 asks if he *may put* a further question to the witness [67:69].... 90
131 So it *may be said* that death was the result [163:152].......... 6
133 something that *may be troubling* your minds. [213:196]......... 1
136 You may have found ... or you *may have* not. [213:196]....... 1
137 anything you *may have heard* outside this court [175:162]...... 21
139 the story ... *may* quite likely *have been started* by the [38:44]... 3
141 You *may* very well *have been wondering* why [193:178]......... 1
144 say that death would not ... It *might* very well. [179:165]..... 4
145 asks his Lordship whether he *might say* that the [75:77]....... 65
147 If there were ... pain, it *might* even *be given* every hour. [113:109] 15
152 Might he not ... have waited? — He *might* well *have.* [136:129] 3
153 anything else ... ? — He *might have given* hyoscine. [129:123] 34
160 Why do more, expose more ... than you *must?* [175:162]...... 3
161 you *must believe* me because I know, it was me, I was [176:163]... 65
163 it *must be shown* where the poison ... came from [12:22]...... 10
165 talk his head off! — *Must be longing* to; wouldn't you? [72:75]... 1

168 your memory was playing you a trick . . . It *mŭst hăve dŏne.* [24:32]   4

169 Mr. Lawrence . . . *must have kept* his eye upon the clock [31:38]. .   23

171 the witness's credit with the jury *must have been impaired* [27:35]   4

176 were disappearing in a way in which they *ought* not *to.* [224:206]   1

177 You might think that you *ought to go* further [224:206]........   7

179 they *ought* only *to be used* in cases of severe pain [107:105].....   2

185 prescribing more than he *ought to have prescribed* [235:215].....   4

187 it was a chance which *ought* properly *to have been taken.* [151:142]   1

193 only the very brave *dare go* near the pressroom. [28:35]........   3

209 I do not think I *need say* more about it than this [227:208].....   3

The *Trial* exclusion of the sequence *be... being* allows only 86 verb forms that are not propredicates; the British preference for very short propredicates favors roughly 34 propredicate forms; the total here is 120. The number of forms found in *Trial* is 80, or 67 percent of 120. But now note that 11 of them were met with only once each. To anyone experienced in statistics, this is a very revealing fact. It immediately shows that *Trial*, with its 8038 occurrences of finites, is still a small sample. It further allows us to estimate that a sample large enough to contain nearly all the English forms would be too large for exhaustive analysis with a tolerable amount of labor; if it contained all but three of them, for instance, it would fill a respectable library with printed books.

On the other hand, it tells us that the sample is large enough for all our present purposes. Here the argument is more complex and moreover relies on something that cannot be clearly presented before the last chapter here, where it will be shown that the choice of fillers for the second position in the schema is not a multiple choice among eight items (WILL, SHALL, . . . NEED) but is instead a set of three either-or choices—like the choice of either using HAVE -N or leaving that position empty, but with the difference that either the second position is left empty or else the complete set of three either-or choices has to be performed. With this point settled, the choice among 224 shapes (or among 172, or among 120 of them) becomes either six or nine dichotomies, and now the statistician's answer is unequivocally favorable: even a much smaller sample than *Trial* would be adequate to confirm the complete finite schema to the point where it is a fair hundred-to-one wager that a library-sized sample would still conform to the schema.

The reader can easily confirm this in one direction, namely that a great many shapes not found in *Trial* might just as well have been employed in it. Thus from the four genuine citations below he can construct the two following sentences by analogy and hear that they sound like *Trial* too.

113 I did not think you *could prove* murder.

121 You *could have asked* this very helpful question

125 they *could* not both *have been telling* the truth

209 I do not think I *need say* more about it than this

217 I do not think you *need have asked* that question.

221 They *need* not both *have been asking* the same questions.

The numbered schema is rather more convenient than any well-organized paradigm as a guide in doing this. But it also does something that a paradigm can't be expected to do: it shows that the English finite paradigm of the twentieth century could not be extended to more than 224 possibilities without either adding more 'markers' (with extension of the schema to more than six positions) or else allowing an alteration in the sequence of them so that this might be English of a later century: 'They could not both be having told the truth.' For today, the schema says this is not English, however good it might be in Serbian.

IV

Basic Meanings and Voice

Category	Tense	Assertion	Phase	Aspect	Voice	Function
Unmarked	Actual	Factual	Current	Generic	Neutral	Propredicate
Marked	Remote	Relative	Perfect	Temporary	Passive	Verb
Markers	-D	WILL *etc.*	HAVE -N	BE -ING	BE -N	SHOW *etc.*

In the preceding chapter, the items in small capitals were exhaustively dealt with as components of *form*. That job has been finished, and its results can be taken for granted from now on. The numbers are no longer needed either, though their arithmetical sequence will govern the order of presentation.

Meanings and Markers

For the remaining chapters, the topic will always be *meaning* in relation to form, and those same items will figure as *markers* of meaning. They will not be regarded as indicating 'components' of meaning, for reasons which will become clear gradually, notably the necessity of distinguishing between lexical meaning and grammatical meaning. In my treatment, the verb or propredicate has meaning as a whole, regardless of how many words it is composed of, and the markers (other than the base) affect that whole meaning without contributing referential meanings to it. I have chosen the term *marker* accordingly, and I am going to speak of 'the tense marker' and the 'assertion markers' and the 'phase marker' and so on, and of the 'unmarked tense' and the 'marked tense' and so on, actually printing -D and the others only when they would contribute to clarity.

For our purposes the term *marker* will be less misleading than any other I have encountered or thought of, except perhaps 'signal.' The markers are indeed signals for categorical meanings, but those meanings belong to the whole verb or propredicate rather than to any fragment of it. I regard this treatment as forced by the data. Some of the reasons have already emerged in the preceding chapter. For example, the simplest English way of insisting on the truth-value of the predication places a primary stress (often called 'emphatic') on the first of two or more words constituting the verb or propredicate. Now can that truth-value similarly be narrowly localized within that sequence? Certainly not, for the truth-value, insofar as it belongs to words at all, belongs to the whole partnership of subject plus that sequence of two or more words; and now if we try at least to find a place where it is particularly strong we are most likely to decide that that place is either in the subject or in the base—and yet neither of these two bears the primary stress, while the base is even missing entirely if the 'verb' is a propredicate! There are other reasons previously encountered, but this will do for a sample.

Base Meaning

The role of the base in determining the meaning of a verb is a double role: by its presence, the base is a marker of verb function (against propredicate function); and by its identity (against all the many thousands of other English verb-bases) the base alone determines the lexical meaning—the referential meaning; that is to say it identifies, within the world of possible topics, the topic now specified by the verb-base for purposes of predication. Now this lexical meaning is again double: it makes an *additive* contribution to the meaning of the whole clause, and it makes a *privative* contribution too. Since in this respect the base differs radically from all other markers, I must try to make this thoroughly clear.

The base, like any other word having lexical meaning, by being introduced into its clause *imports* into the clause the large family of all those references which it has ever had in all other sentences within the experience of the speaker or listener. That is its *additive* contribution: the complete list of all its possible meanings, all the real-world or imaginary items that it might point to, that is, refer to.

Or we can say figuratively that it 'tries to import' them all into the clause; and in that wording the statement is unchallengeable. How does it fail to import some of them? For in each spoken sentence it does fail to import most of them; it fails, in fact, to import all of them except for the one single reference that it happens to have this time. It fails by having some (nearly all!) of them knocked out again by two kinds of fatal conflict. One way is by being in conflict with the known or assumed circumstances; for instance, 'I will *show* you her picture' refers to holding a snapshot in sight for the addressee on one sort of occasion, but on another sort of occasion it refers to putting another reel of film into a projector and starting the machine, and each of these two occasions knocks out the meaning of *show* that it would have on the other occasion.

The other way that a word loses nearly all of its possible references is by their being in conflict with other words, or rather with the (surviving) references of other words, in the clause or perhaps farther away in the context—other words which each have their own families of possible references, most of them similarly knocked out. Utter conflict would knock them all out from every significant word. Before the time when *rope of sand* came into use to mean a political tie that does not bind, it was meaningless for that reason. And we can still say *rigid rope of sand* if we like, and once more each of the three words strips away all the referential meanings from each of the other two that it ever had, so that the phrase can't mean anything at all—until the time comes, if ever (perhaps from reading this page), when it becomes one way of saying 'non-existent item' like that favorite of logicians, the King of France who can safely be said to be bald.

Meanwhile, we take the language as it is. And what we find is that people habitually choose their words, and associate them as context for each other, with sufficient skill so that each knocks out enough unwanted references from others, and what little survives from the original possible importations of each word can cooperate with those surviving from the other words to constitute a useful message. All this has simply got to be done, for without it human communication would be impossible.

Now all this is obvious and hardly deserving of so much explication for its own sake. What I want it for is that it defines *additive* and *privative* as the two aspects of the meaning of a base, now that we are beginning to consider the meanings of verbs and propredicates as wholes. Ultimately I mean to use that distinction in discussing the other finite markers; for the present there is more to say about the meaning and the grammatical status of the finite base.

This will be my last justification for confining our attention, from now on, to the finite verb itself as already defined, finally dismissing all the non-finites, subjects, adverbs, objects, and other complements that have already been mentioned. I do this in two ways. First, I call attention to the fact, plainly visible in the earlier citations and their discussions, that those others either are connected by form and by meaning with the base alone, without correlation to what precedes it, or else they constitute the subject and have already been taken care of in discussing finite predication, or finally they are adverbs inserted to affect the meaning of the following latter words of the finite in ways which we have observed to be again without effect upon the constitution of the finite.

Second and finally, I show what happens if we do try to treat non-finite items together with the base. Doing that is tantamount to locating that material in the final (verb-base) position within the finite schema. When we do that, we find either of two results:

Finite grammar and the meanings of its markers leave that other material unaffected, and vice versa, so that it is idle in that position and can be dismissed again. For example, everything after EXPECT in 'Would you have expected those doses to do her any good?' can be altered without effect on what comes before it:

'Would you have expected any other outcome from such misbe-havior?' And conversely: 'I don't want you to expect those doses to do her any good.' This is the result in general; the one exception comes next and is the next important topic here.

The Copula

How would she describe Mrs. Morell's general condition? "She *was*[1] very weak." *Was*[2] thère anything else she could tell about her? "She was[3] getting[3] duller and duller in every way." Did Nurse Stronach remember anything about her on the last day she *was*[4] on duty, November 2nd, *was*[5] it not? "She *was*[6] rambling and semiconscious." — "Did you ever see any signs that she was[7] suffering[7] pain?" — "She did tell me that she had pains [righteous click] but I considered it neurotic."[8] — Then it *is*[9] the turn of the defence. Interest *is*[10] up. This *is*[11] the first cross-examination, practically the first time the voice of the defence is[12] heard.[12] What line *will*[13] thère *be*[13] to take? On the back benches not much love is[14] lost[14] for Nurse S. Something certainly is[15] expected,[15] though nobody then has any idea of how much thère *is*[16] to come.   [17:26]

"Hóme?" — "In the bag?" — "It *is*[17] a walkover all right!" — "Do you think thère *is*[18] a doctor in England who will go into that box and stand up for heroin?" — "Dr. Douthwaite *was*[19] véry sure." ... — "Wait till Lawrence deals with him." — "Yes; thère *is*[20] Mr. Lawrence." — "An international authority *is*[21] nòt a bunch of nurses who talked too much." — Last night the defence had asked leave to postpone cross-examination till to-day; now, Mr. Lawrence *is*[22] on the brink of it. [117: 113; conversation supposedly overheard; then narrative]

"Well, then, members of the jury, thère *is*[23] a long gap of some six years, and it *is*[24] right that you should[25] be[25] reminded,[25] as Mr. Lawrence re-mined[26] you, that at the end thère *was*[27] no suspicion at all about the way in which Mrs. Morell died. The nurses departed[28] and went[29] about their avocations. The estate was[30] cleared[30] up. The relatives dealt[31] with the legacies and other matters, and thère *was*[32] no suggestion that anything sinister had occurred. It *is*[33] not, in fact, until August or September, the summer of 1956, five and a half years later, that anything is[34] heard[34] of this matter. Then we know that inquiries were[35] made[35] from the nurses by Superintendent Hannam, and they made[36] statements upon which no doubt these proceedings in due course were[37] founded."[37]   [217:200; Judge charging the jury]

Mr. Lawrence submits that the next part of the detective-inspector's evidence *is*[38] damaging to his client while irrelevant to the case, and should[39] not be[39] heard.[39] The Attorney-General submits that it should.[40] The Judge rules that it *is*[41] admissible, and the court also rises.   [76:79; author's narrative]

Then the Judge says, "Mr. Lawrence, *is*[42] this one of the exhibits in the case?" — [Hurriedly, staving it off] "It *is*[43] not, my Lord, but it *will*[44] *be*[44] in due course."   [21:29]

"2 c.c. *would*[45] *be*[45] the normal dose?" — "It *would.*"[46]   [56:60]

"That accounts for the fact that what you said *was*[47] word for word the same?" — "I should hope it *would*[48] be."[48]   [96:96]

"*Is*[49] that part of the regular routine?" — "It *should*[50] *be*;[50] and it *is*[51] my routine wherever I *am.*"[52]   [42:47]

but it *is*[53] the jury alone who must come to the conclusion, Yes or No, it *was*[54] like this or it *cannot*[55] *have*[55] *been*;[55] without their verdict no man in England can[56] be[56] punished[56] for any of the great offences, and their verdict, if it *is*[57] acquittal, *is*[58] irreversible.   [14:23; author's comment]

"Nurse Randall, *are*[59] you *being*[59] frank with me over this business in the train?" — "I *ám*[60] as far as I *cán*[61] *bè.*"[61]   [64:67]

"He *was*[62] most loquacious, and always *hás*[63] *bèen*[63] since I've known him."   [94:93]

In italicizing occurrences of the *copula* in these citations, I am anticipating the results of carefully surveying all the ways of dealing with the data that remain possible after the general notion of a finite schema has been adopted—for the schema, elaborate as it is, is as open to modification as any scientific view is and must be.

The two uses of BE already there in the schema did seem to be distinct by several tests, among them the test of simultaneous use: 'he ought to have noticed when these prescriptions *were being* made that he was prescribing for quantities that were far larger than the quantities which the nurses' books show to have been given' [224:206] has -D BE -ING BE -N MAKE = *were being made*, with BE -ING used to match 'he ought to have noticed when' in the normal English way, and BE -N used because the prescriptions did not make themselves, as they could in certain other languages.

But perhaps a descriptive device could be found for merging them, and then the copula occurrences could be merged with them also to yield a single BE with three uses. No such device was found.

Then it was necessary to test the possibilities of merging the copula with one of the others. Here at least one possibility was found, but the price was too high; further, evidence then emerged sufficient to show that any other possibility would exact a still higher price in the form of confusion of categories and inexplicability of meaning. The device found has two possible varieties. (1) The BE -N marker of passive voice is rewritten BE^2 'BE number two' and the rule is added that BE^2 SHOW $=$ *shown* for every verb-base but that there is no -N suffixation when what follows is not a verb-base: *1, 2,* etc. But now look at *24* and *59:* wrongs are frequently righted in English, and letters are franked. The device fails because in English there is no lexical segregation of verb-bases: what makes a lexical item a verb-base is after all nothing but the maneuver of locating it in the base position in the verb schema. (2) The BE -N is kept as it is, and the rule is added that -N vanishes before anything but a verb-base, as it does before an empty base-position anyhow; this is more tempting, but it breaks down in the same way, and any attempt to rescue the device will result in saying that all the rest of the sentence, however many clauses it may yet contain—and it can be proved that there is no ultimate limit—must be accommodated in the base position of the schema of the first finite of the whole sentence. And it is axiomatic in all sciences that such devices are illicit: this is in fact one of the corollaries of Occam's rule.

One thing remains from this experience. Whatever is usefully recognized as a lexical unit in dictionaries (such as *10* BE UP, *30* CLEAR UP) can easily be accommodated in the base position of the schema, and the suffixation rule applies to *the first word* in use after a hyphened bit; this turns out to be equally valid for all the hyphened bits -S, -D, -ING, -N, and there is thus no extra cost incurred to take care of the copula.

Now the result is that, besides such obvious verb-bases as SHOW, the base-position of any verb schema, finite or non-finite (the gerund schema is on the first page of Chapter III, and by analogy any reader can set up the other non-finite schemas from the data in Chapter II), can contain BE X, with X $=$ an adjective, a noun, an infinitive, a clause, etc., and there is no difficulty because the forms and meanings of X are without influence upon the schema and conversely, so that the surrogate X is all that is needed in the base position and its actual value can be dismissed. Accordingly, where SHOW *etc.* appears in the schema beginning this chapter, the *etc.* can mean BE X as well as any verb-base. Why don't I simply say that this is BE and omit the X? Because plain BE is a separate possibility—an archaic one, but still alive enough to raise difficulties—as in 'Can such things be?'

There is no occurrence of this 'substantive verb' in *Trial;* it is not the copula, and for all such meanings *Trial* instead uses the copula formula of modern English with fake subject *thère: 2, 13, 16, 18, 20, 23, 27, 32:* 'Can thère be such things?' Note that *thère* (also *thĕre* in casual style, and in consultative style when it does not begin the clause; perhaps at *18* for rhythmic balance against the full *is* in contrast to the zeroed form at *17* 'It's a walkover') is not the same word as the invariably major-stressed *thêre* or *thère,* so that *20* 'Yes; thère's Mr. Láwrence' (Mr. Lawrence [also] exists, let's not forget Mr. Lawrence) is readily distinguished from 'Yes; thêre's Mr. Láwrence' (I agree with you that the defense is ready to proceed, for Mr. Lawrence is present: see him?).

The same fake subject is used in sophisticated styles with other verbs too; one example in writing and one in speech: 'Thère has now emerged a pattern in the prosecution's leading' [45:50], 'But thĕre must be sáid in fáirness to the other side that the Doctor displayed a considerable interest . . . ' [232:213]. Presumably because of the rhythmic and word-constitutional identity between this passive voice and the grammatically different copula (But thĕre must be bálm in Gílead), the fake subject is particularly common with passive voice, even in styles which exclude it otherwise than with the copula and in one standing formula: 'Thère cômes a tíme (when patience is no longer a virtue)' and the same with added markers: 'Thère'll côme a tíme when you'll be lonely, thère'll côme a tíme when you'll want me only' [popular song, ca. 1927]. More passive examples in *Trial* will be cited later.

Now there is another reason why we need X in the base position along with the copula BE, and that is the peculiar behavior of the propredicate based on BE X. In general, a propredicate is what is left when just the base (and all that follows it) is omitted, and then words can still be omitted from the end of the propredicate to leave the shorter propredicate which British usage prefers. And when the beginning of the propredicate does not replicate the earlier context's full verb, the propredicate can still be of minimum length without harm. A single example, already treated, will remind us of all this: 'Hê must be longing to; would nồt yóu?' The addressee can take this as ' . . . wouldn't yóu be longing to?' replacing *must* by *would* and taking the rest from before; and if the speaker had said 'He must be longing to; wouldn't yóu bè?' he would have been misleading the addressee: see next.

The copular propredicates follow another routine. To form the maximum copular propredicate, the speaker simply omits X: 'So when you write "awake" on the last afternoon before she died, she *must have been awake?*' — 'She *must have been.*' [38:44]. But whenever, as in this instance, the propredicate replicates the preceding verb from its beginning, it can be clipped to the minimum: *45, 46:* '2 c.c. *would be* the normal dose?' — 'It *would.*' However, when the beginning is not replicated but altered (by using a new auxiliary) the copular propredicate is always maximum, never clipped otherwise than by omitting the X of BE X:

42, 43, 44: "Mr. Lawrence, *is* this one of the exhibits in the case?" — "It *is* not, my Lord, but it *will be* in due course."

47, 48: "That accounts for the fact that what you said *was* word for word the same?" — "I should hope it *would be.*"

49–52: "*Is* that part of the regular routine?" — "It *should be;* and it *is* my routine wherever I *am.*"

54, 55: Yes or No, it *was* like this or it *cannot have been;* . . .

59–61: "Nurse Randall, *are* you *being* frank with me over this business in the train?" — "I *am* as far as I cán bè."

62, 63: "He *was* most loquacious, and always *has been* since I've known him."

This pattern is rigid in all the spoken material in *Trial*, and in nearly all the other material too, for example the one citation above that is not in quotation-marks: *54, 55.* I have found exactly one exception in the whole book:

> He is not, though, as it turns out, one of the expert witnesses, volunteers paid a daily fee whose function it will be to analyse the facts, but a witness who *is* here because he *must.* It is the Doctor's partner.   [99:98; author's comment or narrative]

From the time I first saw this passage, I felt there was something wrong with it; more than a year later, after reading it many times, I found out why it sounded wrong in a book whose tone is otherwise conversational: it is in written English, and spoken English requires 'who is here because he múst bè.'

Incidentally, this strikes me as a neat little example of how subtle the grammatical distinctions may be that even five-year-old children maintain flawlessly while adult learners of a foreign language are baffled—and their teachers at a loss for an explanation. Not that the explanation would help the learner directly; but if the teacher knows what's behind the puzzle he can devise teaching procedures that have a fair chance of success. I was puzzled by this one too, although a native speaker of English since early childhood and a professional grammarian for half my lifetime, when a French friend of mine five years ago said, 'He isn't in town just now but he will Thursday,' and I found myself unable to explain to him, another grammarian, why that wasn't English for the intended meaning *il y sera.* Finding the adequate explanations is largely a matter of luck, of course: this one was found only while preparing the printer's copy of this treatise from rather mature drafts in which the explanation was lacking.

And it is not simply an unnecessary frill, this disparity between passive propredicates and copular propredicates; and indeed as a frill it would be rather surprising in a grammatical system otherwise distinguished for economy of means. Let's look at *48* again: if it had been permissible to shorten an altered copular propredicate, this could have been 'I should hope it would' and equivocal. The disparate rules protect us from this: we all know that a one-word altered propredicate (not replicating the beginning of the antecedent full verb) can't be copular, in the only sense of 'knowing' that really matters, so that if he had said, 'I should hope it would,' the addressee would necessarily have taken this to mean 'I should hope it would account for that fact.'

Passive Voice

Now some more citations, some in passive voice and certain others for contrast, added to those on pages 85, 86:

"Heroin is[64] not often used."[64]   [39:45]

"We must always put down the amount of drugs we use[65] in case we are[66] asked."[66]   [41:46]

"Later she dozed off, but soon became fidgety again, and was[67] given[67] ANOTHER WHOLE GRAIN of heroin."   [46:51]

"When this 5 c.c. injection was[68] given[68] what was her condition?" [48:53]

"Later that night Dr. Harris was[69] telephoned[69] for."   [53:57]

As for the theory of the accumulation of morphia in the body, the whole thing breaks[70] down, doesn't it, because it has[71] been[71] dissented[71] from by two doctors, Dr. Ashby and Dr. Harman.   [197:181; reported speech]

Mr. Lawrence must get full marks for audacity. — He is[72] buckling[72] down. . . . Only the Doctor, one perceives[73] now, still looks[74] smug and pleased. "Let us look[75] at your first day."   [22:30]

The jury does[76] nót look[76] like much, the Judge looks[77] kind (one hardly likes to look[78] at the accused)   [25:33; author speaking the witness's thoughts]

"And in addition to her physical disability she showed[79] signs of cerebral irritation?"   [30:37]

The nurses, the defence suggests, brought a distorted tale to the investigators, and this is[80] shown[80] up by the entries and omissions in their own nursing records.   [57:61; reported speech]

"That was the occasion when you three police officers, Pugh, Hewitt and yourself [it sounds[81] no more gracious than the superintendent's 'you'] went to the house at half-past eight in the evening. [Square look] What were yóu doing at all that night and by what authority?" — Detective-superintendent [if stung, it does[82] not show;[82] quite smoothly] "I was supervising . . ." [92:92]

Some of the seats have[83] emptied.[83] People have crept out into the hall [60:63; author's narrative]

There comes one of the rare moments when the lid seems[84] to fling[85] open and one feels[86] one has at last a glimpse of the workings of the wheels. [65:68; author's comment]

Now Mr. Lawrence has his try. She looked after Mrs. Morell at intervals, he begins,[87] because the nurses kept[88] on changing, "and some of these changes were[89] brought[89] on by Mrs. Morell's own bad temper?" [30:37]

"And I dare say you know this, don't you, that for months and months the regular treatment in the form of morphia and heroin injections hardly varied?"[90] . . . "And it is also quite plain, isn't it, that on that night the usual injection was[91] stepped[91] up?" [53:57]

"After your three years' service as her chauffeur you benefited[92] under her will?" [74:76]

"And on August 24th there was yet another will?" — There was, and this proved[93] to be the last will, and in it the Doctor was[94] left[94] the oak chest with silver and, if Mrs. Morell's son predeceased[95] her, the Rolls-Royce car. — The prosecution leaves[96] it at that [79:80]

The term *passive voice* here refers to the grammatical form that has the marker BE -N; the term *passive meaning* is here used as a rather general term which the examples will have to define for us as they accumulate; but the expression 'the meaning of passive voice' is rather a strict term definable as the meaning, whatever it turns out to be, that is strictly correlated to the use of the passive marker. This hair-splitting is I am afraid somewhat mysterious at this point; the reason for it will emerge later and cannot be anticipated here.

If we begin with *12, 15, 25, 30, 34, 35, 37, 39, 40, 56* (leaving *14* for my readers to cope with as best they can later), we have ten examples of passive voice which no grammarian can quarrel with, either as to form or as to meaning. And it is worth noting immediately that at least three sequences of verbs (*25, 26* and *28, 29, 30, 31* and *34, 35, 36, 37*) here demonstrate how smoothly the passive verbs fit in amid the non-passives; the reason why I do not call the latter 'active' will be evident later.

Now what sort of meaning do these passives have that is not shared by the corresponding non-passive verbs? The pairs *25, 26* and *35, 36* show that the difference *can* be that particular reversing of meaning for which we possess no better definition than just such pairs—and equivalent pairs in Latin and German and many other languages: the *you* with *26* is the victim of the reminding (this is in turn the definition of the term *victim* which I need for our present purposes), and that same victim is designated by the other *you* with *25*. With *25* the designation of the victim is the subject of the passive verb; for identically the same event and the same dramatis personae (only real instead of hypothetical, which makes no difference here) the designation of the victim is in the role of object with *26*.

Since this is the same event and the same victim, there is necessarily a compensatory shift of meaning between the verbs *25* and *26*. Now that shift is customarily ascribed entirely to the passive verb, the non-passive meaning being taken as basic or unshifted, and that custom can serve us here too for the present. Accordingly, we can say: The meaning of such a passive voice is the meaning that *25* has and *26* does not have, with the understanding that precisely that meaning recurs in an indefinitely large number of other pairs. This definition is the best we can get, simply because it is axiomatic: trying to improve on it would be like trying to keep a fire in a wooden stove. If this treatise were written in Tagalog, or in any of a great many other languages, that would be like keeping the fire in a metal stove.

So far, this is only the definition of the *primary* passive meaning. Now the primary passive is the only kind that is in use in most neighboring languages and in classical Latin; and Latin can serve as our typical language of that sort. From Caesar we learn that people *incolunt* 'inhabit' a region and that they *appellantur* 'are called' various names, and we feel sure of grasping how all that works. But then Latin takes us into mysterious regions inhabited by deponent verbs where English can't follow; and English wanders off into another area where patterns are called idiomatic to excuse us from understanding how they work. Instead of calling them that, I will give them names and display their employment; to go beyond that would again be trying to keep a fire in a wooden stove.

From the citations and other sources I construct various non-passive and passive sentences; the labeled display will serve also as a set of definitions.

NON-PASSIVE: She *left* him a car in the will. (-D LEAVE = *left*)
NON-PASSIVE: In the will she *left* him a car.
PRIMARY PASSIVE: A car *was left* him in the will. (-D BE -N LEAVE)
PRIMARY PASSIVE: In the will a car *was left* him.
SECONDARY PASSIVE: He *was left* a car in the will.
SECONDARY PASSIVE: In the will he *was left* a car. (*94*)
NON-PASSIVE: They *gave* her a whole grain of heroin.
PRIMARY PASSIVE: When this heroin *was given*, . . . (*68*)
SECONDARY PASSIVE: She *was given* a whole grain of heroin. (*67*)
NON-PASSIVE: They *telephoned* for Dr. Harris.
PRIMARY PASSIVE: Dr. Harris *was summoned*.
TERTIARY PASSIVE: Dr. Harris *was telephoned* for. (*69, 71*)
TERTIARY PASSIVE: I *was being made* a tool of. [C. P. Snow, *The Masters*, p. 291]
NON-PASSIVE: You *can't sit* down in such a dress.
TERTIARY PASSIVE: Such a dress *can't be sat* down in.

The last example comes from a magazine and accompanied a photograph of a movie actress resting, leaning back against a nearly vertical slant board, probably padded. A strictly intransitive verb can have no other passive than such a tertiary one. There is no *Trial* example. The preceding *Trial* example (*69*) can be called a primary passive only at the expense of saying that TELEPHONE FOR is a lexical unit, a more specific synonym for SUMMON. And when the verb-base is not only surely transitive but is also provided with a designation of the victim, while the subject does not designate the actor but instead an entity involved in the event in a way that has to be specified by a preposition, the result is again a tertiary passive: the Snow citation above.

For the primary passive and that alone, a comprehensive description of the employment could be: The subject of the verb designates
the victim in the event rather than the actor. That would be appropriate to every Latin or German passive; for when there is no
victim there is no subject either: 'Bei Tisch wurde über die Nach-
barschaft gesprochen.'

For all the English passive verbs together, a comprehensive
description has to be made broader by claiming less: *The meaning
of the passive is that the subject does not designate the actor.* This is in
fact all that can be said about the meaning. As for the form of predication, that is to say the partnership of subject and verb, what
we have already learned is still valid: *The subject designates some
entity which is intimately involved in the event.* Then we can cover
the whole range of three passives by remarking: (1) When the subject designates the victim, the pattern is called *primary* passive
voice. (2) If the non-passive clause would designate not only the
victim but also another entity designated without a preposition (or
with the empty preposition *to* of equivalent value: 'They gave
heroin to the patient'), but now the designation of that other entity
is the subject, the pattern is called *secondary* passive voice. (3)
When the subject of the passive verb designates an entity involved
in the event in a way that *has to* be specified by a preposition, the
pattern is called *tertiary* passive voice. The preposition then is
placed after the verb as if it were an adverb.

Remaining designations of entities intimately involved in the
event are placed just as with non-passive verbs with one exception:
the actor-designation is preceded by the preposition *by*, and the
combination is a group-adverb placed as a clause-adverb (*not* as
adverbs are placed that modify the verb alone): *71, 80.* But this
designation is seldom requisite and is most usually omitted. On
the other hand, in a secondary passive clause the victim *must
always* be designated, and its designation follows the passive verb
in the usual object-position: *67, 94.* This situation, paradoxical from
a Latin point of view (What! A passive verb with an accusative?),
together with the adverbial placement of the tertiary passive's

preposition, is presumably what led to the custom of calling the *secondary* passive 'idiomatic' and leaving it unexplained but labeled (for this is its traditional label), and to the customary denial of the existence of the *tertiary* passive: by merging its preposition with the verb-base into a lexical unit, it could be explained away as a primary passive.

To sum up: The English passive is a word-order device. It is marked by BE -N to show that its subject is not the actor, and that is all the device 'means.' The rest is automatic.

Unmarked Passive

The meaning of passive voice (defined by the marker BE -N) has now been adequately treated. One variety of that meaning is *primary passive meaning*. Now if there were in English an exact mutual relation between this form and this meaning, we could say that each is always matched by the other, in every clause where either occurs. We have already seen how that breaks down in one direction: the form has other meanings, the secondary and tertiary passive meanings. Next we observe how it breaks down in the other direction: the *primary* passive *meaning* (defined by the fact that the subject designates the victim) may be effective in the absence of the marker BE -N. At the same time, the examples will define *active* meaning for us:

ACTIVE MEANING: she *showed* signs of cerebral irritation (*79*)

Primary passive voice: this *is shown* up by the entries (*80*)

PASSIVE MEANING UNMARKED: if stung, it *does* not *show* (*82*)

ACTIVE MEANING: one hardly likes *to look* at the accused (*78, 75*)

PASSIVE MEANING: the Judge *looks* kind (*77, 76, 74*)

ACTIVE MEANING: *Can* you *prove* it was murder?   [81:83]

Primary passive voice: in my submission it *is proved*   [200:184]

PASSIVE MEANING: this *proved* to be the last will (*93*)

ACTIVE MEANING: I *increased* the same drugs   [102:101]

Primary passive voice: the usual injection *was stepped* up (*91*)

PASSIVE MEANING: the . . . treatment . . . hardly *varied* (*90, 89, 92*)

Other examples that could be included here are *3, 70, 72, 81, 83, 85, 86, 87, 95, 96,* most of them not in just those sentences but still in other possible sentences, for instance 'it feels rough' for *86.* But in most instances there is the difficulty that we can't be sure how much of this ought to be ascribed to the lexical meanings of the verb-bases and how much to the grammar. As to the meaning of the unmarked passive, little can be added to what the examples more or less clearly show; but it may as well be pointed out that it is the sort of meaning that European languages generally express with a reflexive construction: *it does not show* can be 'il ne se montre pas, il ne se fait pas voir' in French and 'es zeigt sich nicht' in German.

One of our favorite uses of this unmarked passive is rather rare in *Trial,* presumably because situations calling for it are absent from the episodes, common as they are in general. Everyday examples are 'it steers hard' said of a car that is hard to steer because of mechanical friction, 'it buttons in back' said of an old-fashioned dress-shirt, and this in *Trial:* 'It wouldn't wash.' — 'It'd wash better than this' [180:166].

Usually there is an adverb (*hard, in back, better*) for the way the event takes place, and the formula is most convenient for characterizing the victim accordingly. Indeed, for teaching English as a foreign language, the formula could be taught with profit in some such terms. But for what I want to point out next, a single example will serve, or a single pair. The single ambiguous example 'She teases nicely' would serve for certain purposes; but what I need here is a single fairly well balanced pair like this:

They're selling like experts.
They're selling like hotcakes.

The second is equivalent in meaning to the explicit but less ordinary, rather pedantic 'They are being sold like hotcakes.' In all three sentences, *like* signifies that the last word is fairly comparable to the *subject;* and now that that is settled, we can say that experts are of course human and thereby well qualified to be actors in a selling process, while hotcakes are frequently sold and thereby well qualified to be victims, and that that is what settles the choice between active meaning and primary passive meaning for *are selling*. To the contrary, if we say 'They *are being sold* like experts' we must be talking about a slave-market; and thus we see that the natural-victim quality of hotcakes can intervene decisively when the verb is not marked with BE -N, but the natural-actor quality of experts can't prevail when it is so marked.

For general grammatical theory our profit is this: When the verb remains unmarked as to voice, its meaning can be either active or primary passive; but when it is marked, the possibility of active meaning has been eliminated and the passive meaning remains *as a residue*. More briefly: The meaning of BE -N is that it deprives the verb-base of active meaning: the meaning of BE -N is not additive but *privative*. A privative item like BE -N does not have referential meaning (which would be a pointing to components of the world of things spoken of) but rather, to coin a term for use only here, it has 'anti-referential' meaning (which is an elimination of some of the pointing). 'They are selling' points ambiguously both to active components of the referential world and to passive components thereof; 'they are being sold' points only to passive ones; therefore, what BE -N has done is not the adding of passive meaning but only the canceling of possible active meaning.

Privative Marking

Background for this argument was presented early in this chapter under the heading *Base Meaning*, with a first definition of the pair of terms *additive* and *privative*. There it was pointed out that a verb-base or any other sentence-component possessing lexical meaning makes an *additive* contribution of its own possible references to the referential meaning of the whole sentence, and at the same time makes a *privative* contribution by fatally conflicting with most of the possible references of other lexical items in the context—items which in turn make their privative contribution by fatally conflicting with most of the possible references of the verb-base (or whatever) first mentioned here, meanwhile making their own additive contributions.

The meaning of a verb-base, then, is *both* additive and privative; but the meaning of the voice-marker BE -N is *only privative*, not additive. The marked voice is *passive voice;* but its marker does not mean 'passive,' it means only 'not-active.' And that is what all the other markers do too, throughout the whole schema: they are all privative in their effect on the meaning of the verb or propredicate. That will be demonstrated for each, as they are considered one at a time in later chapters. But because the demonstration for the voice-marker has been so very explicit, even verbose, the other demonstrations can be cut very short.

One allusion to a later chapter may still be useful here as an example: It will be demonstrated that the meaning of the tense-marker -D is 'not-actual' rather than positively 'past' or the like. Now since in English 'actual' extends not only over contemporary time but also indefinitely on into real future history, the meaning 'not-actual' has the effect of *confining* the references to the historical past (together with unreal hypothetical occasions: pp. 121–125). This is a confining, not a positive pointing to the past, because positive pointing is otiose: the unmarked tense can adequately point to the past anyhow, as has been repeatedly exemplified in citations here couched in the 'historical present tense,' as it is traditionally called. Accordingly, -D is also a purely privative marker.

Now let's take one last look at the verb-base. In that earlier discussion, before the twin terms *additive* and *privative* came up, I said, "The role of the base in determining the meaning of a verb is a double role: by its presence, the base is a marker of verb function (against propredicate function); and by its identity (against all the many thousands of other English verb-bases) the base alone determines the lexical meaning." In accordance with the privative value of the markers generally, this ought now to mean that the base as a 'marker of verb function' is also a privative marker. Is this view reasonable?

The answer I give is 'Yes,' and the evidence is all there in the preceding chapter where propredicates are discussed. When the verb-base is in use, the references are confined by the lexical meaning of the verb-base alone, so that further references (for example those further references brought in by a following noun designating the victim in the event) can only be brought in by appropriate further words. But when the verb-base is not in use, there is no such confining; there is only the confining that the addressee freely does himself—and it was demonstrated there that his freedom is vast. Thus, just as the privative value of -D could be called a 'confining' above, so also the confining effect of the verb-base actually used is a privative effect on the total meaning.

In its capacity of function-marker, then, the verb-base is a purely privative marker like all the other markers. In that capacity, it exhibits just one noteworthy difference between it and the others. In every other case, the *marked* verb-shape is *less frequently used* than the simpler unmarked shape, as the numbers of occurrences show when they are picked up from the right-hand margin of those pages, late in Chapter III, where all the finite forms are numbered in sequence and exemplified, and are appropriately grouped and added up. The grouping is to be in accordance with the components (1, 2, 4, 8, 16, etc.) of the left-margin sequence-numbers, of course. Now when we add up the occurrence-numbers of the verbs and of the propredicates separately, this is particularly easy: the labeling numbers in the left margin which are odd numbers belong to verbs, the even numbers belong to propredicates. The result here is that nearly 97 percent of the occurrences are verbs, just over 3 percent are propredicates: here and here alone, the marked shape is the more frequently used one.

Considering the mission of language in normal life, there is nothing surprising in this, of course. But there are certain people, for example the present writer, who would regard this as a significant measure of the difference in meaning between verb-bases and all the other markers in the schema. Naturally, this tells us more about such people than it does about the English language.

V

Aspect, Tense, and Phase

Category	Tense	Assertion	Phase	Aspect	Voice	Function
Unmarked	Actual	Factual	Current	Generic	Neutral	Propredicate
Marked	Remote	Relative	Perfect	Temporary	Passive	Verb
Markers	-D	WILL *etc.*	HAVE -N	BE -ING	BE -N	SHOW *etc.*

The meaningful form of an English finite verb derives from the use and the non-use of the markers of the six categories. The function category has dozens of thousands of possible markers, SHOW, etc., including the copula BE X as the most frequently used verb-base of all (28.3 percent of all the finites in *Trial* are based on the copula); the finite lacks this marker (so that its function is pro-predicate) in 3.2 percent of the *Trial* occurrences. The voice category has a unique marker which is employed in 9.9 percent of the finites in *Trial;* the number of finites with unmarked passive meaning is comparable, perhaps somewhat smaller: exact counting is impossible for them because very often the passive meaning could be called lexical (essential to the verb-base) instead of grammatical.

Aside from the non-use of the passive marker with intransitive bases, and aside from the marginal restrictions such as the rules of euphony which prevail in certain personal or local usages, the use or non-use of every marker is independent of, unconstrained by, the use or non-use of any other marker. This has made it possible to complete the discussion of the *function* and *voice* categories without reference to any other category, and again it will be possible to leave the *assertion* category unmentioned until all the others have been discussed.

In theory it is equally possible to discuss each of the categories *aspect, tense,* and *phase* by itself, for they are all similarly autonomous. But there is more than one reason why I choose to cover them all in a single chapter. The discussion of phase can begin late in this chapter, and it will be too short to constitute a respectable chapter by itself. Aspect and tense are best discussed together, not because they are essentially correlated (the perfect autonomy of all the six categories is beyond question) but because the discussion of either would be rather uninteresting if the other were disregarded as we have a theoretical right to do.

Taking them together, we shall see some of the most fascinating details of English idiom emerge, especially a split, unique or almost unique among the languages of the world, between two sorts of verb-base meaning (and of course contextual meaning: the double additive-privative meaning of all verb-bases [Chapter IV] makes this qualification automatic), the *process* verbs and the *status* verbs. In the citations below, the reader should disregard phase for the time being.

The Judge came[1] on swiftly.   [2:13; author's narrative]

". . . You are[2] charged[2] with the murder . . ." — And that, too, is[3] expected.[(3)] It is[4] what all is[5] set[(5)] for—nobody, to-day, is[6] here by accident— yet, as they fall,[7] the words in the colourless clerical voice consummate[8] exposure. — "Do[9] you plead[9] Guilty or Not Guilty?" . . . — "I am[10] not guilty, my Lord." — It did[11] not come[11] out loudly but it was[12] heard,[12] and it came[13] out with a certain firmness and a certain dignity . . . and it was[14] said[14] in a private, faintly non-conformist voice. It was[15] also said[15] in the greatest number of words . . .   [3:13]

Outside in the street, the Old Bailey is[16] sustaining[16] a siege this morning. . . . Here, inside the court, there is[17] more than silence, there is[18] quiet. [4:14]

A trial is[19] supposed[19] to start from scratch, *ab ovo.* A tale is[20] unfolded,[20] step by step, link by link. Nothing is[21] left[(21)] unturned and nothing is[22] taken[22] for granted. The members of the jury listen.[23] They hear[24] the tale corroborated, and they hear[25] it denied; they hear[26] it pulled to pieces and they hear[27] it put together again; they hear[28] it puffed into thin air and they hear[29] it back as good as new. They hear[30] it from the middle, they hear[31] it sideways and they hear[32] it straight; they all but hear[33] it backward again through a fine toothcomb. BUT THEY SHOULD[34] NEVER HAVE[34] HEARD[34] IT BEFORE. When they first walk[35] into that court, sit[36] down in that box, they are[37] like people before the curtain has[38] gone[38] up. And this, one is[39] conscious from the first, cannot[40] be[40] so in the present case.   [4:14]

"A word about this doctor. You will[41] hear[41] that he is[42] a doctor of medicine and a bachelor of surgery, that he has[43] a diploma in anæsthetics, holds[44] an appointment as anæsthetist to a hospital and has[45] practised[45] anæsthetics for many years. With his qualifications and experience, you may[46] think[46] perhaps it is[47] safe to assume the Doctor was[48] not ignorant of the effects of drugs on human beings. . . ." — It goes[49] on in a sort of casual boom. — Now Mrs. Morell was[50] an old woman . . . A widow . . A wealthy woman . . . She left[51] £157,000 . . . She was[52] eighty-one years old when she died[53] in November 1950 in her house at Eastbourne. In 1948, she had[54] a stroke and her left side became[55] paralysed. The Doctor was[56] in charge. She was[57] attended[57] by four nurses; and these nurses will[58] give[58] evidence. They will[59] say[59] they never saw[60] Mrs. Morell in any serious pain. The Crown will[61] also call[61] a Harley Street authority. This medical man will[62] tell[62] them that he has[63] formed[63] the opinion that Mrs. Morell was[64] suffering[64] from cerebral arteriosclerosis, in ordinary language [here the Attorney-General lowers[65] his voice a confidential shade], hardening of the arteries.   [5:15]

Here come[66] detailed figures. The listening mind is[67] pulled[67] up. Figures can[68] be[68] stumbling blocks. These are[69] intended[69] to sound large. They do[70] sound[70] large. Jotted down (roundly), they come[71] to . . . One hundred and thirty-nine grains of heroin into ten months make[72] how many grains, or what fraction of a grain, per day—? . . . — "You will[73] hear[73] that these drugs if administered over a period result[74] in a serious degree of addiction . . . Whý were[75] these drugs prescribed[75] to an old lady who was[76] suffering[76] from the effects of a stroke but who was[77] not suffering[77] from pain?"   [6:16]

"Nearly a year later the Doctor called[78] on Mr. Sogno without an appointment and a conversation took[79] place," a sharp look over spectacles at the jury, "which you may[80] think a very curious one. The Doctor told[81] Mr. Sogno that Mrs. Morell had[82] promised[82] him her Rolls-Royce in her will and that she now remembered[83] that she had[84] forgotten[84] this, and that she desired[85] to leave him not only the Rolls-Royce car but also the contents of a locked box at the bank, a box which the Doctor said[86] contained[87] jewellery. The Doctor went[88] on to say that though Mrs. Morell was[89] very ill, her mind was[90] perfectly clear and she was[91] in a fit condition to execute a codicil. Mr. Sogno proposed[92] that they might[93] wait[93] until Mrs. Morell's son came[94] at the week-end, but the Doctor suggested[95] that Mr. Sogno should[96] prepare[96] a codicil and that the codicil could[97] be[97] executed[97] and later destroyed[97] if it did[98] not meet[98] with Mrs. Morell's son's approval. Was[99] not that," another swift look at the jury, "rather an astonishing suggestion? It showed[100]—did[101] it not?—a certain kéenness?" — The Attorney-General appears[102] to be an earnest pleader. When he poses[103] a rhetorical question, as he frequently does,[104] it has[105] a dutiful rather than dramatic sound. — Once more Mr. Sogno went[106] to see Mrs. Morell, and Mrs. Morell made[107] another will leaving the Doctor the chest of silver and, if her son predeceased[108] her, the Rolls-Royce and an Elizabethan cupboard. "Perhaps you might[109] think[109] it significant and sinister that during the period when he was[110] prescribing[110] for her these very substantial quantities of morphia and heroin the Doctor was[111] concerning[111] himself so much about her will and telephoning[111] her solicitor." [7:17]

The Attorney-General held[112] up an object. It is[113] always slightly startling when an actual utensil of the outside world, not a chart or a document or a photograph of one, appears[114] in a court of law. It does[115] in fact quite often, yet it brings[116] with it a hint of lurid impropriety. It causes[117] what is[118] called[118] a stir; people in the gallery try[119] to stand up and are[120] instantly suppressed.[120]   [9:19]

"Six years later when a detective superintendent from Scotland Yard was[121] making[121] inquiries, he asked[122] the Doctor about this cremation certificate." [10:20]

There is[123] now a definite sense that counsel is[124] building[124] something. He goes[125] on, treading very lightly. "I am[126] thinking[126] of what another of the nurses said[127] when she gave[128] her evidence at Eastbourne. She said,[129] 'I knew[130] what I was[131] injecting[131] at the time but I cannot[132] remember[132] now; but whatever I gave[133] was[134] written[134] in a book and passed[134] on to the next nurse.' "   [20:28]

Before anyone quite realizes[135] what is[136] happening[136] there is[137] somewhere a kind of exercise-book and it has[138] gone[138] from counsel to the usher and is[139] now in front of Nurse Stronach, who at once begins[140] to turn the pages. There is[141] a hovering interval during which the Attorney-General is[142] on his feet but has[143] not said[143] anything, the national Press have[144] leapt[144] their box and are[145] massing[145] by the door, Mr. Lawrence hangs[146] fire and Nurse Stronach is[147] reading.[147] Nobody pays[148] the slightest attention to the Doctor in the dock. Then the Judge says,[149] "Mr. Lawrence, is[150] this one of the exhibits in the case?" [21:29]

"The prosecution wants[151] to finish by Wednesday." [72:75; conversation]

Mr. Lawrence: "My Lord, I object.[152] I do[153] not think[153] . . . the contents of the earlier wills can[154] be[154] evidence unless they are[155] properly proved."[155] [78:80]

"I suggest[156] to you that when you said,[157] 'This is[158] the list . . .' or words to that effect, the Doctor was[159] across the room and just said[160] quite casually, 'Oh, yes?' " [93:93]

"While you were[161] telling[161] my learned friend about the prescriptions and all the rest of it, when you were[162] giving[162] that evidence, you were[163] refreshing[163] your memory all the time from your notebook?" — There is[164] indeed an open notebook on the witness-box. — "Not my notebook. The superintendent's. I did[165] nôt write[165] any notes about the conversation." — Mr. Lawrence, leaning forward, "Am[166] I REALLY HEARING[166] WHAT YOU ARE[167] SAYING?"[167] [96:95]

"Do[168] you call[168] that an independent record?" [97:96]

"Can[169] we put[169] it this way—thirty or forty years ago both morphia and heroin . . . were[170] used[170] . . . ?" — "I accept[171] that." . . . — "I put[172] it to you that they are[172a] not dangerous if properly used?" — "I do[173] nôt agree[173] if you refer[174] to heroin." [125:119]

"I do[175] not question[175] that." [146:138]

"I do,[176] therefore, direct[176] you as a matter of law that there is[177] no evidence . . . " [208:192]

"Another unusual feature—I think[178] it is[179] fair to call it unusual—is[180] that the accused himself has[181] not gone[181] into the witness-box. I say[182] it is[183] unusual, but then in many respects this is[184] an unusual case . . . " [212:196]

"And that last interview at the very end, of which I remind[185] you, at which he was[186] stunned and shocked . . . " [235:216]

"What were[187] the drugs like on the tray?" — Sister Mason-Ellis: "They were[188] very small tablets in very thin tubes like a straw you drink[189] from." — "Táblets?" — "You dissolve[190] them in water . . . before making an injection." [41:47]

"Now watch—I drop[191] the tablet into this warm water, and you see[192] it dissolves[193] quite nicely." [no such occasion in *Trial*]

"The doctor is[194] not obliged[194] to enter anything into that space, if you follow[195] me, Dr. Walker?" [43:48]

"You know[196] that atropine is[197] a kind of antidote?" [46:51; conversation]

"It looks,[198] does[199] nôt it, as if the doctors . . . were[200] coping[200] with the case very well?" [54:58]

"What is[201] the normal dose of paraldehyde, do[202] you know?"[202] — Nurse Randall: "It depends[203] how you give[204] it, but I think[205] 4 c.c. or 5 c.c. is[206] a very large dose." — . . . "Is[207] it a dangerous drug?" — "It helps[208] to make you sleep." [56:60]

"Are[209] you standing[209] there . . . and saying[209] . . . that when you wrote[210] those words . . . they were[211] intended[211] to mean something quite different . . . ?" [59:62]

"I suppose[212] I wrote[213] it down quickly." [59:62]

"Nurse Randall, are[214] you trying[214] to be as accurate as you can[215] be?"[215] — "I am,[216] sir." [61:64]

Temporary Aspect

Plainly we must distinguish between *tense* used (however strangely) as a grammatical term on the one hand, and the everyday word *time*. Now *present* time will serve as our name for a very sharply restricted sort of occurrence: The speaker confines his remarks (or else we can infallibly sort out those of his remarks which are confined) to what is being done, or simply is, there where he can and does report on it currently: *214, 216, 212,* but not *213;* and to make sure of a pure sample we can exclude *215,* for the time being at least, and perhaps exclude it permanently from the category 'present time' because we noted in Chapter II (p. 27) that sharply focussed time is apt to call for 'as accurate as you are able to be.'

Then the first clearly defined group of citations—consistent in form and in meaning both—is a small group here: *166, 167, 209, 214.* One tradition calls this 'progressive' and holds that the specifying done by the marker BE -ING adds the meaning that the action is making headway; but that is preposterous in the face of *209 standing* and others. Another name, more recent and especially in use in Great Britain, is 'continuous'; this emphasizes the point that the other verbs (lacking BE -ING) are apt to refer to isolated acts occurring again and again: *114–120.* There is a grain of truth in this, but there are too many counter-examples: *9, 172,* and many others here. It has been called 'imperfect' with a name borrowed from Latin and Romance-language grammar; but then there are too many counter-examples in both directions: moreover, the English marked aspect is not confined to a past tense as those are. It has a resemblance in form, and a frequent coincidence in reference, with a Spanish (and Portuguese) formula: *lo que Usted está diciendo* 'what you are saying' (*167*). But both this Iberian formula and the Slavic imperfective differ crucially from the English marked aspect: they are specifications of the nature of the event, while the English marked aspect instead specifies something about the predication. I have borrowed the Slavic technical term *aspect* for lack of a better, but the English marked aspect has an essentially different meaning.

I have also anticipated the following demonstration in naming it: I call it the *temporary aspect*. Let me begin the demonstration by transforming all the interrogative examples into statements, thus *166* into 'I am [*or* You are] hearing' and so on for the rest, and taking *216* as 'I am trying, sir.' Now I propose that this means, or rather its use of temporary aspect means: Assuming that the predication is completely valid for the time principally referred to, then it is 99 percent probably valid [a 99-to-1 wager in favor of its validity would be a fair wager] for certain slightly earlier and later times, it is 96 percent probably valid for times earlier and later by somewhat more than that, and so on until the probability of its validity has diminished to zero [the actor then is doing nothing, or doing something other than trying, or is not-trying, or is trying something else] for times sufficiently earlier and later.

This takes so many words to say in this way because it is an English axiom: BE -ING is an elementary signal known to all five-year-old native speakers, and there is no other normal way to say it, so that any attempt at presenting its meaning without begging the question by using it (note that I have not used it above outside the square brackets) inevitably leads to extensive circumlocution.

The temporary aspect does not necessarily signify anything about the nature of the event, which can be essentially progressive or static, continuous or interrupted, and so on; instead it signifies something about the validity of the predication, and specifically it says that the probability of its validity diminishes smoothly from a maximum of perfect validity, both ways into the past and the future towards perfect irrelevance or falsity.

Now once this is understood, I can allow any modification which does not utterly destroy that pattern, and there will be at least once an interesting modification: In combination with marked phase, marked aspect signifies such a probability-diminution only into former times, while towards subsequent times it does not consistently signify anything—so that in this direction the probability can diminish abruptly or not at all: 'I've been watching you.' With all such non-destructive modification allowed (and I must admit that 'You're always bothering me' is a teaser), I sum up this whole exposition with the single term *temporary aspect*.

In Chapter IV it was shown that the voice marker has only a privative meaning, and the promise was made that the other finite markers would turn out to behave the same; all of them have purely privative meaning. The unmarked aspect, that is to say, could then equally well predicate with temporary validity, so that 'You are not feeling well?' [25:33] in the temporary aspect could instead be said in the generic aspect: 'You don't feel well?' And this is indeed equally idiomatic English, with no shift of meaning at all: to feel well or not feel well is something which we all assume is temporary anyhow, so that Mr. Lawrence's temporary solicitude is here expressed redundantly, and the temporary aspect of his verb is exactly correct but unnecessary. Accordingly, we must not be disconcerted when we later find that the temporary aspect marker is often omitted, especially when the reference is not strictly to present time.

First, however, let us complete the survey of present-time verbs and their meanings, especially as their profiles of validity along the time-scale differ from the temporary-aspect profile. For this comparison, a consistent graphic representation may be useful, and for all readers who have a visual habit of thinking (like the present writer and in fact the majority of the population) this device will be most illuminating.

The graphs have been assembled on one page in the Appendix. The left-to-right spread of each graph represents the passage of time, earlier time to the left and later time to the right of that central point which belongs to the exact time for which the predication is principally valid. Graph A expresses just what I first defined the temporary aspect to mean. As in all the graphs, the solid base-line represents zero validity (perfect irrelevance or falsity), and the greatest height reached by the dotted-line validity-probability graph represents perfect validity (100 percent probability) while lesser heights represent proportionately diminished probability that the predication is valid for other times than the principal time. No specific time-scale is needed. The full width of the graph, or somewhat more (since there may not be room on the page for everything, but the rest can be imagined by the reader) represents the span of time of interest in each utterance—say two seconds or less in some sentences, many millennia in others: 'History teaches us that man *is growing* no wiser' at one extreme, and 'It'*s breaking!*' said of a chair at the other extreme.

The only four present-time temporary-aspect verbs in the citations (*166, 167, 209, 214*) have now been taken care of, and the obviously temporary-aspect propredicate *216*, which needs no completed marker BE -ING because its -ING has vanished with the missing base TRY, as explained in Chapter III.

Generic Aspect

Most often the unmarked or *generic* aspect has the monotonous profile of Graph B: *74, 114–120, 155, 189, 190;* that is to say, most often in *Trial* as a whole or in any unbiased large sample of English; the citations above are a deliberately biased sample exemplifying one other meaning of generic aspect as fully as convenient. The eleven examples, so far, fitting Graph B are what has most often been entirely misleadingly called 'present tense for universal time' or the like, meaning for example (*74*) that addiction resulting from these drugs is being reported equally for all times of interest. That this piece of folklore is false to the constitution of English communication is easily shown. It can be refuted from both directions.

First, universal-time reporting in English is not done that way, but instead like this: 'You now understand that you must not discuss with anybody at all the evidence you *have given or are going to give*' [49:54] with a gap that is regularly filled when requisite without using the generic aspect: 'have given or are giving or are going to give,' or with *and* instead of the *or* that is there brought in by the negative *must not discuss*. The statement about those drugs in our normal universal-time formulation would be: 'these drugs if administered over a period have always resulted in a serious degree of addiction . . . ' most likely without going on to say with pedantic precision ' . . . and must be expected to continue doing so.'

Conversely, it is clear that 'They were very small tablets in very thin tubes like a straw you *drink* from . . . You *dissolve* them in water . . . ' (*188–190*) does not actually impute any drinking or any dissolving to any actor, not even to the *you* that is *on* in French and *man* in German. Presumably such drinking and such dissolving had occurred, for otherwise she would not have said that; but that is a material implication (from knowledge of how things happen in this world) and not a grammatical implication. Sister Mason-Ellis cannot be held responsible for the past events, for what she was doing was not reporting events but characterizing things: such a straw and those tablets.

This is the meaning here, and in fact most often the meaning, of the generic aspect in referring to what is happening, or simply is, there where the speaker can and does report on it currently: the 'present generic aspect'; and it is used similarly with references outside of this 'present time,' as will be shown later. This is the *characterizing* generic aspect, represented by Graph B with a level line of dots representing constant maximum probability of validity for all times of interest. This does not mean that the events which the verb-base, in this context, are apt to specify have always occurred and still are occurring and always will; it means *characteriz-*

ing, for the time principally referred to (here the speaker's tenure in the witness-box), by specifying *hypothetical* events that are adequately characteristic. For understanding this point, it may be helpful to remember that when such characterizing is confined to a certain previous era the formula USED TO is employed, as described in Chapter II, the last item under the heading *Quasi-Auxiliaries*.

When, instead of characterizing, the speaker *reports* an event that is entirely confined to the time of speaking, he uses the generic aspect. Nearly always, he is able to report it with utter confidence because he *is making the report valid* while uttering it: *9, 152, 156, 168, 171–176, 182, 185 I remind you*. We note that the Judge could have said 'I am reminding you'; and that would have meant that the reminding was not necessarily entirely confined to the act of speaking these few words: some of the reminding may have been spread out earlier and later within the paragraph, or in fact all of it could have been delayed yet a while: 'I am reminding you of that again this evening' said in the morning to one's spouse.

When the speaker is himself responsible for the event, as in the citations listed just above—and this is true under the usual understanding that we have a right to transform a question (*168*) into a statement 'I call that . . . ' and a negative statement (*173*) into a positive one 'I agree' before we scrutinize it for our present purposes—the meaning is utterly specific and exact: it is what I call *asseveration*, meaning that the speaker makes his statement valid *by* speaking it.

An easy relaxation of this strict condition gives us the use of generic aspect for *demonstration*—the mode of speaking which we have learned to describe more or less in Shakespeare's wording: "Sute the Action to the Word, the Word to the Action." Since the courtroom episodes in *Trial* are pretty thoroughly confined to speaking of what occurred elsewhere (note the message at *112–120!*), I have had to supply a plausible set of examples, *191* and *193*, and, if you like, *192* also. There is a gradation of meaning here, of course, with *191* at the opposite extreme from *192*, but we see that it makes no difference in the choice of aspects.

Privative Aspect Marking

Both the above-described asseveration and demonstration uses of generic aspect are adequately represented by Graph C, or, if you like, the topmost dot of the vertical column: printed alone, that would not have been sufficiently conspicuous, and furthermore it is possible without disturbing the purport of my message to argue whether the single dot or the whole column is the adequate graph.

In any case, we now have two graphs (B and C) for the meaning of the generic aspect—and we must not be surprised if we can establish still others. These two already seem to contradict each other. But this is not a conflict, not an antinomy. There is no contradiction between meanings because the generic aspect *has no meaning of its own*. It gets its meaning entirely from the context; and for our purposes the 'context' includes the lexical meaning of the verb-base, so that for example the asseverative use is confined to 'verbs of saying.' Again, for the moment it is unnecessary to argue about whether *195 if you follow me* fits Graph B or Graph C.

Another example: I have suggested that 'I don't feel well' can be adequate for the explicitly temporary message of 'I'm not feeling well' on occasion, and similarly 'I feel dizzy' for 'I'm feeling dizzy.' This means that the validity-probability Graph A, which is specifically appropriate to the temporary aspect, is one of the possible graphs for the generic aspect. That is, of course, why I call it *generic*.

Now it has become clear what the marker BE -ING of the temporary aspect does: from among all the possible aspectual significances of the generic aspect, it singles out one *by obliterating all the others*. In one word, its significance is *privative* as defined early in Chapter IV. And, as suggested before, we ought to be ready for this, since we have already seen in Chapter IV that the *voice* marker has only privative significance, and even in Chapter III that the verb-base itself (with respect to its use or its non-use in the propredicates, though not quite in the same way with respect to its identity) is purely privative as a *function* marker.

Choice of Aspect

How—or if you like 'from what motives,' for our observation of how this is done is as close as we shall ever come to determining human motives—how does the speaker choose between the aspects? A complete answer must await consideration of tense at least, but we already know enough so that we can answer for present-time use, that is, for contemporary comment.

It appears that when such a temporal limitation of the validity of the predication as Graph A represents—a limitation in terms of probabilities rather than any absolute limitation (for instance that of Graph C)—is requisite, the speaker uses the temporary aspect. What he accomplishes thereby is a *framing* of his predication's validity: he says that the extent of its validity fits some such frame, filling it up but not spilling out beyond it.

The frame is both broader than the instantaneous duration of the validity in asseveration or demonstration and narrower than the enduring validity in characterization; moreover, it is not a strict but a probabilistic frame. This latter characteristic is perhaps not entirely clear to such readers as are not accustomed to reading probability-graphs. The best I can do in that case is to offer Graph A in another version but with identical significance: Graph A' in which the diminishing probability toward times aside from the time principally referred to is represented by the diminishing density of a cloud of dots. The two mean exactly the same.

The difference between this, the privative significance of the English temporary aspect, and the Iberian formula already mentioned (p. 107) or the Romance-language imperfect tense or the Slavic imperfective or 'durative' aspect, aside from the fact that they all characterize the event while English here characterizes the predication, is that in those others the duration is primary (and in the Iberian formula the intensity of commitment of the actor to the event) while in the English temporary aspect it is the probabilistic *limitation* in time that is the primary significance. The meaning of our temporary aspect is *limitation of duration*.

Basically this limitation is in terms of probability; but it can be converted into a pair of strict time-limits by adequate context: 'during the period when he *was prescribing* for her these very substantial quantities of morphia and heroin the Doctor *was concerning* himself so much about her will and *telephoning* her solicitor' (*110* and *111*). The pair of limits, already provided for probabilistically by the temporary aspect, is here sharpened into precise limits by *during the period when*. Compare *35–37;* the timing is equally exact there, but there is no pair of limits. We can return to this later; here we still have a chance to find out more about the use of the aspects with reference to present time.

When such limitation is requisite, the speaker uses temporary aspect. It is a limitation on the temporal span of validity of the predication. Often no such limitation is requisite; even more often it would be positively harmful: the message would be spoiled. Clearly there are two converse cases in which this is true.

(1) The message would be spoiled if the validity were not allowed to spill over the edges of every such frame: *194–199* and many other examples, of course including all the *characterizing* uses of generic aspect. After all, such characterizing would necessarily be weakened if any time-limit were set.

(2) Sharp focussing on a single time is part of the message; allowing the validity to spread out within a temporary-aspect frame, however narrow, would then spoil the message: *asseveration* and *demonstration* uses of the generic aspect are obvious cases.

The first case is not always so obvious; in fact, our experience with adults learning English as a foreign language shows that it is one of the most difficult peculiarities of the language. There is a long list of verb-bases—apparently some hundreds but presumably fewer than a thousand—whose most usual lexical meanings are incompatible with the temporary aspect; and unfortunately for the foreign learner it is very difficult to see the reasons for that incompatibility. Of all the books that have come to my attention, W. Stannard Allen in his *Living English Structure* [pp. 78f] does the best job with such verbs:

Certain verbs are practically never used in the Present Continuous [present temporary aspect], even when describing the real present. — These are mainly verbs of condition or behaviour not strictly under human control; consequently they go on [their referents occur] whether we like it or not. Take an obvious example: "I *see* a man outside; he *is looking* at me." — Although these are both "real" present, the verb "see" [in this sense] is never used in the continuous form. I have no control over what I see; I see all the time my eyes are open; but I can decide what to look at . . . — The following is a fairly complete list of these verbs not usually found in continuous forms. — see, hear, smell, recognize, notice; remember, forget, know, understand, recall, recollect, believe, trust (=believe); feel (that), think (that); suppose, mean, gather (=understand); want, wish, desire, refuse, forgive; care, love, hate, like, be-fond-of, adore, be-angry, be-annoyed, be-pleased; seem, signify, appear (=seem), belong-to, contain (=hold); matter, possess, consist-of; have, be (except in continuous passive [temporary passive]). — In general these verbs are only found in the continuous form when we wish to give special emphasis to their particular application to this very moment [not so: that is rather the meaning of that Iberian formula]; more rarely as an immediate future. Most of these exceptional uses are more frequent in spoken English; notice in particular the present continuous with "always" or "forever," meaning "at all times, but especially now at this moment." — *Examples:* "You're always seeing something strange." — "Your mother is forever refusing to do something or the other." — Here are a few more exceptional continuous forms. — I'm seeing him tomorrow. — We are certainly not recognizing such a fantastic claim. — I was just thinking it might be a good idea . . . — Are you forgetting your manners? — Are you supposing I'm going to take you out? — How are you liking it (=enjoy)? — We are thinking of going out. — Now you're just being silly.

The insertions in square brackets are of course mine. Now Allen's treatment is good as far as it goes, but it needs to be cleaned up and extended. The "fairly complete list" is deceptive both in size and in complexion. When I first saw it, I sat down and doubled the list off-hand in about half an hour of musing; that brought it up to eighty-five, and I have reason to believe that there are surely over two hundred of them. Allen's list is deceptive in complexion, in that most of the words in an extended list resemble in meaning a small minority of those in his list, namely his *seem, signify, appear, belong-to, contain, matter, possess, consist-of, have, be.*

Status Verbs

It is from the greater part of the extended list that I take a name for all those that are repugnant to the temporary aspect; and it is among them that we can find those few which reject it until absolutely forced to accept it—I don't really mean to anthropomorphize them: I say it this way for brevity. Such a verb-base is RESEMBLE. Apparently there is only one way to use BE -ING with such a base: there has to be context which makes the validity equivalent to an *intensity* of resembling, so that the temporary validity opposes a greater or lesser intensity to those at other times or else so that the intensity either increases or decreases (not both) throughout the temporary span: 'The baby is resembling his father more and more' or 'rather less now.' Some speakers (I have no idea of what share of the English-speaking world they constitute, for lack of data— after all, the diagnostic situations are so rare as to afford little opportunity for observation) reject even this sort of use of BE RESEMBLING; and I have never known a native speaker of genuine English to employ it beyond that limit, either with RESEMBLE or any other of the verbs of this semantic class, numerous as they are.

Years ago I called some of them 'private verbs,' too narrow a term. Since writing this chapter I have seen them called 'statal verbs,' in Akira Ota, *Tense and Aspect of Present-Day American English*, Tokyo: Kenkyusha, 1963. I call them *status verbs;* I am still looking for a better name, but this one is adequate. Beyond certain coincidences, this has nothing to do with the technical term *stative verb*, a term used in describing many of the world's languages, notably Chinese. The English verb-bases which, like RESEMBLE, are used only as status verbs are relatively few. Vastly more numerous are the verb-bases like SEE, HEAR, MATCH, CONTAIN, which are used both as status verbs and as *process* verbs, in the latter use joining the dozens of thousands of verb-bases which are always process verbs. The process verbs can be thought of as 'ordinary' verbs needing no separate and segregated discussion; the status verbs, and the verbs used both ways on various occasions but now being considered only in their use as status verbs, need a thorough one.

Take HEAR as a typical verb-base used both ways. As a *process* verb it has a number of fairly distinct meanings, as in 'The Judge is hearing a case just now; you'll have to wait,' 'I hope to be hearing from him soon,' and as many others as we care to distinguish. But as a *status* verb it seems to have exactly one meaning, the same in 'I can hear it now' and 'You will hear that the maximum quantity of heroin which should be prescribed in a period of twenty-four hours is a quarter of a grain' [11:20] and 'At certain assertions his mouth compressed slowly and hard, . . . as if prompted by an inner vision that did not correspond to what he had to hear' [6:16]. The Allen description of such a meaning, quoted earlier, is perfectly adequate, as it also is for verbs like CORRESPOND which do not necessarily involve any person in their reference; there is no compelling reason, moreover, for not carefully adjusting and spreading his description of that sort of meaning over the whole list of status verbs, and it wouldn't matter if his original formulation vanished meanwhile. Yet there is no need to do that here; it will be enough if we hold fast to the single label *status verb* and let our notion of its class-meaning develop without strict control, since our principal concern is with the outward grammatical form.

Of course we are concerned also with the class-meaning of status verbs; but our concern is essentially satisfied when we have noted that it is regularly a *single* meaning for each status verb, no matter how many meanings the same verb-base may have when used as a process verb. Those two *Trial* citations for the status verb HEAR come from a courtroom scene, but it is clear that neither of them suffers even the slightest deflection of meaning on that account, for instance towards that one of the other HEAR meanings which is found in 'The Judge is hearing a case just now.' Again, the second citation contains also the status verb CORRESPOND, and there we make another negative observation: there is no trace of the process-verb meaning that is found in 'They correspond regularly—weekly letters, in fact.'

In the further discussion we can therefore safely merge the exclusively status-verb list that includes RESEMBLE with the status-verb meanings (one for each verb-base) of the bases available to both uses. For these latter bases, it is incidentally interesting how widely divergent, in most instances, the unique status-verb meaning is from the various meanings the same base has as a process verb, and it seems only fair to say that English has here achieved a triumph of economy in the exploitation of its vocabulary resources.

From now on, *status verb* in this discusssion indifferently means either a verb-base like RESEMBLE or else the single status-verb meaning of a verb-base like HEAR or CORRESPOND. One grammatical peculiarity has been noted so far. A status verb in the temporary aspect necessarily refers to an *intensity* of meaning that is either temporary or is temporarily waxing or waning, and this derived meaning *replaces* the basic meaning of the verb. This may be thought sufficient evidence to transfer the verb in such use into the other class and lodge it among the process verbs, but I need not press the point.

Another similarly specific relation between form and meaning of a status verb is that it cannot have future reference without an explicit time-shifter such as WILL or BE GOING TO. With substantially any process verb we can say things like 'Don't worry: he leaves next week'; but 'Don't worry: the baby resembles his father next year' is not English. This turns out to be a fairly economical criterion for sorting out the status verbs when we need to.

Finally, a rough semantic subdividing of the status verbs. There seem to be two main groups: (1) psychic state, including the specific perceptions (SEE, HEAR, etc.) and the intellectual and emotional attitudes (BELIEVE, UNDERSTAND, HATE, LIKE, REGARD, etc.); (2) relation, such as the relations of representing, depending, excluding, and so on; it seems interesting that HAVE and the copula BE are status verbs of this sort, so that possession in English is a status: 'He has a farm' and 'He is a farmer' are usually synonymous.

The Allen list quoted on an earlier page consists mostly of status verbs of the first kind, and just after quoting it I sorted out his status verbs of the second kind. Others of the latter kind are: *make a difference, fill, complete, suit, resemble, extend, reach, adjoin, border on, fail, differ, include, exclude, preclude, comprise, complicate, vitiate, demonstrate, show, intersect, be supposed to.*

Now a certain interest surely attaches to the standing these words have in English-speaking culture and for the members of it. My supplementary list are mostly rather mature words, yet not esoteric ones: the member of the culture has a fair chance to learn substantially all of them by the time he reaches voting age (though for most people not much earlier) while no normal person learns half the process verbs (*hydrogenate, scarify,* etc.) in his lifetime. Again, new ones are hardly ever invented except by mathematicians, the specialists in *relation.* The *psychic state* verbs begin to be learned in earliest childhood; in more mature years one adds only their learnèd synonyms to the personal vocabulary: *perceive, comprehend, detest.* In short, learning the status verbs is tantamount to learning the ropes of English-speaking culture.

For relation verbs it is obvious, and for psychic-state verbs it is now not too hard to see, that the (single!) meaning of each status verb is such as to reject the time-limited validity of the temporary aspect. 'That makes no difference' is not a process, not an event that essentially proceeds but is now frozen for our inspection; it is instead a relation between 'that' (whatever it is) and the whole world we live in: it doesn't happen, but simply *is so.* Equally truly, 'I drop the tablet into this warm water, and you *see* it dissolves quite nicely' (*192*) is not a process of seeing; it doesn't mean seeing is proceeding within time so that it could be made temporary by using the temporary aspect. Instead, this perception, a kind of psychic state if you like, is a sort of *relation* between the beholder and the dissolving tablet.

Thus the sorting-out of status verbs into relation verbs and psychic-state verbs is perhaps an expository convenience but not a logical necessity. Again, there is evidence of this sort of equivalence in what psychologists call the 'projection' which leads from 'I feel warm' to 'This fur coat feels nice and warm,' so that the seemingly private meaning of 'I feel good' is now perhaps unmasked as a relation between one component and another component (or others) of the ego.

We need no more of this sort of speculation for our further purposes; rather, it is time to close the books by listing the status verbs from the citations we have been using. They are: (1) *12, 24–34, 41, 73* HEAR; *19* BE SUPPOSED TO; *39* BE CONSCIOUS; *46, 80, 109, 153, 178, 205* THINK; *48* BE IGNORANT; *60, 192* SEE; *69, 211* INTEND (projected into the other group by passive voice?); *85* DESIRE; *130, 196, 202* KNOW; *151* WANT; *195* FOLLOW; *212* SUPPOSE. (2) *4, 6, 10, 17, 18, 37, 40, 42, 47, 50, 52, 56, 68, 89–91, 99, 113, 123, 137, 139, 141, 142, 150, 154, 158, 159, 164, 177, 179, 180, 183, 184, 186–188, 197, 201, 206, 207, 215* BE; *43* HAVE; *44* HOLD; *70* SOUND; *71* COME TO; *72* MAKE; *87* CONTAIN; *100* SHOW; *198* LOOK; *203* DEPEND. Now even without counting in the copula, these outnumber the occurrences of process verbs; the copula occurs just about as often as the other status verbs together (a couple more occurrences); and the psychic-state verbs occur nearly four times as often as the relation verbs. The sample is somewhat biased, having been selected partly to illustrate everything about aspect, but even so these statistics are revealing in what they suggest about normal communication.

Tense

Form always dominates in these discussions, and meanings are subordinated to form in the sequence of topics, though with an occasional reversal for convenience. Now tense is our category in which a finite verb (non-finites can have voice and aspect and phase, but not tense) is either marked with -D or lacks that marker. Then by definition there can be only two tenses.

In the folklore, an English verb has a good many tenses; this notion does not derive from our 224 or (neglecting function, assertion, and even voice) at least eight, but instead from Greek, Latin, and Romance-language grammatical tradition. The corresponding reaction to our dichotomy is that we are disregarding the tense-paradigm of the English verb.

What we are actually doing is making adequate use of the term *tense* at last. This is not my invention; for over a century grammarians have been saying that English (like the other Germanic languages and Russian and many others) has only two tenses: past and non-past. That is not quite our dichotomy, as we will see; but a maximally useful dichotomy has to be recognized somehow and we need a name for it. If we took over the folklore sense of 'tense,' we would have only occasional rather literary uses for it, and another name would have to be invented for the dichotomy which is our proper topic.

The unmarked tense will be called *actual* and the marked one *remote*. The latter name fits the meaning precisely. The modern English remote tense has the categorical meaning that *the referent* (what is specified by the subject-verb partnership) *is absent from that part of the real world where the verb is being spoken.* In some languages, there are several kinds or degrees of such absence; for instance, on the time-scale alone, apart from other kinds of absence, French and many other languages have two possibilities: past time and future time. On this scale, English has only one, for English treats future time as not remote from the present occasion, and remoteness in time in English is always categorically past time. This is one English kind of remoteness, to be discussed presently; first it is expedient to clear away the other kind: *unreality.*

The modern English remote tense has exactly the same form, no matter whether the meaning is unreality or past reality, with a single exception: replacement of *was* by *were* when the meaning is unreality. Cultivated American usage (except for some archaic class or regional usages) is rigorous about this replacement. The corresponding British usage is not rigorous in the same simplistic way, but I am uncertain about all the details. There is many an 'If I was you' in print, but such evidence has been impossible to evaluate because I have found it only in creative writing, including the journalistic. From listening to British speech I feel able to offer only one tentative generalization: *vivid* presentations of unreality freely use *was*, while a technical-philosophical unreality calls for *were:* 'If I was you' but 'If I were in your place.' C. P. Snow, *The Masters*, has 'It looks as though I was being made a tool of' [p. 291], supposedly spoken by a mature academic man.

Hyperurbanisms are roughly equally common in British and American usages. The commonest type is created by wording a real past condition as if it were unreal and contemporary: 'Yes, I admít she was in my room; but what if she wére?' instead of the 'what if she wás?' used when not suffering from insecurity—either a temporary insecurity on such an occasion or a persistent habit deriving ultimately from the insecurity of some mentor. The only example in *Trial* is in reported speech, so that we can't determine whether the Judge or Mrs. Bedford is responsible for it: 'The Judge says that if the book *were* going to be evidence the Attorney-General *had* a right to see it' [21:29].*

Unreality specified by using remote tense consists in a posited substitute for accepted reality being essentially in conflict with the reality. The conflict is mutual—each contradicts the other absolutely. But in that conflict the accepted reality of course prevails—the English constitution provides that we do not live in a dream-world but rather in a world of accepted realities, including the Electoral College and the Stewardship of the Chiltern Hundreds, and our literature singles out for blame those people who take refuge in the subjunctive. This normal resolution of the conflict banishes the posited substitute into the kind of remoteness called 'unreality.' This is not a shift on the time-scale and therefore cannot be graphed in the Appendix; for that matter, neither has it anything to do with truth or validity or probability.

* Conceivably this is a trace of Mrs. Bedford's background and derives from the German subjunctive of reported speech (indirect discourse); but that is altogether unlikely in view of my being unable to find even one other trace of German influence in her English—if anything, there is at worst a faint trace of French in it here and there, but that is to be expected in cultivated British English anyhow. The Penguin edition of *Trial* (Penguin Book No. 1639: *The Best We Can Do*) has this inside its front cover: "Sybille Bedford was born in Charlottenburg, Germany, and was privately educated in England and France. Most of her life has been passed in Provence, London, New York, and Rome, but she is at present living in England and working on a new novel."

Unreality, then, emerges vanquished from the irreconcilable conflict with reality, and the reality prevails without needing to be put into words separately. This means that the exact contrary of the referential meaning is strictly implied by every unreal clause. Thus if Mr. Lawrence had spoken the following sentence by itself, he would have been prevaricating; for his *we* subsumes the addressee, and he in fact possesses the reports and 'can see the truth' adequately, while this bare sentence strictly implies that we do not possess the reports and further that we can't see the truth: 'If only we *had* these reports *now* we *could* see the truth.'

Now that is exactly what he said; but does that make him a liar? No, it doesn't. He is indeed trapping the witness, his addressee; but he is doing it legitimately—he is not 'entrapping' her, which would never be permitted in an English-speaking court—for he is employing that exact wording within a confirmation-question offered by him as a fair interpretation of what she has been saying all along:

Nurse Stronach: "We reported everything, a proper report is written day and night." — Mr. Lawrence [speed again] "As distinct from your memory of six years later, these reports would of course be absolutely accurate?" — [Sturdily] "Oh yes, they would be accurate from each one of us." — "So that if only we *had* these reports now we *could see* the truth of exactly what happened night by night and day by day when you were there?" — "Yes. But you have our word for it." — Mr. Lawrence: "I want you to have a look at that book please." [20:29]

Since, with one exception (which does not figure in this citation), the identical remote tense forms serve both for real past and unreal contemporary meaning, the question naturally arises how the two are kept apart in English. The answer is a clear though not particularly neat example of the general English habit of economy of means and devices.

First, the remote modals *would, should, could, might,* as explained in the next chapter, more often have unreal contemporary than real past meaning. Therefore the listener's expectation, based on his experience, is in favor of unreal contemporary meaning when he

first hears any one of them, and he will shift to a real-past interpretation only when forced by contextual evidence; indeed, in
modern English communication he never shifts to reality as a
possible interpretation of *might*. Second, in a two-clause sentence
like the one cited, the simple *if* matches the interpretation of the
one-word remote-tense *had* to the unreal *could see;* also, quite
often the unreality is forced, as it is here by the *now* used to exclude real-past meaning.

There are other equally efficacious frames. One is *as though* (nowadays more often *as if* in American), which both forces a following
remote verb to be taken as unreal and allows the other verb to be
taken as real (in either tense), for example in the sentence with
which I introduced that typical hyperurbanism. The same is true
of *What if . . . ?* and *It's time . . . ;* the latter usually with *high
time* in British English and *about time* in American, oddly reversing
the usual rule for allocating understatement and overstatement to
the two regions.

But the commonest pattern of all is the two-clause sentence in
which the conclusion uses an unreal modal, as in the citation. That
could serves perfectly; *might* is commoner; *would* is the one used
most. Edited English introduces *should* to replace *would* when the
subject is *I* or *we*. There is just one *Trial* example of such a *should*
[240:220], and I have never heard one from an Englishman in my
hundreds of hours of listening (for instance, I once shared lodgings
for two months with a man from whom I certainly would have
heard it if it were authentic English), but I have been privileged
to hear it from Americans as a marginal usage (specifically what
we call 'affected') and it is established in one kind of New England
usage. For the complete theory and demonstration of why 'If she
were here I should show it to her' is not to be expected in modern
British English, and numerous examples of the pattern 'If she
were here I would show it to her,' see Chapter VI.

Occasionally we make sure of unreality in the *condition* clause by
introducing an unreal modal there too: Mr. Lawrence: 'If this
sleeplessness *would have been allowed* to go on, she would have col-

lapsed' [127:122]. In popular American usage, this is routine. The other extreme would consist of not using a modal in either clause: "If the bowl *had been* stronger, my tale *had been* longer." This is now obsolete; any present-day use of it ranks with using Latin words midway in an English sentence, except that it can still be recognized in the petrified unreal conclusions *had rather* and *had better*. In active use, then, our unreal conclusions today always employ an unreal modal, and our unreal conditions are more likely to have one (nearly always *would*) in less cultivated usage—and perhaps also in the relaxed speech of certain cultivated persons, which may be the explanation for the Lawrence example last cited. It is unique in *Trial*.*

Past Tense

Remote tense with real past meaning is all that is left of the remote tense after the unreal meaning has been cleared out of the way as I have done above to keep it from interfering with further discussion here. For convenience, I will use the non-technical term *past tense* in any discussion where it must be mentioned frequently, though I do this with considerable fear of being misunderstood as subscribing to the popular fallacies about tense in English. To do the same with 'present tense' is impossible, as will be made thoroughly clear later on; I will stick to the term *actual tense*.

Even more than in European languages generally, past tense is the normal narrative pattern in English; in *Trial* it is the pattern for detached narrative: *1, 50–57, 60, 64, 75–77,* most of *78* to *111, 112, 121, 122.* It mixes in comfortably with the actual tense: *126* to *134,* serving then to keep all the times distinct: *156* to *160; 169* to *174; 185, 186; 187* to *190; 198* to *200; 209* to *213.*

But when the speaker gets so deeply involved that he forgets where he is as he speaks, and tends to place himself rather at the scene he is narrating, the actual tense may be used with the exact meaning of the past tense:

* Perhaps that is why it got a unique response from Dr. Douthwaite—see page 51, citation [128:122], spoken thoughtfully as if to himself.

Dr. Harris [quite at ease now; almost with animation] "One *wóuld have* to consider the long-term effects, but it *is* not always easy to know how long that length of time *is going* to be. . . . In a case where one *is* oniy *going* to see the patient for a few days one *would* not *change* the treatment that *had been instructed.*" [107:104]

Mr. Lawrence [wholly second violin] "Looking at the nursing notes up to the spring of 1950, what *do* you *say is* a fair summary of the position?" — Dr. Harman [trenchant and urbane] "I *should say* she *had recovered* from her stroke as far as she *is* ever *going* to; that she *hås reached* a stage at which one *might describe* her as being partially crippled, but there *are* no signs of anything further about to happen." — Mr. Lawrence: "What *do* you *say* about the continued medication at that period . . . ?" — [Lively] "The clearest thing about that *is* that by that time it *has been going* on for a year and some months . . . It *would* certainly *have* to be continued even if it *was producing* no good. I can see no evidence it *was producing* any harm." [172:160]

We note that this mixture of tenses is what we get from two educated and urbane British physicians when either of them is "at ease" and speaking "almost with animation" or "lively." This means that Mrs. Bedford's use of the same device is not to be dismissed as somehow foreign to English narrative, as perhaps a slavish imitation of the 'historical present' which is at home in French and the languages of the Continent generally.

Narrative Aspects

But this English version of 'narrative in the historical present tense' is not simply a speaking of the past as if it were the present, as if the narrator were on the spot reporting on the current events by synchronizing his speech with the action and giving it to us just as radio sports announcers do but now with the trifling difference that the 'radio' link is not only measured in miles but also in years. It will take me four pages to demonstrate this, but the proof will be rigorous.

If this were almost any language but English, no such proof would be possible. But English has the category *aspect;* further, although Slavic aspect would be of no use for such a proof because it characterizes the events themselves, English aspect does serve as a criterion because it instead characterizes the distribution, along the time-scale, of the probability that the predication is still valid when the attention is shifted to earlier and later times, as has been pointed out on earlier pages of this chapter.

Specifically, the result is that there are two different sets of habits for choosing whether or not to use temporary aspect. When the speech refers to the things going on at the time of speaking, the choice is made as previously described. But when it instead refers to things that happen in the authentic past (when the aspects are chosen for normal past-tense narration) there is a notable alteration in the habits of choice.

This can be stated as a simple transformation rule, thus: Every generic aspect of here-and-now reference remains generic with real past reference; but the temporary aspect is changed to generic aspect *for each event that advances the plot* of the narrative and remains temporary for each event that is rather *background to the plot-advancing events* without itself advancing the plot.

Plainly this cannot be an automatic alteration such as could be managed by an electronic computer, for the narrator is a living person who exercises Free Will in assigning the events to these two roles; indeed, we can't always penetrate the narrator's motives for the particular choices, and yet the evidence is clear enough to show that the above transformation rule corresponds exactly to the resultant meanings: contemporaneous but background events in the temporary aspect, plot-advancing events in the generic aspect, as well as the generic aspect used as always for characterizing rather than narrating and the generic aspect that is obligatory with status verbs.

Naturally, when asseveration is narrated instead of being quoted it remains in the generic aspect because its meaning is unchallengeably plot-advancing: 'He pronounced them man and wife' so that they could live happily ever after.

On a certain occasion later reported in *The Times*, certain things took place in the house of Dr. Adams which a detective spying on them could have reported currently, say by private wire to a colleague, in these terms:

"Superintendent Hannam is examining the cupboard. Behind his back the Doctor is watching him. He seems to think that the superintendent won't notice what he is doing. He is starting to walk slowly across the room. Ah, I see: there is another built-in cupboard on the left-hand side of the fireplace. Now the Doctor is opening the centre compartment and putting his hand inside. I'm afraid the superintendent is watching after all and can see what I see: the Doctor is taking out a couple of things and putting them inside his left-hand jacket pocket."

The superintendent told his version of this scene at a magistrate's hearing, in what wording we can't guess, though of course he used the official "two objects." The hearing was reported in *The Times*, and its report of this episode, quoted in *Trial*, begins with "While the witness was examining . . . ," which I will replace with his name.

While Superintendent Hannam was[217] examining[217] the cupboard, the Doctor walked[218] slowly across the room to an identical built-in cupboard on the left-hand side of the fireplace, opened[219] the centre compartment and put[220] his hand inside, then he took[221] out two objects which he put[222] inside his left-hand jacket pocket.   [84:85]

Now from this we know that five events occurred in the same sequence as their five narrations here, *218–222*, and that this sequence *began* while Hannam was examining the cupboard; quite surely, however, it ended after Hannam had quit examining his own cupboard to give full attention to the Doctor. When did Hannam's first occupation cease? We don't know for sure; but it can do no possible harm to place this betweeen *220* and *221*, where the *Times* report seems to place it by printing *then* there.

This calls for some sort of graph like those in the Appendix; but there is a logical difficulty in matching the other graphs: Graph A does not say that an event gradually begins and gradually ends; it says that the probability that the predicating of the event *would be valid* also for earlier and later times diminishes as they are chosen more and more apart from the time principally referred to.

The difficulty vanishes when we carefully distinguish between the two points of view. (1) Graph A is defined from the point of view of the speaker whose time principally referred to is identical with the time of speaking; from his own standpoint *at the center* of Graph A he can look backward and forward in time and see diminishing probabilities that he would still be telling the truth with reference to those other times. (2) The *Times* report looks at everything from the outside—from a far later point in time, as a matter of fact, but *in effect* as if looking at the episode *from above*, from a point of vantage that is outside the inexorable flow of time. This is the conventional point of vantage in our literary tradition—not in all literary traditions, but in the principal European ones and certain others—and it enables a narrator to go so far as to use the past tense in writing of the future: one such tale is even entitled *Looking Backward!*

Now consider what the superintendent's examining of the first cupboard looks like from this other point of vantage. Now it has acquired a definite beginning and a definite end: it is *essentially* limited in time with precise limits. Either or both of these precise limits can be specified as exactly as the narrator's command of English *vocabulary* affords him adequate means, with items like *just then* and *no sooner* and all the rest. So much for that; we can dismiss it after noting that English verb-grammar has, so far as we have yet observed, afforded no devices at all for doing the same job.

What the finite verb's grammar does offer is the temporary aspect as represented by Graph A. How does the narrator use it? He *does not* rely on it to do *that* job; he does as much of that as he likes by other means, for instance the *while* that begins the citation and further the words *and*, *then*, and *which*. From what Graph A means he uses just what is usable here, namely the notion of *duration that is not eternal* but *is sufficient to qualify the event to serve as background* for the principal events (*218–222*) that advance the plot. He even finds it unnecessary to say how long it lasted; and that is the equivalent, for his purposes, of the *essentially indefinite* duration-meaning of present-time comment in the temporary aspect as in

Graph A. It is a reinterpretation, but that can do no harm: the point of view is different, and everybody knows that and makes his own adjustments.

Now we are ready to represent the cited episode in a graph suitable for printing on that same page as Graph A. It should be remembered that Graph A′ is the more realistic one, with the following decisive effect. Suppose we make a graph similar to Graph A; then we would place *218* roughly at its center, *219* just to the right of that, and so on until *222* is rather far outside to the right. Then Graph A will either seem to cut between two of these numbers, or else will cut through one of them; and such effects are illusory, for the graph still represents probabilities of truth, not event-limits however vague. Now, however, the reader can do his own correcting.

Finally, let me go back to the fourth paragraph of this section and tabulate its transformation rules:

Contemporary ⎫
Comment in   ⎬ ...... *Transformation Rules* ...... ⎰ Narrative in
Actual Tense ⎭   ⎱ Actual or in
                                                       ⎱ Remote Tense

GENERIC ASPECT......................... GENERIC ASPECT

Status verbs: all.   Status verbs: all.
Process verbs: Process verbs:
   characterizing,   characterizing,
   demonstration,   etc.; *but also*
   asseveration.   plot-advancing.

TEMPORARY ASPECT....................... TEMPORARY ASPECT

Process verbs: Process verbs:
   temporary   temporary
   validity, back-   validity serving
   ground or not.   as background.

Narrative Actual Tense

Now let me go back to the *Times* report and alter it in just one detail; all I do is drop out each use of the tense-marker -D:

While Superintendent Hannam is examining the cupboard, the Doctor walks slowly across the room to an identical built-in cupboard on the left-hand side of the fireplace, opens the centre compartment and puts his hand inside, then he takes out two objects which he puts inside his left-hand jacket pocket.

This is still past-time narrative, but it is the narrative use of actual tense. This is the English equivalent of the French 'historical present.' A reader or even a radio listener, by the time he hears the third verb, realizes that the *aspects* are being used exactly as they are in past-tense narrative and thereby determines that this is *narrative*—that is, it is *not* a running comment on what is happening before the speaker's eyes like this:

"Hannam is examining the cupboard. Now the Doctor is walking slowly across the room to an identical built-in cupboard on the left-hand side of the fireplace. He is opening the centre compartment and putting his hand inside; now he is taking out two objects and putting them into his left-hand jacket pocket."

From citations given a few pages back we have learned that the narrative actual tense has a firm basis in speech, where the use of actual tense for past events comes naturally to the lips of a man who gets himself involved in what he is talking about. This does not yet mean that narrative past tense is identical with the man's performance; for that man will *always* use enough past-tense forms, mixed in with his actual-tense forms, to reassure the listener that he is 'keeping his feet on the ground'—something that has a high value in English-speaking cultures.

It has such a high value, in fact, that even Mrs. Bedford dare not make full use of her poetic license for the sake of the vividness and involvement that narrative actual tense procures, but mixes in narrative past tense too. She does not do it as haphazardly as those witnesses did, but rather with a novelist's sure touch.

Narrative actual tense is used in English for stage-directions in printed dramas. Newspaper headlines differ from this pattern principally in that they usually also delete the aspect marker BE -ING; but this is marginal to English usage and needs no discussion here. No doubt there are other variations too; but for our present purposes just three possibilities are of any interest: (1) contemporary comment, (2) narrative past tense, (3) narrative actual tense. The three possibilities have been demonstrated on the *Times* story appearing in *Trial* as (2). Let us see what we can do with (3) *135–150*.

> (1) *contemporary comment:* I'm afraid I don't quite realize what is
> (2) *narrative past tense:*   Before anyone quite realized what was
> (3) *narrative actual tense:* Before anyone quite realizes what is

happening. There seems to be a kind of exercise-book. Now it has gone
happening there was somewhere a kind of exercise-book and it had gone
happening there is somewhere a kind of exercise-book and it has gone

from counsel to the usher, and now it's in front of Nurse Stronach. She is
from counsel to the usher and was then in front of Nurse Stronach, who at
from counsel to the usher and is now in front of Nurse Stronach, who at

beginning to turn the pages. Nothing much seems to be happening. Well,
once began to turn the pages. There was a hovering interval during which
once begins to turn the pages. There is a hovering interval during which

the Attorney-General is on his feet but hasn't said anything; the national
the Attorney-General was on his feet but had not said anything; the national
the Attorney-General is on his feet but has not said anything; the national

Press have leapt their box and are massing by the door. Mr. Lawrence is
Press had leapt their box and were massing by the door. Mr. Lawrence
Press have leapt their box and are massing by the door. Mr. Lawrence

hanging fire. Nurse Stronach is reading. Nobody is paying the slightest
hung fire and Nurse Stronach was reading. Nobody paid the slightest
hangs fire and Nurse Stronach is reading. Nobody pays the slightest

attention to the Doctor in the dock. Now the Judge is speaking to . . .
attention to the Doctor in the dock. Then the Judge said, 'Mr. Lawrence,
attention to the Doctor in the dock. Then the Judge says, 'Mr. Lawrence,

Aspect, Tense, and Time

When this passage goes on to finish the Judge's question, 'Mr. Lawrence, is this one of the exhibits in the case?' the top line of the triplet fades out. If it were being converted into sign-language by the companion to a deaf and blind person, of course, it could continue and would then be identical to the quotation as included in either narrative tense. But the institutions of English communication make no provision for echolalia. Narration in both tenses is, however, known to us all, and most of us can do it both ways on occasion.

It is not, in either case, something to be learned entirely separately. The reason is that the *narrative* rule for choosing between the aspects is also the rule for *all other uses* of verbs, *apart from* the contemporary comment upon which my first discussion of aspect and of process and status verbs was based. In narrative and in all those others, the process verbs are in the generic aspect unless they are specifying the background. This is true of all the non-finites, of course; since they do not assert at all, they have no use for plot-advancing temporary validity. However, when the non-finite is governed by a quasi-auxiliary or the like, the dependent non-finite is usually the bearer of the aspect marker: 'Nothing much seems to be happening' with the meaning 'Seemingly nothing much is happening.'

Again, unless there is an analogous reversal of functions between a main clause and a subordinate clause, *subordinate clauses* follow the narrative rule for choice of aspects, namely temporary aspect only for background to plot-advancing verbs; otherwise generic aspect.

93: "Mr. Sogno proposed that they *might wait* until Mrs. Morell's son *came* at the week-end, . . . "

103: When he *poses* a rhetorical question . . . it has a dutiful rather than dramatic sound.

121: "Six years later when a detective superintendent from Scotland Yard *was making* inquiries, he asked the Doctor . . ."

The last example is background, we see; the first two are not. 'We *are waiting* until Mrs. Morell's son comes at the week-end' is comment with the normal temporary aspect. And the latter part similarly becomes 'Mrs. Morell's son *is coming* at the week-end' by itself. Again, the posing of rhetorical questions is clearly not characteristic of this actor, so that *poses* is not the characterizing use of generic aspect; the crucial thing is that it is in a subordinate clause without serving as background to any plot-advancing statement. By itself, this must become 'He *is posing* a rhetorical question.'

We next consider the use of actual-tense forms with real future reference. There are few if any examples in *Trial*, because planning and prophecy are not at home in its episodes; but it needs treatment here because of its great importance in English. Like all the Germanic languages, English refers to the future with the actual tense of its finite verbs. In *Trial*, BE GOING is used 28 times with future meaning, and is in fact the only colorless way of prophesying: 'You now understand that you must not discuss with anybody at all the evidence you have given or *are going* to give . . . ' [49:54].

The above formula was discussed in Chapter II under the heading *Quasi-Auxiliaries;* in Chapter VI the use of WILL for another way of viewing future time will be discussed, and SHALL too for that matter. Here we are concerned rather with future reference without any such adventitious devices. Unfortunately, I have not picked up even one unchallengeable example in *Trial*.

When there is a separate reference to the future, what is most noticeable is that the generic aspect has something like its characterizing meaning and is used for a future event that is part of an established program: 'His ship *leaves* tomorrow'; with the temporary aspect this factor drops out, and 'His ship *is leaving* tomorrow' leaves us to guess whether that sort of thing has ever happened before or how long ago this departure was determined upon. At first glance, it now seems that it is the generic aspect that has the privative significance, contrary to our expectation from our experience with marked and unmarked forms. Let us leave that as a warning while we consider further.

We note first that the generic aspect can hardly have future reference without a separate reference to the future like *tomorrow*. Such a negative proposition is verifiable only by accident, of course; but it does seem that hardly any accumulation of context will do the job if there is nothing remotely like *tomorrow* in it: 'I understand he has his orders to leave immediately and he *leaves* by the first available transportation . . . ' still doesn't quite seem to be English. And it has already been pointed out that even *tomorrow* is inadequate if the verb is a status verb. But with temporary aspect there is no difficulty: 'He's leaving' as a complete sentence is good enough for future reference, with one simple proviso: that the leaving itself *is known not to be occurring at the time of speaking*.

Then 'We're having a picnic' has two sets of interpretations depending on its basic meaning. (1) With literal reference, signifying having an open-air meal without domestic conveniences, it is (1*a*) contemporary comment if spoken on the occasion itself, perhaps to an inquisitive police officer, (1*b*) narrative (with past-time reference) if there is context revealing that the aspects are being chosen appropriately (for instance, in 'We're having a picnic when this policeman comes along, stops, and asks what we're doing'), (1*c*) prophecy for the future if spoken in any other circumstances. (2) With transferred reference, signifying the same as 'having fun, having a ball, having a good time,' it is (2*a*) contemporary comment if apposite at the time of speaking, and again if meant ironically, (2*b*) narrative as above, (2*c*) nonsense otherwise, since having fun can't be prophesied this way in the local idiom.

Now either this is one of those hopeless messes called 'idiom' as an evasion of the responsibility to describe it, or else the explanation is essentially simple. 'We're having a picnic' has temporary validity. Its time-reference can be anything at all. We listeners assume that if the reference were to real past history there would be contextual evidence for that, especially the choice of aspects in the context but of course any adequate evidence will serve. Lacking that, we are left with contemporary time *and* its automatic extension into future history: English *grammar* has *no device whatever* for cutting future time away from the time of speaking. Then if the hearer has sufficient reason to believe that the sentence would be false if taken to apply to the time of listening, he subtracts that too, as well as past time; now he has left—and he *always will* have this left as a solid residue—reference to future time.

Since the evidence for subtracting past and contemporary references automatically stops short here—it can't extend beyond that small extension of time into the future within which the circumstances still forbid having a picnic—this way of speaking has been called the 'immediate future' of English. Very well; but we must not forget that there is no standard time-scale inherent in the temporary aspect: its span of validity can be measured in seconds in one social situation, in centuries in another. The crucial feature remains intact. To the literal-minded, 'I'm speaking German' is one way of lying in English; but there is nothing dishonest in this transaction: 'Are you sure of getting your message across to an Austrian audience?' — 'No need to worry: I'm speaking German.' This is future reference, perhaps for tonight, perhaps for next year.

Accordingly, if the Judge, instead of asseverating, 'I therefore discharge each of you from jury service for the rest of your lives' [241:221], had said 'I am therefore discharging . . . ' the jury would have understood him to mean that he undertook to accomplish that in writing and soon enough so that he couldn't forget.

Now it has become possible to explain something that ought to have been worrying us ever since the tabular diagram was printed for the rules for altering the choice of aspects between contemporary comment and narrative. The dotted lines converge at two points in a way that means 'ambiguity.' In listening to or reading narrative, the same generic aspect is to be interpreted either as characterizing for all times of any interest or else (and these two exclude each other) as narrating a plot-advancing event. This is one of the two ambiguities. Thus 'I sang bass' is characterizing if it refers to the fact that when I was a member of the choir that was my regular function, my assignment; but if 'I sang tenor' refers to my habit in part-singing a song of three verses in a small social gathering, namely that I like to sing bass through the first and last verses but tenor through the verse in the middle, 'I sang tenor' becomes the narration of a single event when it answers the question, 'Why did the second verse sound different?'

The other ambiguity consists in the identical temporary aspect being used in contemporary comment no matter whether it is background or plot-advancing. The discussion of future reference, with its implications for the situations where future reference would not be a reasonable interpretation, has cleared this up: the ambiguity does no harm because the addressee is a competent witness and can sort things out for himself.

But in the narrative situation the addressee or other hearer or reader is presumably not a competent witness, and occasionally he needs to have the first-mentioned ambiguity resolved for him. Skillful speakers can anticipate this, and English has three ways of providing the requisite information. One way falls outside the limits of the present discussion: it consists in the multifarious ways of including enough information throughout the narrative so that the hearer or reader can safely guess which is meant: characterization or single plot-advancing event. Another method employs two devices belonging to the verb-system in the larger sense. Both of them characterize, so that the hearer or reader is left to assume that if neither is used the narrator means a plot-advancing event.

One has been treated in Chapter II, namely the quasi-auxiliary USED TO; and now we see that it doesn't need to have any 'present tense,' for in contemporary comment the addressee doesn't need its message and in narrative using the actual tense the narrator can drop back into remote tense if USED TO is requisite. Its significance, I remind you, is that the past era as a whole, or some character active within it, is being characterized by a favorite deed: 'Victorian juries used to grow quite restive.'

The other device is not confined to the past tense, for it is simply the past-tense equivalent of 'John *will* fall asleep in church.' This is *would*, not with its commoner unreal contemporary meaning but as a real past:

Did the Doctor ever write the prescriptions in her presence? — Nurse Stronach: "He often did." — The Judge: "Was that because someone had told him that the supply was running out, or because he found out himself?" — "He *would* probably *ask* and we *would tell* him how the drugs were going." — "He *would write* out a fresh prescription and *would give* it to the nurses?" — "Yes, and we *would give* it to the chauffeur, Price, who *took* it to the chemist. And when he *brought* them, they *would be taken* in by the cook; she *would bring* them to the dining-room to the nurse on duty who *would put* them away. The nurses had charge of the locked cupboard in the dining-room where the drugs were kept. If the Doctor *wanted* drugs from the cupboard he *would ask* for them and we *would produce* the key; but he usually had his own drugs from his bag." [29:36]

The difference is that *used to* matches the events to the whole era, while *would* matches them singly to their separate occasions. No other kind of characterizing seems to be needed, so that no problem remains.

Our last topic under this heading can be the simple reminder that we have seen that both aspect-marking and tense-marking are *privative*: the marked temporary aspect cannot be non-temporary in meaning, but the unmarked generic aspect can easily have the temporary meaning; the marked remote tense cannot have real contemporary meaning, but the unmarked actual tense can have past meaning—and will have it with narrative aspects.

Phase

This privative character of all the markers is curiously different in the case of the phase marker HAVE -N, as we shall see presently. But first the meaning of *phase* has to be explored. It was given this untraditional name some fifteen years ago by George L. Trager and Henry Lee Smith, Jr., *An Outline of English Structure*. The name derives from the special relation between cause and effect signified by verbs in the perfect phase.

Any event is not only sure to have a cause, though sometimes its cause may be difficult to ascertain; it is likely to have effects too, and here the relation is clearer or even obvious. A finite verb will hardly be used to specify an event unless there are effects; it is fair to say that language is not organized for entirely idle talk but is rather well adapted to mentioning things *because they matter*. Let us take it as axiomatic that the referent of a finite verb is regularly the cause of certain effects—unknown perhaps, often unforeseen, but in any case not assumed to be non-existent—since otherwise the finite verb would be idle, otiose, and rather left unused.

Now in all this chapter so far we have been concentrating our attention upon verbs in the current phase (lacking HAVE -N); and both here and previously when voice was discussed in the preceding chapter, the effects of the specified event have either been simultaneous with their cause (this event) or have been not substantially delayed: 'The Judge *came* on swiftly' is the beginning of *Trial*, and the simultaneous effect is that he *is seen* to come, the immediate effect is that he *is there*, and later (perhaps delayed) effects can be taken for granted. Using the terminology borrowed from electrical circuit theory, used there for cyclically recurrent causes and effects, the cause and the principal effects are 'in phase with each other,' as the amount of moonlight is in phase with the phases of the moon (the two waxing and waning together) and the visibility of the moon is in phase with its being above the horizon time after time (the two occurring together cyclically), the effect never delayed behind the recurrent cause. In its English grammar use, the regular cyclic feature of that electrical *phase* drops out, though of course recurrence does not drop out with it: after all, the reason why items are in the vocabulary and in the grammar of English is that they are kept alive by recurrent use, and the events that they designate are not unique. For our purposes, then, the sense of *phase* is adequately defined so far by the one example.

So much for *current* phase: the principal effects are in phase with the specified event, their cause. Now consider the very first appearance of the *perfect* phase in *Trial:*

The high-backed chair *has been pulled, helped* forward, the figure IS SEATED, *has bowed*, and the hundred or so people who *had gathered* themselves at split notice to their feet RUSTLE AND SUBSIDE into apportioned place. [2:13]

This is not simply a narration of events in sequence; instead, certain of them (*is seated, rustle and subside*) are presented as *effects* (or at least the possibility of their occurrence is an effect) of the earlier-in-time events stated in the perfect phase. Their presentation as effects is not marked in their own verbs; that marking is done by the perfect marker on the verbs for the precedent events. The perfect-marked verbs are there specifically *for the sake of the effects* of the events they designate, and that is the essential meaning.

True, the events designated by perfect verbs may be interesting in themselves, and may have simultaneous effects, but all that is now treated as uninteresting; the focus of attention is entirely on the *delayed* effects which remain uncertain until separately specified by other verbs. It is this focus of attention that determines what effects will figure as *principal* effects. The name *perfect* is traditional and entirely misleading; the essential point here is that the meaning of perfect phase is that *the principal effects of the event are out of phase with it*, which of course can only be true if they are delayed.

Now the effects may in turn be prepared-for events, or they may be simply new opportunities for events. In any case, the same Graph D or D' will serve: see the Appendix. As before, a dotted line represents the distribution, along the time-scale, of the probability that a predication is valid. In these new graphs, a dotted line belongs to the verb in the perfect phase. But now its dottedness takes on a further significance, never in conflict with the other: now it reminds us that the perfect phase means that the event is *not mentioned for its own sake* but for the sake of its consequences.

The perfect phase has removed our attention from the event which it itself presents, and has relocated our attention on the subsequent opportunities for events, now that they have been prepared for. In the new graphs, the solid-line half-curved frame represents these new opportunities, and the prepared-for events will be accommodated within it. There is room for them, for they are never such as require representation according to Graph B. The room does not extend (to the left of the solid vertical straight line) into any period earlier than the principal time of this new frame. The room diminishes into the future: the hundred or so people had better *subside* into apportioned place promptly, now that the Judge *has bowed*, or they will lose their chance and be ushered out.

The vertical dotted line is placed at the principal time of the event belonging to the perfect predication. It represents either an instantaneous event like 'He *has pronounced* them man and wife' as in Graph C, or else an event essentially of the limited-duration sort like 'Hannam *is inspecting* the cupboard' that is now (like any plot-advancing event in narrative) viewed from afar so that its duration has shrunk into insignificance: 'Hannam *has inspected* the cupboard.' The high level dotted line represents any status verb or characterizing use of a process verb like 'He *practises* anæsthetics' (Graph B), and in Graph D it fits 'he is a doctor of medicine . . . and *has practised* anæsthetics for many years' (45).

The curved dotted line represents an event essentially of the limited-duration sort (Graph A) like '*is inspecting*' or 'another nurse *is waiting* her turn,' but this time the duration *has not shrunk* into insignificance: 'She IS FOLLOWED at once by another nurse, the sixth prosecution witness, who *has been waiting* her turn outside the court' [29:37]. Because of the words *at once*, this fits specifically Graph D, and this *is followed* fits the beginning of the new frame (with room in the rest of the frame for her to be sworn, etc.). If instead it had read 'After a considerable delay she is followed by another nurse who *has been primping* in the Ladies' Lounge,' Graph D′ would have been appropriate.*

---

* The meaning of BE GOING TO (Chapter II, heading *Quasi-Auxiliaries*) turns out to be the exact reversal, in every detail as far as I can see, of the meaning of perfect phase: it simply exchanges 'previous' and 'subsequent' on the graph (D or D′), but it is safer to keep the standard time-direction and draw a new mirror-image graph.

Then the solid-line curve is the frame around the occasion of saying 'I'm going to show it to her' (we gradually get ready to say it; and once we've said it the frame terminates abruptly), and the dotted curve frames (or the vertical dotted line marks) the time of showing. The level dotted line belongs to 'I'm going to like her' (status verb) and to 'We're going to live there' (characterizing generic aspect), but now that part of the dotted line lying above the solid-line frame has to be erased: this is what is known as *entropy* in Physics, which forbids absolutely reversing time.

A still longer interval, so that the dotted curved line had sunk to an insignificant level of low probability, would have induced Mrs. Bedford to write *had been primping*, no doubt. But that is not the reason for the remote perfect in the citation which we first started considering on page 140. Those people's gathering themselves at split notice to their feet had no effects or consequences specified by any *verb* in this citation: the effect was that they were *on their feet* waiting for the Judge to bow; and now any of us can choose whether to say that that was the reason for not writing 'have gathered' or rather to say that this is just Mrs. Bedford mixing tenses within a narrative. In any case, it does no harm.

Quite early in this section I said, " 'The Judge *came* on swiftly' is the beginning of *Trial*, and the simultaneous effect is that he *is seen* to come, the immediate effect is that he *is there*, and later (perhaps delayed) effects can be taken for granted." That is to say, if the later effects of an event are of great interest, that does not in itself *require* that precedent event to be presented in the perfect phase; it may be enough for the addressee to know that it did take place, and when later another, thus prepared-for event comes along, he can make the connection himself. That is substantially all a French or German perfect usually does. We can do that with an English past tense just as well as with an actual perfect:

"Morphia and heroin are drugs outstanding in their variability of effect. I *made* researches into histories of addicts in hospitals . . . The highest daily morphia injection I *could discover* was 77 grains every day, and the highest dose of heroin 40 grains."   [179:165]

This witness is speaking of how he has prepared for his turn in court as an expert witness. If he had made the connection himself, he would have said: 'I *have made* researches . . . The highest daily morphia injection I *have been* able to discover was . . . ' Both ways are grammatically sound; this is a choice among messages, the messages differing in the explicit versus implicit presence of the connection between his researches and discoveries on the one hand and the purport of his testimony on the other hand.

In immature English usage, the connections generally remain implicit; that is, the perfect phase is used very little or not at all. In *Trial*, where the usage is nearly always mature, the perfect marker is used in only 10.9 percent of the finites, though there were opportunities to use it considerably oftener. Some more citations:

> This medical man will tell them that he *has formed* the opinion that Mrs. Morell was suffering from cerebral arteriosclerosis . . . [5:16]

> "Nearly a year later the Doctor called on Mr. Sogno without an appointment . . . The Doctor told Mr. Sogno that Mrs. Morell *had promised* him her Rolls-Royce in her will and that she now remembered that she *had forgotten* this, and that she desired to leave him not only the Rolls-Royce car but also . . ." [7:17]

> there is somewhere a kind of exercise-book and it *has gone* from counsel to the usher and is now in front of Nurse Stronach . . . There is a hovering interval during which the Attorney-General is on his feet but *has* not *said* anything, the national Press *have leapt* their box and are massing by the door . . . [21:29]

> Mr. Lawrence: "I will begin at the beginning. You *have seen* the Cheshire reports? Are you prepared to condemn or not to condemn the use of morphia during her stay in Cheshire?" [172:159]

> "Another unusual feature—I think it is fair to call it unusual—is that the accused himself *has* not *gone* into the witness-box." [212:196; Judge to jury, after the witnesses have all been heard: no more chance for the accused to do that]

It is only because this medical man *has formed* an opinion that he will tell them anything. Mrs. Morell could not have remembered unless she *had forgotten;* and she could not have forgotten her promise unless she *had promised*. This necessary antecedence is the reason for the 'rule' that a past tense is transformed into past perfect in indirect discourse: 'I REMEMBER that I *forgot*' gives 'The Doctor TOLD Mr. Sogno that . . . she now REMEMBERED that she *had forgotten*'; and this medical man said either 'I *formed* the opinion' or 'I *have formed* the opinion,' but the Attorney-General now says, 'This medical man WILL TELL them that he *has formed* . . . ' The 'rule' is not a necessity; if it were, we would have to read 'The Doctor told Mr. Sogno that she *had* now *remembered* . . . '

The meaning of perfect phase is equally clear when it is negated. That exercise-book can be in front of Nurse Stronach only because it *has gone* from counsel to the usher; the national Press can be massing by the door only because they *have leapt* their box; and equally the word *but* is in order because the Attorney-General *has risen* as if to speak but *has* not *said* anything. Similarly, in the last citation the feature can be called an unusual feature only after the last chance for the accused to testify has passed and still he *has* not *gone* into the witness-box.

If these citations are a fair sample of mature English, then the one citation which can best serve as an epitome of them all is the second-last. Seeing the Cheshire reports is preparation for condemning or not condemning the use of morphia there; and that, in the opinion of your witness, is exactly what the English perfect phase means. Once in *Trial* it is used ornamentally: 'They were addressed to Miss Lawrence, and if she *has* not *heard* them it was because she was turned away from him' [95:94].

Before leaving this topic, it is appropriate to mention some of the things that the English perfect phase *does not mean*, either because they appear in many books about English as misinterpretations of it or because they are meanings or uses of the similarly-shaped perfects of other languages such as French and German.

First, the English perfect does not mean that the specified event occurred previous to some other event specified with the current phase. That is a possible interpretation of it, but it is not what it means, just as many other kinds of utterances can be interpreted into messages that they do not intrinsically mean: 'How do you do?' meaning 'I'm pleased to meet you' but interpretable as an inquiry about health. The previous occurrence is at most a *connotation* of the perfect phase; its *denotation* indeed contradicts that by telling us that the event presented in the perfect phase is not being presented for its own sake but only as a means to a separate end, and its denotation positively is that we must look elsewhere for the important message. 'You have seen the Cheshire reports' is not a past-tense message; it belongs solely to the actual or 'present tense.'

Conversely, the English actual perfect *cannot be used for narration:* 'I have seen him yesterday' is not English. The nearest thing to it is 'I have seen him. Yesterday.' But this is two separate messages, the second in a one-word sentence without a verb.

Second, a French or a German perfect does not mean that the specified event is uninteresting in itself, which is always part of what the English perfect means. In both those languages it is a narrative tense, used for presenting events interesting for their own sake; and to the extent that those events can serve as preparation for later affairs the English-perfect meaning can be read out of them—but *only as a connotation!* As we have seen, the English past can do that too; and we can also say, 'As we saw . . . '

Finally, by virtue of all such connotations in all languages, and other connotations too, it is possible to employ any west-European perfect to convey to a reader or listener a complete sequence of events and lay out the sequence into at least six different times of occurrence. But, for reasons which ought to have become clear by now, that does not mean that the English perfect formulas are *tenses* in any sense of the term, however loose.

Privative Phase Marking

Of course we now expect the phase marker HAVE -N to have only privative significance like the others. This is true to a conspicuous extent only in one respect as far as I have noticed: It deprives its verb of narrative value—it says that the event does not advance the plot or anything like that, but only prepares for other possibly plot-advancing events.

The other markers previously considered were not requisite for their usual messages, for example the passive message of 'They are being sold' comes through equally well without BE -N in 'They are selling like hotcakes.' But if the message of HAVE -N is taken as *preparation* we find that equivalent preparation cannot emerge from simply zero, the absence of any marker. Instead, we find the tense-marker serving as a kind of substitute for HAVE -N or for such a zero, for example in the case of that expert witness.

It is really a curious thing about English that its perfect phase, which is roughly a millennium old, should be so unstable today, while the temporary aspect, half that old or less (and brought to its present stability only in the nineteenth century with the emergence of 'his house is being built' for only slightly earlier 'his house is building') is as firm and symmetrical as anything in the language. But the curious thing is historically and structurally not entirely mysterious. With most verb-bases, including I should think more than half the commonest ones, 'suffixed' -N and -D lead to exactly the same word-form: -N LIKE = *liked* = -D LIKE.

Starting out, then, from the majority verbs like *liked*, the perfect marking seems to be not an abstract element HAVE -N but rather the mere insertion of completed words *have, has, had*, into completed verbs; for example, 'They *have shot* President Kennedy' seems to be 'They *shot* President Kennedy' (which is the exact wording in which the grim tidings were brought to the billiard-room of the University Club at the University of Wisconsin that day by a member of the faculty) plus an extra *have* too pedantic for such an occasion, that is, too frivolous.

I say "insertion into completed verbs" to cover such instances as 'You *could put* it here' and 'You *could have put* it here,' for PUT, SET, CUT, COST, HIT, HURT, SHUT, SPLIT, SPREAD and rarer bases together form an imposing and surely somewhat influential group. This and the other sort of influence together are probably contributing strongly to the occasional (and in popular usage prevailing) treatment of the perfect marker as simply *have, has, had*, which makes it a privative marker in the fullest sense, like all the others.

VI

Assertion

Category	Tense	Assertion	Phase	Aspect	Voice	Function
Unmarked	Actual	Factual	Current	Generic	Neutral	Propredicate
Marked	Remote	Relative	Perfect	Temporary	Passive	Verb
Markers	-D	WILL *etc.*	HAVE-N	BE -ING	BE -N	SHOW *etc.*

There are especially two reasons why *assertion*, with the markers
WILL, SHALL, CAN, MAY, MUST, OUGHT TO, DARE, NEED, for the *relative* assertions that have no truth-value as to the event, in opposition to the unmarked *factual* assertions, is the most difficult to
discuss among the six categories of the English finite verb—one
essential and one adventitious reason.

First, when English is learned natively the meanings of those
eight modals are learned so extremely early—necessarily before the
child is ready for kindergarten—that as an adult one has left them
buried deep in the subconscious where they are inaccessible to rational scrutiny by anyone but a ruthless professional analyst of
languages; and when they are seen laid out and dissected as they
will be here,* we are bound to feel that we are witnessing the anat-
omizing of our own flesh and blood.

For one thing there is the entirely natural feeling that nothing of
the sort can be done at all. When a four-year-old child asks,

---

* Parallel jobs have been done on relatively defenseless languages, but never on a
European language. Even Hans Glinz, *Die innere Form des Deutschen* [Bern:
Francke, 1952; 3rd ed. 1962 with 154 new notes and two-page glossary], after doing a
beautiful analysis of form and meaning through all the rest of German grammar,
skirted around the modals *wie die Katze um den heissen Brei* and left their inner
form untouched.

"Daddy, what does *must* mean?" and a quick-witted parent answers, "Well, for instance your duty is what you must do," the child can only take that as a definition of *duty* and not one of *must*. The sense of *must* is as axiomatic to him as it is to his father. It is not a meaning that can be *paraphrased*, for English has no more elementary words to paraphrase it with. And when a linguist undertakes to *describe* that meaning, there is an aura of illicitness about the undertaking reminiscent of the days when students of human anatomy had recourse to grave-robbers to procure their primary data: the fatal result is that the end seems to be vitiated by the means.

For another thing there is the equally natural feeling that nothing of the sort ought to be done at all. We are in our daily lives so dependent on mutual understanding by means of modals—even in *Trial* 16.7 percent of the finite predications are accomplished by those means, and it is certain that 'with their aid' would be an entirely false way to put it—that we have a visceral feeling that any thoroughgoing scrutiny would damage the mother tongue. It seems rather like taking a perfectly good typewriter apart at the risk of mislaying the first letter of the alphabet forevermore. The Appendix will explain why there is no such danger, and more besides.

That is the essential reason. The adventitious reason derives from the complete solidarity and symmetry of the English system of modal markers for relative assertion: they offer no starting-point, such as we always were able to find when tackling each of the other categories, where the presentation could be arranged in a sequence of topics that could serve as a sequence of discoveries.

Here I must almost reverse that procedure. This time, the citations are all grouped together and printed in the Appendix to keep them from disrupting the present chapter. And instead of developing the meanings of the modals in sequence, I first present their whole meaning-*system* at once in advance, in a somewhat cryptic summary; and then I proceed to verify their meanings singly and in pairs from the citations. The meaning-system presented in advance is only the modern one; the archaic counterparts are added later.

Modal Summary

First a list of reminders of what has been established so far in dealing with the finites; the list ends with the modal category that still remains to be elucidated:

Verb Function (marker: SHOW, etc.): None of the predicate's message is to be guessed-in by the addressee.

Passive Voice (marker: BE -N): The grammatical subject does not designate the actor.

Temporary Aspect (BE -ING): The validity of the predication vanishes outside a certain span of time.

Perfect Phase (HAVE -N): The specified event is not interesting for its own sake; its interesting results are opportunities for events.

Remote Tense (-D): The specified event is absent from the scene of the asserting: it is in the historical past, or it is unreal.

[Factual Assertion (unmarked): The specified event itself is asserted, and the assertion has truth-value: it is true or false.]

Relative Assertion (WILL, etc.): There is no such truth-value with respect to occurrence of the event; what is asserted is instead a specific *relation* between that event and the factual world, a set of *terms of admission* for allowing it real-world status.

There are eight of those specific relations, and each relation is asserted by using one of the eight modals. There are three kinds of difference in meaning among the modals. Each is either *adequate* or *contingent*, and either *casual* or *stable;* and each either *assures* the event or specifies that it is *potential*. Readers with a visual habit of thought can easily place the modals at the eight *corners* of an abstract semological cube; here I will list the four belonging to each *face* of the cube:

Casual modals (WILL, SHALL, CAN, MAY) *take* that relation from the *minimal* social matrix of events, where the determining factors are the resultant of chance and whim operating upon the items that populate the factual world of accepted reality; but the

Stable modals (MUST, OUGHT TO, DARE, NEED) *find* that relation in
the *maximal* social matrix of events, where the determining factors are eternal and omnipresent: they are the community mores.
Accordingly, stable modals exclude remote tense.

Adequate modals (WILL, CAN, MUST, DARE) derive their force from
completeness in the set of determining factors; but the

Contingent modals (SHALL, MAY, OUGHT TO, NEED) get their weak-
ness from some *deficiency* in the determining factors.

Assurance (WILL, SHALL, MUST, OUGHT TO) comes from *penalties* for
failure of the specified event to occur; but

Potentiality (CAN, MAY, DARE, NEED) comes from *immunity* in case
the actor brings the event to completion.

To start from the end of this: The penalties and the immunity are
of two kinds, depending on whether the modal is casual or stable;
and again the completeness or deficiency is found in two kinds of
determining factors for the same reason: whether the matrix is
minimal or is the maximal one. This beginning of the above list of
oppositions gives the clearest survey of the whole system, starting
with the minimal matrix of events.

Here the background is the world of accepted reality which one is
aware of gradually learning about, throughout one's life up to
senility. This awareness means that one expects to find the nearest
areas differing from time to time as one ages (second by second and
year by year) and moves about, for what is nearest depends on
where one is at the moment. Not that whole background is the
minimal matrix, but only whatever is near; that is why I call it
'minimal.' The minimal social matrix of events *always has a center*,
and the occupant of the center determines its extent and boundary.

A factual statement is made at the risk of telling a lie; but casual
relative assertions are made at the risk of 'being wrong' as we say in
English (to the puzzlement of the Europeans who 'have reason'
when they are right) and the penalty is a reputation for not being
well oriented in the circumstantial world—for misjudging how
things are going to turn out. One who is thoroughly at home in this

world makes assessments that can even be treated as prophecies: 'I hope I shǎll finish all these inquiries soon, and we wîll probably have another talk,' says Superintendent Hannam, and we have a feeling that that talk is indeed part of future history. But this police officer is by no means utterly confident of when the end of the inquiries is going to arrive: his assessment tells him that *not all* the determining factors are in favor of 'soon,' and so he says 'I hope' and uses the *contingent* casual assurance modal SHALL.

The *maximal* matrix of events is the polar opposite (not negative, not contrary, but rather the extreme counterpart) of the minimal matrix. To begin with, one is not aware of having learned anything about the community mores, and a suggestion that something remains to be learned is an insult. All questions and answers using a stable modal are devoted to ascertaining the relation between the specified *event* on the one hand, and an *actor* on the other hand. This actor is presumed to be a proper member of the community; and now the question is whether he is in jeopardy, in danger of forfeiting that status; and if he is, whether that can be evaded. 'Must I answer that?' says the witness [33:40] in something like desperation, and when the Judge instantly says, 'Yes,' the French newspapermen may imagine that they have heard him issue a command but then they would be utterly wrong. Sister Mason-Ellis was inquiring about the relation between herself, a loyal member of the community, and that answering; the Judge, one might almost say, ruled in her favor: he gave her the information, not in the popular sense of *authoritatively* but instead in the technical sense *utterly knowledgeably*. The contrary false information would have been 'You need not answer that,' with that particular stable modal which is the polar partner of MUST. But if a hitherto undetected impostor on the bench had said, 'Answer the question,' the lawyers would have been shocked right out from under their wigs. What happened this time is that Sister Mason-Ellis, as if glad to escape from the position she had been maintaining for a number of minutes—heroically refusing to tattle—instantly answered that question, and truthfully; if the Judge had instead commanded her to answer, there's no telling how much longer it would have taken. Finally, the *actor* here is *not* necessarily the entity designated by the grammatical subject of a non-passive verb: 'Dr. Douthwaite must be six foot six' [109:106] makes *the order of nature* the technical actor for our purposes, and now we see that 'A member of the Queen's Own Guards must be six foot six' is not a moral assertion, that is, in the popular sense it is not, though of course it is a 'moral' thing in the sense that it derives from the mores of that total community in which even the order of nature is a *member* like any other: 'It ought to rain before long,' we say, and 'It mustn't rain on our picnic.' In short, the *maximal* matrix *has no center:* all are equal before the Common Law.

Readers have been warned that a survey of the whole modal system would precede the verification of any of it; accordingly, it must be understood that I have been very cautious, very careful not to say anything in these pages which is not verified by the data in *Trial*. Before proceeding to the verification, let me summarize the summary; this sort of 'putting it in a nutshell' is naturally done with symbols such as are used in mathematical logic. Not many symbols are needed; they are easy to understand and remember; and each symbolic proposition reads off naturally as a sentence.

E means 'event'—what would be specified by the whole clause minus the modal—the deed considered as done, the state as factual.

$\overline{E}$ means 'non-occurrent event'—the deed left undone.

A means 'actor as a proper member of the community.'

$\overline{A}$ means 'actor in jeopardy as not a proper member.'

C means 'all the circumstances, none neglected.'

c means 'some of the circumstances *but not all.*'

o means 'is consistent with (and vice versa).'

$\overline{o}$ means 'is inconsistent with (and vice versa).'

$R = \Sigma E$ 'Reality is the sum of events already known.'

o stands between two other symbols. This is the definition of *finite predication.*

$\overline{E} \ \overline{o} \ E$ does not define a privative marker. This is the definition of the assertion *category.*

Only one bar goes with the same symbol. This is the definition of *negation*. The usual paraphrase is 'two minuses make a plus.'

An even number of bars will be used here; zero is even. This is the definition of *affirmative* assertions.

R can stand in a consistency relation only with E. This is the definition of English *realism*.

C and c are exempt from bars: 'circumstances can never be excluded.' This is the definition of English *pragmatism*.

C and c can stand in a consistency relation only with E. This is the definition of the *minimal* social matrix of events.

A can stand in a consistency relation only with E. This is the definition of the *maximal* social matrix of events.

When these definitions and restrictions are applied to the elementary symbols, exactly thirteen symbolic propositions can be written. The first eight define the markers of *relative* assertion; the next one defines the significance of *factual* assertion, either *unreal* or not; the remaining four define the modes of *belief* which I believe I have encountered so far in my experience; the last one, for example, is related to that well-known theorem in mathematical logic which says that any proposition whatever can be proved from false premises, and all four can be verified from *Othello*.

$\bar{E}\,\bar{\mathbf{o}}\,C$ WILL: adequate casual assurance

$\bar{E}\,\bar{\mathbf{o}}\,c$ SHALL: contingent casual assurance

$E\,\mathbf{o}\,C$ CAN: adequate casual potentiality

$E\,\mathbf{o}\,c$ MAY: contingent casual potentiality

$\bar{E}\,\bar{\mathbf{o}}\,A$ MUST: adequate stable assurance

$E\,\mathbf{o}\,\bar{A}$ OUGHT TO: contingent stable assurance

$E\,\mathbf{o}\,A$ DARE: adequate stable potentiality

$E\,\bar{\mathbf{o}}\,\bar{A}$ NEED: contingent stable potentiality

$\bar{E}\,\bar{\mathbf{o}}\,E$ (no marker): factual assertion

$\bar{E}\,\bar{\mathbf{o}}\,R$ belief: 'the assertion *must* be true'

$\bar{E}\,\mathbf{o}\,\bar{R}$ belief: 'the assertion *ought to* be true'

$E\,\mathbf{o}\,R$ belief: 'I *dare* say the assertion is true'

$E\,\bar{\mathbf{o}}\,\bar{R}$ belief: 'the assertion *needn't* be false'

Verification

It will not have escaped the attentive reader that the negation-patterns of the definitions of *belief* are identical with those of the definitions of the *stable modals*, in the same sequence as the stable modals are used above in the paraphrastic definitions of the four modes of belief. Now it will be verified later that the stable matrix is where morality, moral certainty, or absolute logic is at home, and that these are only three names for what English relative assertion treats as one and the same thing. Meanwhile it is worth while to point out what is meant by *verification* in any science.

Verification is not logical proof; it is an accumulation of experience sufficient for belief. The witness to a verification procedure, if he is qualified to be a member of the jury, starts out from a suspension of disbelief such as is symbolized by the last-named mode of belief here; as the process continues, he gradually climbs the ladder towards the top of the four: he becomes convinced. Whether or when he achieves conviction is his own affair; human nature is so variable that an advocate must content himself with convincing twelve good men and true, and he must leave the rest of the community to believe as they like—because he must.

The process begins with a scientific *hypothesis*, that is to say an essentially verifiable statement; and by that is meant a statement worded in such a way as to imply what kinds and amounts of factual data would suffice to refute it. Or in one word, a scientific hypothesis is a *vulnerable* statement. After verification (and only the jury can define *after* in each case) the hypothesis is a *theory*. In due course, the theory will be refuted in turn; then it may be abandoned and it may still survive to serve in all but a tiny minority of cases. Thus Newton's theory of gravitation still serves on all but the largest and the smallest scale of cosmic events, but it has been refuted and at the two extremes replaced by Einstein's theory; specifically, Newton's theory is taken as absolutely precise in ballistics and in computing the Nautical Almanac's tables of lunar and planetary motions, but Einstein's theory is used when the scale of the cosmic events is calibrated in light-years and again (within any atom-smasher, for example) when the velocities are comparable to the speed of light or the distances are of atomic size. Ptolemaic astronomy was vanquished by Newton's theory three centuries ago, and that was the sequel of a verification procedure; but it survives to serve our astrologers, whose usefulness is attested by the money they earn. But it was not vanquished within a single verification process, for that is not the way those things happen; it lost out in a comparison between two verifications.

This is the second and final essential feature of verification, no less important than the first. Verification does not consist in pitting a hypothesis against a theory. It can't, for the reason that the new hypothesis and the old theory in general will both stand the test of verification over a considerable middle range of phenomena, as already exemplified, and this middle range typically comprises nearly all the factual data. The outcome of verification therefore cannot be made to depend on a majority of the items of data. Yet it must be admitted that a new hypothesis can be verified, for if that were denied there could be no progress in science, and it is an axiom of the modern period that progress is essential to survival. If this sounds like a dilemma, let me point out that the verification-rules of present-day science are the same as in the English-speaking courts of law.

The one essential rule here is that there is a pair of stipulations. (1) The proponent of a new hypothesis stipulates that a hypothesis *cannot be proved* but can at best survive a vigorous try at refuting it. (2) The defender of the old theory stipulates that *only one case is to be tried at a time*. If either party refuses to enter into his stipulation, he is ruled out of court. Since I am here playing the role of proponent of a new hypothesis, it is my duty to submit that my opponent (I will give him a name later) is false to his stipulation if he requires my hypothesis to be verified by texts that have been *either* edited *or* interpreted in accordance with some other theory, and that I undertake to cite *Trial* data without any misbehavior beyond excusable oversight.

Casual Assurance

Citations for all the eight modals have been assembled in one series in the Appendix. I have counted 1340 occurrences of modals in *Trial*, exactly one sixth of all the finites; the completely detailed statistics have already been given late in Chapter III. The verification begins with *will* and *shall*, the actual tense of WILL and SHALL. There are 121 occurrences of *will* (including *'ll* [see pp. 162–163] and *won't*) of which this sample includes all the 13 whose subject is either *I* or *we;* one of these 13 is in the 'I will see you in heaven' whose several repetitions are counted among the 121 separately but only once here so as to leave the opposition all the statistical comfort they could get from *Trial*. The 20 occurrences of *will* with other subjects cited bring the total for *will* up to 33, or 27.3 percent of the 121 in *Trial*. All the 11 occurrences of *shall* are cited; two of them have subjects in the 'third person' (one of them *the accused* and the other *that answer*) and the others have 'first person' subjects (5 times *I* and 4 times *we*).

The textbook theory says that *I shall, you will, he will* are normal, and that *I will* is reserved for 'intention, volition, choice, etc.' There is not one shred of evidence in *Trial* in favor of that hoary theory, and adequate counter-evidence to refute it.

Will: At the time of speaking (since this is the actual tense) there is *adequate casual assurance* of eventual occurrence: the event is assured by everything the speaker has not overlooked; its failure to occur is inconsistent with all the cogent circumstances.

Shall: At this moment there is *contingent casual assurance* of eventual occurrence: the assertion is heedful of circumstances and is worded with this modal to allow that events assured to such an extent have failed to occur; failure is inconsistent with heeded circumstances while perhaps consistent with others.

The end of this is the definition of *contingent*, which does not mean 'conditional'; clearly *conditional* sentences use *will:* see next. As before, italic numbers refer to the citations as numbered where they are assembled in the Appendix. To begin with, a condition could hardly be clearer than *Don't you say that or you will get me into trouble* (*70*). Others are: *if you are wise* (*98*); *stop the drug and* (*165, 167, 168*); *the nearer . . . the more* (*203*); then *264* is the condition for *272, 273*, and *as far as . . . can go* (*278*); that makes nine of the twenty *will* examples in the Appendix without *I* or *we*.

There is no sharp division between clear conditions and the remaining *will* uses, no matter what the subject. The essential point, which unites them all, is that the speaker has selected *will* because of his prudent confidence in the event's eventual occurrence. Once that is clear, we need not be surprised either at being unable to guess all the grounds of his adequate assurance or at his use of this modal ironically, as at *118*. There the ultimate basis was a promise made at the start of the First World War by the Government and tauntingly echoed through the rest of it. The echo was revived, with characteristically British rueful irony though seldom with the same bitterness, two decades later; and at the epoch of *Trial* this speaker was not alone in using it as a sort of classical allusion.

Generally the basis of the adequate assurance is *knowledgeability: 119, 143, 169, 172, 199, 255, 325, 349, 355*. Mr. Lawrence is utterly knowledgeable at *264*. And this gives us a firm bridge to *266 I will*. Assuming that we are not committed to the tradition that 'futurity' is the sense of *shall* or of *will*, with some violent shift of meaning for *I will*—that is, under the stipulation that only one case is to be tried at a time—it is crystal-clear that *264* is not significantly different from 'I will call Dr. J. B. Harman as our first witness.' And this is what we find throughout the 13 occurrences of *I will* and *we will: 20, 41a, 80, 91, 117, 134, 157, 178, 251, 266, 294, 339, 346*). (There are only nine of *I shall* and *we shall* together, and *will* means the same here as before.)

The first of this list (*20*) will be postponed to the end of the *shall* survey. At *41a* the meaning is unchallengeable: No matter which way things turn out, that is what we will see; the speaker is perfectly safe because he has not specified which of two or more events he is assuring us of. If he had specified one of them rather exactly, and assuming he speaks like the other persons in *Trial*, he would have said *we shall* to protect his reputation (not for good grammar but for factual knowledge!) as at *68* and *345*.

When the subject of *will* was neither *I* nor *we*, we found some occasional specifications of the basis for the adequate assurance; when the subject is *I* such specifications are routine: *at this rate (80), I adhere to that (117), certainly (134), not my affair (157), certainly . . . if you say so (178), more likely (251), if you do not want to answer (294), and then (339), probably (346);* with respect to the last of these I must remind certain of my readers that although an American may say *probably* when he means 'perhaps,' a typical Englishman says it when he means 'It's an odds-on bet' and his *probably* means 'probatively.' Some of the specifications are of course 'clear conditions' as before, notably at *80, 157, 178, 294, 339.* Others that I have cited are of course only manifestations of the fact that the conditions are clear in the speaker's mind, rather than literal specifications of what the conditions are.

At any rate, we have found no occasion to depart from the position that there is neither prophecy nor resolve in any of these, but only prudent confidence based on adequate assurance of the event. One particularly clear case is that in which the speaker has been in a sense *invited* to do just what he says he will do: *91, 266.* The whole routine of the courtroom provides for these very things to be done freely and on any slightest impulse of each speaker-actor, and if he didn't feel that, he would not be at home there as these lawyers are: we remember that these two men are the principal counsel for the prosecution and the defense respectively. Precisely parallel to this is the case of the superintendent at *346*, for he knows that he can invite himself at any time to 'have another talk' with the Doctor and can afford to let the time of it depend on when the inquiries are finished: the Doctor will naturally be available then too. Incidentally, there is ample reason to believe that if he had said 'we shall' the Doctor would have taken that 'we' to mean 'myself and another police officer.' Such considerations are *real;* schoolbook grammar is not.

At this point it's about time to dispose of the notion that *will* is a 'future tense' auxiliary. Like *every* modal, and simply because 'time will tell' whether the asserted relation of the specified event to the real world suffices to bring about its occurrence, it has a *connotation* of futurity; but *no* modal has a *denotation* of futurity. For *will* this is particularly easy to demonstrate; what I am going to show is that the denotation of futurity, if it had one, would be damaging in specific cases. One will suffice.

Consider *165, 167, 168*. We all know Dr. Douthwaite by this time. Another man might have contented himself with the plain facts as he knows them: 'You can stop the drug and the tolerance *disappears* in a week or two; or you can increase the drug and immediately you *overcome* the tolerance and *satisfy* the craving. [What *are* the results of stopping the drug?] The patient *becomes* [or *is*] terribly ill and *has* acute pains in the limbs and *collapses*.' Not Dr. Douthwaite. He goes further: he underlines the reliability of his testimony by introducing three times the *will* which signifies that *he* has *adequate assurance* of those events. It is a neat and economical way to do that, for *will* three times applies to *six* verb-bases in all. On the other hand, he would have thrown away as much as he (from his peculiar point of view) thinks he is gaining here *if* our English *will* had a denotation of futurity, and in a way even more. It would have been a bad bargain, for *futurity* would shift the impact of his testimony right out of the courtroom into quite different places (hospitals, for example) and later times. Here in the courtroom is where he achieves his triumph, if at all; and as a matter of fact he does procure a temporary advantage, as even the newspaper men seem ready to agree (see near *169, 170*); but because this advantage depends on the validity of his own assurance it is all the worse when he is finally routed (see *239*) and the jury are left aghast at such inflexibility.

But now if this is not the English future, then what is? Well, a good many languages get along without any, but not English. Besides the use of future-time adverbs (He leaves tomorrow; He is leaving tomorrow) whose equivalents are found in all languages as far as we know, English has the *quasi-auxiliary* BE GOING TO. What it means has been carefully explained in the footnote in Chapter V under the heading *Phase*, with cross-reference to where BE GOING TO was first dealt with and cited a few times. It is used 28 times in *Trial*, 10 times looking ahead from a past epoch ('The superintendent told the accused that he was going to charge him with murder' [81:83]) and 18 times looking ahead from the present time—which is what we mean by *future*. Of these, seven are in the first person:

"I *am going to* suggest to you that he never said these words."   [95:94]

"I cannot remember the details, and I *am* not *going to* discuss it." [97:96]

"is not for me to say and I *am* not *going to* say it."   [149:140]

"If we *are going to* talk about instructions . . ."   [158:148]

"I *am* not *going to* help you"   [196:180]

"I *am* not *going to* deal with them. What I *am going to* tell you is simply this"   [213:196]

Simple futurity with subject *I* or *we* is not often requisite in a text like *Trial*, of course; but *casual assurance* with the same subjects is equally of course needed a good deal oftener in those surroundings: *adequate* casual assurance 13 times and *contingent* casual assurance 9 times. These nine occurrences of *shall* are *68, 100, 126, 245, 254, 274, 311, 345, 351;* and these are now to be considered. In contrast to the firm grounds for using *will* that have been quoted—such contexts as *if you are wise, knowing, probably, certainly*—we find *shall* based on soft and uncertain grounds: *I think (68, 245); I hope (345);* these never introduce *I will* or *we will* in *Trial*. That seems clear enough; but things can get a good deal more subtle, and indeed contingency and subtlety are not far apart.

Consider the contrasting reactions of the Attorney-General at *91* and at *126*. At first glance, the situations are identical: Mr. Lawrence has just objected to what his opponent was about to do. The first time, the Attorney-General "remaining urbane" promptly complies, and we see that he has lost nothing thereby. The second time, he says 'Very well,' which is an English institution: it is our way of seeming to comply while reserving one's right to alter one's course of action in the future. Thus when he goes on to say 'I shall not ask about the contents of the earlier wills' it is plain to see that if on a later occasion he finds it expedient to ask about those contents he will first see to it that 'they are properly proved' and then ask whatever he chooses to ask.

The converse case comes up at *100*. This judge "looks kind" [25:33] and as a matter of fact he is, as we see again and again. This time, what he is saying is this: 'Because if I do {God forbid} have any grounds for complaint I shall {unless I get soft-hearted, and I say it this way because I'm afraid I often do get soft-hearted, and then I don't} take a very serious view of it.' Contingency is precisely this: the recognition that circumstances alter cases.

This can give the impression that *will* serves best when the anticipated time of the event is near at hand (and indeed it was, in nearly every case), while *shall* is used when the interval is capacious enough to provide for alterations, frustrations, loss of opportunity —or, when *shall* is negated, emergence of an unforeseen opportunity: *254, 274, 311 at the end, 351:* the last of these plainly because the accused could not be sure of holding to his chosen course of action come what may.

These nine are all the first-person uses of *shall* in *Trial*, and we have seen that this is even less of a 'future' than *will*. This point is likely to be hard to grasp by people who, like Americans generally, have been taught to think that *shall* is a particularly solemn, impressive, and therefore presumably *forceful* word: they are apt to associate it with the proverbial 'an Englishman's word is his bond' or with its archaic use in the drafting of documents and ordinances. Instead, we have seen that among people who use it freely, as they also use *I will*, in either case because that is what they mean rather than because of what it says here in this grammar-book (blowing the dust off it and then searching in the index), the distinctive feature of *I shall* is not that at all but almost the reverse: *diffidence*, distrust of eventualities that depend on one's own consistency to bring them about.

Contingency is an old story to any frontiersman, and diffidence is not going to get us summoned before the Committee on Un-American Activities, so why don't we say 'I shall lecture on Milton in the fall semester'? Because it's not in style. The symmetries of the English modal system could bring it into style at any time; what has prevented that, so far, is presumably the feeling that it's schoolbook stuff.

To return to our Englishmen. I promised to deal with *20* at this point. When we stand off and look at it, it becomes plain that diffidence as defined above would be out of order here: it would mean 'I am on my way to heaven and expect to get there eventually if nothing unforeseen intervenes.' Instead, the message is an expression of something like prudent confidence: 'I look forward to seeing you again, if not soon, then in heaven.' This is as modest a message as the other would be immodest. For the parallel *I would* we have Mrs. Bedford's word for it: The Judge "modestly" says, 'I would like to ask' at *181*, in contrast to the closely following expression of diffidence in the face of contingency (for he can't be sure of being able to assist the jury) at *184*.

It seems that everybody concerned in the trial has the same interpretation of *20*, and this is the evidence: We do not hear the Doctor say it; we instead hear it reported over and over again by various persons, *in three versions:* 'See you in heaven' and 'I'll see you in heaven' and 'I will see you in heaven'—the last being what was written down officially in the police officer's notebook. Yet nobody speaks up to correct anyone else's version. The rule governing omission of the early part of a sentence has been given before, in Chapter III at the beginning of the section *Finite Predication:* in casual style, any minor-stress words can be left unspoken from the beginning of the sentence up to the first major-stress word, here the word *see*. The only possible interpretation of the courtroom tolerance is that everybody takes it for granted that the Doctor said 'See you in heaven' and that everybody knows, as we native speakers of English all know, that that is necessarily 'I will see you in heaven.' This is also the proof that *'ll* is *will* and not *shall*, so that there was no risk of error when I cited *41a* (*We'll* in *Trial*) as *will*. I have included every *'ll* among the instances of *will* in the statistics.

Of course there is also the folklore theory in the schoolbooks which says that *I'll* is 'colloquial' for *I shall* as well as for *I will*, but that is nothing but a measure of desperation, an attempt to save the rule where it conflicts with the facts of usage in standard British English. Nowadays, people who bear a substantial burden of responsibility for realistic English teaching have turned their backs on those books:

> Whether *I'll* represents *I will* or *I shall* is perhaps an academic question. Who knows? We often say *I'll* and then have to write down what we say: when we put pen to paper, we then find ourselves wondering whether we should write *I'll, I will* or *I shall*. In reaching our decision, we are usually guided by the "rule" that prescribes *I shall, you will, he will* and we therefore turn *I'll* into *I shall*. Personally, I agree with Daniel Jones, and think that if one uses *shall* meaningfully (and not simply because a pedantic rule prescribes it) then the weak pronunciation becomes *shăll*. [R. A. C. in *English Language Teaching*, Vol. 27, No. 2 (January 1963), p. 95]

This is the leading British journal devoted to the scholarly guidance of the teaching and learning of English overseas; it is published at Oxford University; this excerpt is taken from the section which answers worried questions from foreigners of all complexions. In quoting this piece, I have changed one detail in an inconsequential way: the last word was printed there in the International Phonetic Alphabet with symbols showing that this *shăll* is the same as the last syllable of *official*.

To summarize so far (though I must still discuss *295* and *356*), casual assurance is the sole meaning of both *will* and *shall*, the first for adequate assurance and the second for contingent assurance. Future reference is freely possible, but there is no evidence that it is ever anything but secondary: not a message but only a useful interpretation on *most* occasions *though not all*. There is no control over the choice between *shall* and *will* according to whether the subject is or is not in the first person; there is only—and apparently only for *shall*, with no effect whatever upon *will*—an automatic reinterpretation (see below on *295, 356*) when the speaker is not also the actor so that the actor is somewhere else in the matrix. This happens to make *shall* relatively rare with subjects other than *I* and *we;* but that is not a grammatical fact, it is merely a matter of how often various messages are useful. In short, these doctors and lawyers are none of them slaves of schoolmen's grammar; they just say what they mean, and we are lucky to have their words unedited.

Two of the eleven occurrences of *shall* remain to be discussed. It may very well be that 'you will now consider what that answer shall be' *(356)* is an ancient and traditional courtroom formula; but there are two things to say on that point. For one thing, from this one example we have no way of guessing what the ancient meaning of *shall* may have been; but from the rest of *Trial* we have learned that the modern meaning is not out of order here, for what could be more contingent than a jury's verdict? If it had not been, there would have been either a plea of Guilty or else a dismissal. The other point is that later on, when an appropriate time has come for suggesting what the ancient meaning of *shall* was, we shall see why that doesn't matter: the rule of linguistic change is 'Business as usual during alterations.'

The remaining citation, 'the question arises, shall the accused go into the witness-box?' *(295)* is the only use of *shall* in *Trial* that would take no American by surprise, though in immature American usage even that is routinely replaced by *should*. We also say 'Shall I shut the door?' anywhere in North America, though I think less commonly today that when it was the first thing my little sister said, after more than a year of silence, when she finally decided she had learned the language.* This is simply the *actual tense* corresponding to the *remote* tense *should* in the employment which I will explain below as its commonest use.

Outside of questions with subject *I*, *we*, *John*, etc. (never *you!*) people in my part of the world seem to have no use for *shall* in unedited English, admitting that some of us edit while speaking; its principal employments arise out of the drafting of documents, and I am putting a couple of delightful specimens in the Appendix.

* See *The Five Clocks*, p. 47.

Remote Assurance

In the tabulation next, the first figure is the total number of occurrences in *Trial*, the second is the number cited in the Appendix and accounted for in this chapter:

will 121/33   *shall* 11/11   *would* 338/94   *should* 98/36

Citation and discussion will be exhaustive not only for *shall* but also for *ought to* (15 occurrences) and *need* (3) and *dare* (3). For all the others, I have made sure that all uses are represented, and in fair proportion. This section begins with *should* for reasons which will become clear soon enough, and then covers *would*. Both still represent casual assurance; the heading here is not misleading because the stable modals are not split into actual and remote tenses, and it may be helpful as a reminder that what has been learned from the *actual* casual modals is still valid for the *remote* ones though not vice versa in general.

In these citations the commonest use of *should* is parallel to the rarest use of *shall*, namely that in *295 shall the accused go into the witness-box?* Now it would be possible, with the help of a long spoon, to equate this to the common use of *shall* (9 occurrences) as in *295* to signify contingency, either manifesting diffidence or reserving one's right to alter a course of action as already explained. To equate them, it would be necessary to call the *should* clause the expression of an unreal conclusion whose hypothetical condition has not been stated in any coordinated clause. Examples:

3 But they should never have heard it before.

7 in terms of what should or could be given?

46 "All experienced nurses do it?" — "They shóuld dò."

123 evidence is damaging . . . and should not be heard.

124 The Attorney-General submits that it should.

The suppressed condition for the last of these would presumably be 'If this were a well-behaved court'—and we have to dismiss this explanation because that would be contempt of court, and analogous objections can be raised to all the other examples.

What we have to do, I submit, is to recognize a consistent and well-defined meaning that is not explicitly provided for in the system of modal meanings that I have presented as the hypothesis to be verified. This well-defined meaning can be approximately paraphrased in various ways: 'But they are not supposed to have ever heard it before' and 'in terms of what ought to be given' and 'The Attorney-General submits that it is proper evidence,' or 'submits that the court must hear it if he chooses to present it.' The impossibility of finding exact paraphrases suggests that this is a primitive meaning, a modal meaning like the others that have been verified for *shall* and for *will*, but in conflict with the others.

The resolution of this dilemma comes from the recognition that we have here two competing systems of meaning for the same words, and it will turn out that we need the same two systems for all of *shall*, *should*, *may*, and *might*, though for no other modal. History supplies names for the two systems: I will call them the *archaic* system and the *modern* system of modal meanings. The modern system has prevailed since around 1700; its firm establishing coincides, surely not merely by accident, with the emergence of England's parliamentary democracy; before that time American English had definitively split off from British English (Benjamin Franklin's usage is unmistakably different) with results that will concern us later. The archaic system prevailed past Shakespeare's day, but his plays show the characteristic features of the modern modal system occasionally. For the examples, I take the first three occurrences of *will* from his very early *Two Gentlemen of Verona*, all archaic, and the first *will* in *Tempest*, probably his last complete play, as showing the modern meaning:

Commend thy grievance to my holy prayers, for I will be thy beadsman, Valentine. — And on a love-book pray for my success? — Upon some book I love I'll pray for thee. . . . 'Tis true; for you are over boots in love, and yet you never swum the Hellespont. — Over the boots? Nay, give me not boots! — No, I will not, for it boots thee not. [I, i, 17–28]

BOATSWAIN: You are a Councillor. If you can command these elements to silence and work the peace of the present, we will not hand a rope more;

use your authority. If you cannot, give thanks you have lived so long, and make yourself ready in your cabin for the mischance of the hour, if it so hap. [I, i, 23ff.]

Now the archaic system lacked *ought to* (at that time the past indicative of OWE) and *need* (noun, adverb, and impersonal verb); but our casual modals were already the terms of a two-dimensional sub-system of the same orientation as today; the difference is that each term had different senses. It is a little hard to read this off at a distance of more than three centuries, but I believe the archaic and modern sub-systems match up like this:

WILL $\begin{cases} \text{Authoritative Probity} \\ \text{adequate assurance} \end{cases}$ SHALL $\begin{cases} \text{Subservient Probity} \\ \text{contingent assurance} \end{cases}$

CAN $\begin{cases} \text{Authoritative Freedom} \\ \text{adequate potentiality} \end{cases}$ MAY $\begin{cases} \text{Subservient Freedom} \\ \text{contingent potentiality} \end{cases}$

Only one of the polar terms needs explication, namely Freedom. This word is to be understood in the medieval sense, when there was no abstract *freedom* but only countable Freedoms, each bestowed, none inherent, all subject to forfeiture. The *Tempest* passage still shows the archaic meaning of CAN: note how the boatswain bases his correction of the Councillor on the medieval theory but bases his estimate of what the seamen will do on his own adequate assurance.

Over a substantial middle range of sentences, both the archaic and the modern meaning-systems will give the same first-order effects in the communication situation. This middle range covers all but the rarest uses of WILL and CAN, and the extremes can be safely neglected even in a text as long as *Trial*. As to SHALL and MAY (of course including *should* and *might* as well as *shall* and *may*) the situation is far more complicated. The nine *Trial* examples of *shall* with first-person subjects all can be taken, as I took them all, as having the modern meaning *contingent assurance*. Yet roughly half of them are also open to interpretation in the archaic sense Subservient Probity. One example will be enough (*126*): 'Very well,' says the Attorney-General, and these words are already ambivalent in exactly the same way, 'I shall not ask about the contents of the earlier wills'; and now Subservient Probity makes this a faithful promise good for all time, while *contingent assurance* claims the modern democratic right of letting circumstances alter cases.

I can safely leave the reader to sort out for himself just which others of those nine first-person *shall* occurrences could have the archaic sense, always of course side by side with the modern sense which is valid for them all. It is certain that this can't be done for quite all of them; certainly not, for example, at *351*, where the Judge has explained through close to a hundred preceding words why this is not archaic: when he speaks of the natural thought of England, he means only modern England, for the right to evade self-incrimination did not exist in the medieval theory of justice.

Before considering *should* (and eventually *would, could,* and *might*), I must reconsider the significance of *tense*. In Chapter V the unmarked tense was named *actual*, the marked tense *remote*, with explanations which should be reviewed for background to what must be said next. There the marked tense was the one of strictly limited significance (either historical past or unreal contemporary), while the unmarked tense was equally good for any time whatever. The validity of this distinction is obviously related to the fact that unmarked (factual) assertion was envisaged throughout that chapter.

In relative assertion, the tense can be marked only with the casual modals WILL, SHALL, CAN, MAY, giving *would, should, could, might*. The matrix is always the minimal one: see under *Modal Summary* above. Now the value of unmarked tense is that the very moment of speaking dominates this minimal matrix. For *will* and *shall* so far, it has been clear that only the circumstances of just the moment of speaking (*C:* all of them; *c:* some of them) could be circumstances of the minimal matrix, which is as much as to say that they dominate it, for they alone constitute it. What is

new about remote tense in turning to the modals is that the domi-
nance drops out; in the remote tense of factual assertion the whole
present scene dropped out. In factual assertion, remote tense blots
out present reality; with modals (in relative assertion) remote
tense does this only part way.

The remote tense of a modal generalizes, so that present reality
becomes a minor fraction of the total possible reference. The result
is that the present scene becomes a small sample of all the possible
scenes meant, real and unreal together, future, present, and past
together. When this small sample is in the focus of attention, it
thereby is more important than the rest; when it is not, it is subordinated to the rest; it can even drop out, so that only unreality
or only real past time is meant: but this is rather rare, in contrast
to the remote tense in factual assertion, where it always drops out
completely. A few typical results thus are:

(1) The real present scene is most important, but remote tense
is used to signify that it is only a sample of what is generally true:
187, 177 (compare *178*).

(2) Generalization dominates, and the real present scene is not
allowed to be an exception: *33, 44* (compare *54*), *13* (compare *9*).

(3) Past reality is meant: *10, 63–67, 77, 95*. The examples are
few.

(4) Unreality is meant: *187–194* and many others.

This brief survey of the remote tense of modals is sure to be
deceptive at this point; it has been given only to help clarify somewhat the peculiar definition of modal remote tense given just
above, or rather give it some substance instead of leaving it entirely
abstract. From here on, the remote tenses of the four casual modals
will be considered in turn, beginning with *should* in its archaic
meaning: *3, 7, 46, 123, 124, 159, 174, 265*.

The meaning is Subservient Probity *generalized*. Take *46:* Nurse
Stronach [righteous click, light snap, defensive, satisfied tone,
click, shutting-out tone] says, 'That is quite correct,' and a little
later, 'It is the usual thing when you are nursing. It is the proper
thing to do.' And then we have Mr. Lawrence's next question and

her response: 'All experienced nurses do it?' — 'They shóuld dò.'
There it is. If we have ever wondered what Subservient Probity,
the righteous consciousness of duty well done, is good for, we can
rest easy: Nurse Stronach has told us, and in certain moods we
may wish there were more of her. [Sturdily].

Next, citations showing preservation of this sense in subordinate
clauses; American English does the same thing freely but not quite
as often, for the first citation could be, and in formal American is
more likely to be, worded without *should* to make 'suggested that
Mr. Sogno prepare a codicil,' and similarly with certain others:
11, 16, 82, 127, 129, 176, 195, 205, 247; now we have covered
roughly half the *should* citations. This is enough to make *should*
quite a frequent word, and frequent use has caused the bad odor
of Subservience to pretty well evaporate from the word. In both
British and American English, *should* is accordingly a frequent
replacement for *must*, and its modern *contingent* value makes it a
handy replacement for *ought to* also; finally, Americans are apt to
interpret documentary *shall* into *should* when memory of the official
wording has become hazy. Thus we feel right at home with *279*
and probably interpret it very close to what Mrs. Bedford meant.

In the United States, *127* is a New England provincialism and is
rapidly dying out there; it has acquired an aura of vulgarity or at
least bucolic quaintness. And *141* is evaluated as quaint and
literary; our normal equivalent is 'and who do you suppose walked
in.' On the other hand, *186* is interpreted by Americans exactly
the same as *3*, though I must doubt whether this is what Dr.
Douthwaite meant. My guess is that he meant what we can say as
'Why not reduce the heroin?'

In other words, *should* can be used to signify nothing but sub-
ordination—not a very considerable departure, after all, and
plainly not a contradiction of the basic archaic sense. In this function, we find *should* in *263* 'not desirable for him to comment';
300 'not desirable for judges to express'; *302* perhaps 'inevitable
that reports appear' in formal American. Each *should* is possible
American.

From here on, the remaining 13 of these 36 *should* citations are all marginal to American usage, and the reason is plain: they all have strictly the *modern* British sense of SHALL, not the archaic sense which is the only one known to American English by continuous tradition since the split in the seventeenth century. This marginal status has more than one effect.

First, it leads to misunderstandings when an Englishman says *should* in the modern sense and an American takes it in the archaic one. Let me paraphrase both what I take to be the *Trial* message and the possible American misinterpretation: *45* 'What I diffidently say is that it was due . . . ' misinterpreted as 'I feel an obligation to say' and the same at *107, 139, 146, 184, 261, 267, 271, 292, 299, 361;* this makes eleven possible misunderstandings already among the thirteen. The actual results vary, of course. At *184, 299* the combination with *like* practically forces the correct interpretation, and it is distinctly encouraged in certain others— though seldom, to an American ear, at all strongly. On the other hand, hardly any American could guess that *77* means 'Made me think "I'm going to be dismissed." '

Second, the modern British sense was brought to New England by Yankee seafarers, and encouraged by local schoolteachers there; the first influence was strong until it ceased almost abruptly at the same time that the railroads became a stronger force (around 1845), and the second influence still continues today though diminishingly. The odd result is that what is modern in Great Britain is represented in American tradition by a handful of frozen archaisms:

I shouldn't wonder.
I shouldn't be (a bit *or* the least bit) surprised.
I should think so.
I should hope so!
I should hope not!
I should say so!
I should say! [approximately 'goodness gracious me!']
I should sáy nót!

This list may not be quite complete, but the point is that the list is essentially closed. It is possible to add *at all* after *wonder* or *surprised*, but not possible to replace either by *be amazed; think* and *hope* are replaced by *presume* only by those few who love antique furniture; none can be freely extended to form longer sentences. All are fading out rapidly, but in an odd fashion: feeling them to be archaic, we would like to drop them, but in accomplishing that we limp into makeshift employments of wordings that we know mean something else: 'I'm not (*or* I won't be) surprised; I hope so, I hope not.'

Of course *361*, following as it does right after the *360* that seems right and proper to us, is inevitably misinterpreted (or can it be that Mrs. Bedford meant this too?) like this: 'I really ought not to be here at all!'

Third, with the recent efflorescence of American education there has been force-feeding of *shall* and *should*, with the predictable result: everything from flat rejection to galloping hyperurbanism. It makes one secretly hope that *87* is a hyperurbanism too, as *252* strongly suggests: it is exactly the sort of thing that happens when an American has learned about SHALL, WILL, and *one*.

Remote Adequate Assurance

It is something of a relief to turn to *would* and find nothing un-American there, and everything American. We have to remember that what R. A. C. said about *shall* and *will* very largely applies here too, as the *Trial* statistics confirm: the SHALL that is absent in American is less frequent in standard British English than the WILL that is condemned by prescriptive grammarians.

In *Trial* the central or normal vehicle for remote assurance is *would*, with 338 occurrences against 98 of *should*, and with no elusiveness of meaning whatever; the statistical difference is far greater than the ratio of frequency of other 'persons' to 'first person,' and the occurrences of *I would* are plentiful and easily compared with *I should* to establish the modern British distinction between them.

Both *should* and *would* are in the remote tense, and we know that in factual assertion this nearly always means 'past time,' occasionally 'unreality.' When *would* has real past-time meaning, it corresponds exactly to *will* at *165, 167, 168;* one result is the series of ten uses of *would* at *58–67*. With *will*, the meaning is *characterization* (see under *Generic Aspect* in Chapter V) with adequate casual assurance. Now with *would* this meaning becomes narrative-past, regularly in the generic aspect (temporary aspect is provincial, specifically Irish), freely either characterizing (*58–61*, perhaps *62*) or plot-advancing (Chapter V, end of the section *Narrative Aspects* and beginning of the next) as at *63–65*, perhaps *62*.

But the plot can be advanced without it, so what is *would* good for? Without it, the plot can be advanced only in steps, in sequence one after the other; the specific function of *would* now is to present a step as simultaneous with its fraction of the occasion, and that is the same meaning as the use of *will* for the consequence of a 'clear condition' (John will fall asleep in church; You know you won't not drink when you're there) and once more underlines the point that futurity is not a denotation of WILL, that its meaning is adequate assurance *at the time.*

That fraction of the occasion may be represented by its own verb (between *62* and *63: took* and *brought*) or it may be implicit: *62, 64, 65*. When the occasion is not thus fragmented, we find things like the whole sentence between *65* and *66*. This is indistinguishable from factual characterization, and why shouldn't it be? Beautiful; and there are equally admirable devices in every language. This one derives from the adequacy and casualness of assurance with *would*, as the other one did with *will*. And let's not have any more fustian about intention, volition, choice, etc., if we can help it.

This fitting of the event to a fraction of an occasion is evident also when the generalizing remote tense *would* is not real-past but unreal and contemporary. The unreality then is a manifestation of *urbanity*. Exactly the same urbanity inheres in *should* in that modern British sense discussed at the end of the preceding section, and the present discussion is partly a footnote to that page: it was postponed to this spot to facilitate comparison between British *should* and *would*. Examples:

33 On these points . . . would seem to rest the weight

42 "That would be after you yourself had given her . . ."

43 "Mrs. Morell would be fairly dopey and half-asleep . . ."

47–51 "And whatever you wrote in that book would be accurate because it would have been done right at that very moment?" — "It would." — . . . [speed again] "As distinct from your memory of six years later, these reports would of course be absolutely accurate." — [Sturdily] "Oh yes, they would be accurate from each one of us." {urbanity enough for export}

83 "Would you mind reading us out the whole of the completed form?" {this is taught in early lessons in English in Belgrade as the normal request formula, to the intense bafflement of the forthright Serbs, who never do quite figure out what *mind* could possibly signify here or in the response 'I don't mind'}

104, 105 "and you said, 'No,' and that would not be quite right, and again for the same reason, would it not?" — Nurse Randall [resigned tone] "No." {not the only time Mr. Lawrence has blended urbanity with litotes and reversed the tag-question; what could Nurse Randall *do* but resign?}

The remaining citations which can be completely explained in this way are: *22* (compare *21*), *120a* (comradely), *140* (compare *45*), *175, 177* (compare *178*), *181* (compare *184*), *192, 194, 232, 250, 256, 286;* some of these can also be treated as unreal conclusions: see below.

Our next step will make a clean sweep of the rest of *would*. It has been pointed out that *would* has the function of *matching* or *fitting* the event to the occasion: as a real past it fits it to a fraction of the occasion, as an unreal contemporary relative assertion it fits it to the urbanity of the occasion. Fitting is a relation; relative assertion is what is needed for that, and WILL is the cheapest marker of relative assertion, so everything is in order so far. When the occasion is connected to the present scene (which in English stretches indefinitely into future time), *will* is the form; when it does not (and urbanity is not a part of the scene, not being forced on the speaker but rather issuing from within him) the form is *would*, unless contingency replaces it with the rarer *should*, or else the editing rules for the use of SHALL and WILL.

Now for the last use of *would*. Referring to the event itself (no longer to the fact that the speaker is fitting it to something) *would* fits any *unreal* event (contrary-to-fact, as the books say, or not contrary; that is not the point) to anything whatever. Remembering that this or any language is designed for speaking of things *because they matter*, this means that *would* fits any unreal event to anything that matters. Having disposed of two sorts of things that matter—real-past *would* fitting to fractions of the occasion, and unreal contemporary *would* fitting to urbanity—we are left, by definition, with *hypothesis* as the adequate category of things that matter.

That hypothesis may be as real, factual, circumstantial as you like; or it may be as utterly inaccessibly unreal as you like; none of that makes any difference. Again, the *would* event may be utterly certain, or it may be utterly unreal and fanciful; the only requisite for *would* is that the event must *not* be treated as *contingent*, that is, dependent on evading frustrations, which would call for *should* instead—naturally then in the first person because only one who is both speaker and actor can specify that he both foresees and means to evade.

Returning to that hypothesis: it may be expressed in the immediate context or not; and it may be expressed with or without a verb; and this gives us probably the best way to subdivide the citations.

Hypothesis unexpressed in the close context; but of course the speaker has taken some hypothesis as his basis for asserting the unreal conclusion: *40* 'Wouldn't you think he could have taken his pick?' We can guess that the hypothesis was that the addressee is an Englishman, a sufficient determinant of a way of thinking; this could have been cited before under *urbanity* along with the comradely *120a*. Similarly *22, 33, 39, 110, 128, 154, 190, 191, 193, 215;* in general, these can be distributed among the others.

Hypothesis expressed in the context but not in a clause with its own verb. Here we can to a degree distinguish between (1) prior or causal hypothesis, and (2) posterior or teleological hypothesis. Since there is no verb expressing the hypothesis, it is often impossible to guess whether it was conceived as real or as unreal. Examples: (1) *78, 112, 130, 142, 147, 160–162, 236, 238, 281–284, 293, 360;* (2) *36, 208, 235.* The subdividing is subject to considerable error, but it roughly indicates how human motives have their basis in recent events, in foresight, and in mixtures and confusions.

Hypothesis expressed by a non-finite verb, so that it is generally impossible to distinguish between a real and an unreal hypothesis: *84, 150, 152, 155, 156, 270.*

Hypothesis expressed by an actual factual verb ('real condition') or by a remote factual ('past tense') verb that seems to refer to the real past: *114, 115, 145, 220, 331.* These are traditionally presented as a minor aberration among 'conditional sentences,' though it would be hard to find a more misleading treatment: an unreal assertion based on a real hypothesis is not conditional.

Hypothesis expressed by an unreal remote verb, factual in well-behaved English. Here at last is the famous 'conditional' of the school grammars. It is a minor use of *would* in *Trial;* it is outnumbered, roughly half a dozen to one, by those majority uses which tradition treats as aberrations. The few examples can still be usefully subdivided.

(1) The unreal hypothesis is contemporary; that is, treated as associated with the same scene rather than with one remote from it; the unreal *conclusion* is then in the *current* phase: *133, 187, 217, 218, 226, 227, 312.* The expression of the *hypothesis* splits the English-speaking world roughly into British and American, with Dr. Douthwaite on the American side: *217; Trial* otherwise uses the quasi-auxiliary BE TO substantially wherever possible (not with the copula: *133*); in American, this is rather precious and our norm would be: *187* 'if you made application,' *218* 'If another doctor said,' *226–227* 'if the Doctor went,' *312* 'if you regarded.' Commonly in American (and possibly in British? and is this archaic?)

the unreal hypothesis employs *should:* 'If another doctor should say . . . ' There is no *Trial* example.

(2) The unreal hypothesis is remote, usually but not necessarily referring to a previous time: *188, 189, 336, 337.* The unreal *conclusion* is then in the *perfect* phase. This is requisite in the unreal hypothesis too, but can drop out as if it were redundant: *113, 234.* Conversely, *would* may be introduced into the unreal *hypothesis: 179–180.* In popular American usage this is routine, and presumably also in British usages that are somehow marginal; my data are too scanty to allow me to be specific.

I have undertaken to deal with forms and meanings both. Within the limits of descriptive linguistics, or indeed of any single book, such a topic can be exhausted only in one direction: by listing under each form all its attested meanings. The other direction, which starts out from all possible meanings and presents suitable forms, opens infinite vistas: not linguistics but literature.

Finally—and it does seem peculiarly appropriate to the heading of this section—an *envoi* to casual assurance and my last respects to the schoolbook theory and to H. W. Fowler's astrology. In his classic essay on mathematical invention Henri Poincaré explains that a mathematician can be weak and confused in simple arithmetic; he, for example, can seldom add a short column of figures correctly; and continues with this:

> Je serais également un fort mauvais joueur d'échecs; je calculerais bien qu'en jouant de telle façon, je m'expose à tel danger; je passerais en revue beaucoup d'autres coups que je rejetterais pour d'autres raisons, et je finirais par jouer le coup d'abord examiné, ayant oublié dans l'intervalle le danger que j'avais prévu.

> In the same way I *should* be but a poor chess-player; I *would* perceive that by a certain play I *should* expose myself to a certain danger; I *would* pass in review several other plays, rejecting them for other reasons, and then finally I *should* make the move first examined, having meanwhile forgotten the danger I had foreseen.*

* This translation, by George Bruce Halsted, is most easily accessible in *The Creative Process*, ed. Brewster Ghiselin (University of California Press, 1952; now in the New American Library as Mentor Book MP383).

Referring in the Appendix to this page, I quote Fowler, who would call this "elegant variation" and rightly to be contemned; and I would agree if it were. Instead it is exactly what we have been observing all along. It is fortunate that the standard translation I quote was made by an Englishman of superior education and strength of character though only moderate literary talent, and that he understands Poincaré as one mathematician understands another. For our purposes, then, either or both is the 'speaker.'

This speaker has adequate casual assurance (casual in that it is based on self-knowledge and on having watched a little chess and perhaps played some for fun within his family) which makes him prudently confident both of this perceiving and of this passing in review. But for each time he says *should*, it is brilliantly clear that he cannot foresee the event with more than contingent assurance: (1) he might turn out to be an excellent chess-player, though for unforeseen reasons, if he ever tried it (he never seriously did, I have been told); (2) it might very well not be a danger at all, or one easily met; (3) it is surely not certain that the ultimate move would be identical to the first one. We have seen exactly these same things happen in *Trial*.

French says nothing whatever in its verbs about this contrast. Three times, Poincaré couldn't care less: he can trust his readers. Once he uses *bien* for something very much like our adequate assurance; once he uses the *vivid present* tense *je m'expose* for a *hazard* felt strongly enough so that an Englishman in his place would use instead the expression of *contingency*. But British English packs all of this into the finite verbs. We Americans would employ *would* all five times; but we would occasionally parallel the French *bien* with one or more of these: 'I would *most likely* be a poor chess-player,' 'I would *practically always* notice,' 'I would *be likely to* expose myself,' 'I would *then* pass in review,' 'I would *end up by* making the very move I had first rejected.' Not all five, of course; that would be too much clutter even for an American. And Fowler would throw the baby out with the bath-water, for five times *should* is no better than five times *would*.

Casual Potentiality

The tabulation on page 167 and the accompanying discussion can be used as background for this section too. Aside from that, however, most things come out differently when we examine CAN and MAY. Here grammarians say practically nothing (Fowler has no entry on these modals) and the background is left mysterious; censure of 'incorrect English' is no less vigorous but is in all other respects different. The parent or teacher who meets 'Can I?' with 'No, you may not!' seemingly has no theory about it at all: the child's *can* simply was incorrect and *may* the correct word and that's that. The child knows better of course—he is by profession a learner of the community language and simply can't be fooled about such matters; what's more, he is a student of sociology, before he gets to kindergarten, and promptly figures out that *may* has two employments of which one is the function of substituting for *can* and *might* when the speaker feels the need to impose or acknowledge authority—the acknowledging may be ironic, the imposing of course not. This peculiar institution seems to be approximately as old as schooling in more or less modern patterns. Since among adults (except teachers of rather young children) the whole matter is sedulously avoided as a topic for open discussion, the history cannot be reconstructed; my guess is that it is around two hundred and fifty years old, and that makes it all the more mysterious: why should the situation be exactly the same in England and in America, while the old shift from archaic to modern meaning-structure for WILL and SHALL splits the two regions apart so cleanly?

No American needs to explain anything about CAN and MAY to any Englishman, nor has the Englishman anything to teach an American: both have known about this since they were babies. I will therefore explain things especially for the benefit of readers who are learning about English from some other starting-point; that is, my description will read somewhat like an anthropological field-worker's report. The natural beginning is a set of paraphrastic definitions; the two origins, archaic and modern, do not split the CAN definition:

CAN: either Authoritative Freedom or *adequate potentiality:* the event is entirely possible in that no cogent factor stands against its occurrence: the event is consistent with all the circumstances.

MAY: (1) archaic sense: Subservient Freedom: the event is authoritatively allowed, and the assertion is worded with this modal to signify that the actor is hardly free to desist.

(2) modern sense: *contingent potentiality:* the event is allowed by some but not all circumstances, and the assertion is worded with this modal to allow for contrary circumstances to perhaps prevail.

There are 261 occurrences of *can* in *Trial,* of which 63 (just over 24 percent) are cited in the Appendix to make them available for discussion here. The meaning is so transparent that the discussion need not go beyond showing what the various employments are.

First, the six instances *24–29* show the essential meaning of *can.* The picture is the same six times, yet in about four variations. What is the same is that a 'line of sight' is conceptually defined by its two extremities, both named; one is the eye of a beholder (or the ear of a listener: *29*) and the other is the object seen or not seen (heard or not heard); the line is geometrically straight (except *29*); and now the question is whether it is interrupted by at least one obstacle: if interrupted by one, it doesn't matter how many others there are: 'at least one obstacle' answers the crucial yes-or-no question. Such an answer is, however, susceptible of numerous ramifications; and it is out of these branchings, these subdividings of the 'yes' or 'no' answer, that the 'variations,' the various exploitations, arise.

Exactly once among these 63 examples, the variation is a matter of degree, so to speak: *hardly* (*75*) seems to speak of an intensity that is smoothly variable. This will be commented on later. In the other 62, it is always a countable or 'discrete' matter, as mathematicians say. Let us look at the six examples *24–29* again. Here *24* and *28* say that there is no obstacle to the seeing. Now just after

The prisoner can look (*24*) there is its counterpart 'the Judge sees him' which says that the Judge not only can see him but does. The difference is that the prisoner has no duty to see, while it is the Judge's office to see what he can; similarly (*28*) all can see the Judge if they choose, but they have no office or duty to do so.

At *25, 26, 27, 29* we have fractional or total negations of potentiality, always countable: *few* (*25*) uses our substitute word for small numbers; *none* (*26*) and *no one* (*27*) remind us that 'zero' is a number, and both are associated with further numerical specifications: *26* with [*both*] *at one time*, *27* with *at all* which is our intensifier for 'zero' wordings such as *nothing, nowhere,* and the like; and *not . . . by everyone* (*29*) is similar. In the last of these, the negation is placed in another clause, separate from the *can* clause but linked to it; in the others, it is the subject of *can* that is wholly or fractionally negated; none of them has the negation applying directly to the *can*.

But *can* is negated directly with *not* in 18 of the 63 occurrences in this sample; the result is printed as *cannot* in every instance but one, but of course we know that a good many of these represent *can't*, and in the Appendix I have printed *cannŏt* for some that I am reasonably sure of. The list is *4, 17, 31, 54, 71, 73, 132, 149, 173, 204, 207, 209, 222, 228, 275, 290, 316, 330*. To these 18, we can add the two confirmation-questions that received negative answers (*201, 246*), the two statements governed by negative clauses (*29, 125*), the four with negated subjects (*26, 27, 32, 99*) and the one with negative object (*249*); that makes 27 times that *can* is effectively negated, and once (*25*) fractionally.

Now from the 63 examples of *can* in the Appendix we can subtract the five unanswered confirmation-questions *18, 35, 352, 363, 364*, and the two information-questions *163, 358*. That leaves just 56 uses of *can* that were open to negation at all, and we have found 27 of them effectively negated. This is as near as we could expect to come to exactly half of them. Imposing theories have been built upon foundations no stronger than that; for instance, when Newton set up his inverse-square law of gravitation he used a figure for the distance from here to the moon that was no closer to what his theory demanded than this 27 is to half of 56. In this instance the point is that 'one half' (like 'two') is a very simple number, the next-simplest after 'zero' and 'one,' and such simple numbers are always matters of intense interest when they turn up in scientific observation. The custom then is to say that it 'ought to' be exactly 'one half,' and thereafter to find appealing paraphrases for this 'one half.' Here are some possibilities:

We might say that *can* is like an honest coin, as likely to fall 'tails' as 'heads' when you toss it. Again, we might say that native speakers of English are especially likely to say *can* when they judge the probability of eventual occurrence to be about half; that is, when the probabilities are about evenly balanced between occurrence and non-occurrence. Third—this time quite a hazardous speculation—perhaps it is true that when the probabilities are sufficiently unbalanced, they (at least the British ones) say *shall;* when very strongly unbalanced, *will;* when utterly unbalanced, not relative assertion at all but factual assertion is used instead, without a modal; finally, *may* must await further investigation. Why do I draw just these possible conclusions? Because each negated *can* can be replaced by an affirmative one by replacing some context wording with its opposite, as when *4 cannot be so* is replaced by 'can only be false.'

But before going any farther with such tentative conclusions, it is wise to scan the neighborhood for more solid pieces of data. I go no farther in this book; instead, I turn my back on negated *can* after one more remark. I simply point out that negated *can* is quite often left without explicit argument, without stated justification for the impossiblity: *71, 73, 132, 316.* When there is a justification, it is often very weak: *17, 54, 173, 204,* and others. Of course the justification can also be strong; at its strongest, it is tautological: *149 great* (after *not . . . much!*), *207, 209,* and others. This full range of possibilities becomes particularly interesting when it is compared to what we find with affirmative *can,* which in this sample is *always* tautological!

Before marshalling the evidence, let us remind ourselves of the definitions which underlie my hypothesis for the meaning of *can*, beginning with the first description of the minimal social matrix of events, page 150. For every statement (assertion that is not a question), the center of the minimal matrix is the speaker. It is this personal center that determines just how much, and which particular items, of the factual world are to be included within the minimal matrix to constitute 'all the circumstances.' It is an essentially casual, a free-will determination. The person at the center is presumed to determine this responsibly; that would be the reason why he is normally not challenged when he negates *can*, but is rather assumed to have his good and sufficient reasons for saying *cannot, can't*. Now turning to affirmative use of *can*, what we see is that he shows us how responsibly he selects 'all the circumstances' from among all the content of the factual world. In general, he does this by making his selection tautological to the scope of his *can*. He trims R down to a C that is exactly right so that *can* will be valid; and in general he does it tautologically by using *can* to do the trimming. This may not be equally clear from every group of examples; but when any one of the following paragraphs has been understood, it will help with the understanding of the others.

A particularly interesting group is *few (25)*, *[some] mistakes (55)*, *any (170)*, *a (216)*, *any (246)*, *any (315)*: all these crucial context-words have the identical component of meaning, called 'indefinite,' which is the sole meaning of *a* at *a valid contrary view (216)*. Speakers of west-European languages use such expressions to segregate, delimit, circumscribe without specifying, within the factual world R just that C which is wanted for the occasion; this is always successful by definition, for the assertion (here, the *can* assertion) specifies the C.

The corresponding adverb is *only: 88, 211, 219, 237, 262*. The grammatical difference is inconsequential. Sometimes the segregating is easy because other context has already trimmed R into the shape of a line-segment having two ends; then the speaker can start at one end and stop wherever he likes short of the other end. The trimming down to *C* is then done by means of *as far as: 96, 116, 277;* or *before: 89, 182.* Or he can select a shorter segment excluding both ends; *where: 216.* If the line is not continuous but rather constituted of countable items, one way to do it is to say *about which: 315;* and similarly with other prepositions. The most abstract way of doing this is with *if: 233, 327;* or with its contrary *unless: 37.* An appeal to the addressee to do it himself is made by replacing *if* with *supposing: 257;* or it can be done cooperatively with *suppose.* The reader can now do what he likes with *hardly* (75).

When the speaker is not sure that his trimming or selection of *C* will be allowed, he protects himself with a tag-question: *206–207.* This can also be done with a tentative negative: *209–210.*

The even balance already noticed is evident in *equally well (269)*, which doesn't need to be taken quite literally: in idiomatic English, if *P* can be true and *Q* can also be true, we say that *P* and *Q* can 'equally well' be true. Sometimes this holds true by convention; thus the jury is expected to say either Guilty or Not Guilty: *31.* Similarly, when *164* and *166* are linked by *or*, the speaker, not knowing Mr. Lawrence's plan, can't guess which alternative is going to be pursued; his ignorance balances the alternatives. This is also fairly comparable to the way *333* is followed by *334*. Now consider *212.* Here the *might (213)* and the *equal eminence* together make the *can* tautological.

One curious detail remains, almost overlooked because it is a blank: it is the absence of a detail. Among all the ways of trimming *R* down to leave the *C* that will exactly fit *can*, there is not one instance in *Trial*, among all the 384 occurrences of *can* and *could* together, where the trimming is done by specifying a clock or calendar time. I suggest that the reason is contained in the definition of the minimal social matrix of events: its content and boundaries are determined by *where* the personal center is *at the moment*. Now this appears to have exhausted time as a determinant of *C;* and if time is to come into the picture again it can only affect the verb-base and the rest of the predicate, no longer the modal, so that *R* has to be trimmed in some other way to leave the *C* that is to be adequate to the *can*.

For one thing, this verifies once more the thesis that no modal can have a *denotation* of futurity, allowing that futurity may be a *connotation*. For another, it reminds us that we have already seen what happens when exact time is prominent: see BE ABLE TO under *Quasi-Auxiliaries*, Chapter II. And this in turn reminds us that *before* often trims *R* to leave the right *C* for a *can*, but *after* never does, at least not in *Trial*. Do we ever say anything like 'I can understand him since that evening'? I for one would have to say 'I have been able to understand him since then,' or possibly 'I am able . . . since then.'

There is nothing to add with respect to *could:* the 21 in the Appendix (and so I suppose the 123 in *Trial*) all behave as we must expect by now. The meaning is real past at *93* and perhaps a very few other places; otherwise it is unreal contemporary with all the familiar employments: urbanity at *44* in comparison with the straightforward *54;* unreal conclusion at *52;* and so on. It would serve no real purpose if I presented the survey here.

Contingent Casual Potentiality

The CAN discussion is still wide open at both ends: both the first paragraph of the preceding section, and its last paragraphs, call for the data and discussion on MAY. First its modern sense: the event is allowed by some but not all circumstances, and the assertion is worded with this modal to allow for contrary circumstances perhaps prevailing.

We have seen that responsible use of *can* meticulously excludes *all* the contrary circumstances; to accomplish that, an almost elaborate machinery of contextual sorting devices is employed; and when it has not been thoroughly done, Mr. Lawrence speaks another sentence after *55* to serve as a clean-up device. Then what are we to expect of *may?* Well, it would seem to be the word to use when that can't be done: when the speaker doesn't see how to specify which are the favorable and which the contrary circumstances,

when he must admit that frustration or failure lurks in unidenti-
fiable spots in the matrix, he leaves the contrary circumstances indeterminate by using *may*. It follows that there can be no such
even balance of probabilities as with *can*, and what 'may happen'
has an uncontrollable probability of happening; but to the extent
that a rough estimate has been made, the speaker can say things
like *may perhaps* near one extreme and *may very well* near the other:
I do not recall finding *can* or *could* in either of these combinations
in *Trial*.

Our sorting then naturally begins with *perhaps: 9, 14.* At this
point in the trial—the prosecution's opening address to the jury—
nothing whatever can be taken as settled, and I suppose (I don't
know the British courtroom rules, but the speech as a whole reads
accordingly) there may even be a rule enjoining extreme care in
avoiding prejudicial assertions: it is all right for the Attorney-
General at this point to say, 'She was attended by four nurses;
and these nurses *will* give evidence. They *will* say they never saw
Mrs. Morell in any serious pain. The Crown *will* also call a Harley
Street authority. This medical man *will* tell . . . ' [5:16; reported
speech] and the Judge and jury *will* allow the factual 'She was
attended' because if false it would easily be refuted in cross-
examination, but they won't allow anything like a flat 'She never
was in any serious pain.' This *perhaps* is what we call 'bending
over backwards' in the effort to be upright and fair.

Usually, however, *may* is found either unsupported or in this
sort of company: *partly (196); I don't know (197, 198); if you like
(319)*. Mostly, the speaker treats *may* as clear enough by itself:
*15, 69, 72, 72a, 131, 185, 202, 230, 243, 244, 253, 296, 304, 309,
310, 338.* All but two of these would mean exactly the same after
inserting *perhaps*, so that the Attorney-General's *perhaps* was
redundant.

Those two would not be deflected by *perhaps*, only disturbed:
it would be unidiomatic. They are the two with *what: 69, 202.*
English treats contingent casual potentiality as a close fit to vague
and hence potentially excessive generalization with that word and

its congeners: *whatever* (*56*) is the other example here, and *6* has
exactly that sort of meaning but those other words are excluded
by *all*. Finally, *34* looks like a bridge to our next topic.

Might, the remote tense of MAY, never has real-past meaning in
modern English; its remoteness is that of *unreality*. It is of course
used in unreal conclusions as *would* is used: *317*. That one followed
as a consequence of an unreal *could* hypothesis; but usually *might*
takes almost anything else, perhaps unstated, as its hypothetical
basis: *23, 94, 148, 151, 213, 214, 223, 231, 239, 259, 260, 303, 359*.
These could use some sorting, but I needn't allow that to inter-
rupt us here.

Such unreality, we know, is available as a manifestation of
urbanity, here perhaps rather to be called tender-mindedness. We
have seen that *may* is a safer word, a more non-committal word
than *can;* the next step in this direction is *might: 13* (compare *9!*),
239 (Dr. Douthwaite hedging at last!), *287, 288, 289, 306, 322*
(compare *319!*), *340–350* (the last with a special kind of remoteness, an extra expression of horror: 'Far be it from us!'), *357* (compare *319* again, but somewhat differently). As with *should* in
indirect discourse, 'We may wait' softened to contemporary 'We
might wait' gives *10*, still unreal. This exhausts our *might* uses with
the modern meaning.

That was another bridge to our next topic, the *archaic* meaning
of MAY. One background is the first paragraph introducing *Casual
Potentiality*, the mysterious correctness of 'No, you may not!'
Another background is the definition of Freedom on page 167.
Now the definition of the archaic meaning of MAY; this is repeated
here for convenience:

MAY: archaic sense: Subservient Freedom: the event is authoritatively allowed, and the assertion is worded with this modal to
signify that the actor is hardly free to desist.

So archaic, not to say ancient, that only courtroom custom could
maintain it, is the inverted word-order with imperative effect
(note the last few words of the definition above) at *2*. Very much
like that is (*1*) the formulaic use with *hope* and a few synonyms.

The principal employment today is the use to impose a formal chill upon the social interaction; the method is to replace logical *can* and logical *might* (unreality when signifying tender-mindedness) with the arbitrary *may*. Everybody knows this subconsciously, certain mature people can see through it, nobody understands it rationally: we just react. As teachers, we are capable of rationalizing: we say then that *may* properly signifies permission, *can* mere ability. 'Mother, can I go out to swim?' — 'Of course you can if there's a place to swim that you can get to; but you're supposed to ask for *permission*, like this: "Mother, *may* I go out to swim?"!' On the surface, this is a correction of a lexical misunderstanding: Mother as dictionary. Underneath, it is an imposition of maternal Authority. The reader may have fun sorting out the channels (there are two obvious ones, and a Small Prize is offered for the third) through which it is imposed. My English friends assure me that all this goes on at home exactly in the same patterns as I have told them of from America.

Straight from the schoolroom is *276* against *275*. Perhaps it is indelicate to suggest that Mrs. Bedford is speaking to us *ex cathedra;* but these things appear in print, after all, at the author's risk, and she is known to have other words to protect herself with. To make sure of the meaning this time, note that we are supposed to be in the courtroom with Mrs. Bedford and that this is spoken to us while we are watching the proceedings. How is it marked to show that the meaning is not the modern *may:* 'is likely to do it sooner or later but I can't guess the probabilities'? Very plainly. Why do I say plainly? Well, if you are a native speaker of English, you were not in doubt when you read it, were you? The marking must have been plain. The marker is the indefinite article: 'a judge,' not 'the judge.' Even quite small children know this; it is never pointed out in school, because everyone knows it and nobody knows that he knows it.

What is subtle about archaic *may* is the way its effects depend on 'tone of voice.' Any urbanity can be used ironically; politeness can be a cruel weapon. This *may* belongs to what used to be called 'the small civilities.' From a modest pretense of subservience we get *171*. It can be further weakened to the doubly urbane 'Might I,' and either of these may underlie the indirect-discourse use at *138*. It is of course possible that the Doctor did not use either word but instead said something like 'Do you mind if' or 'Would you mind if' or 'Is it all right if I ring up my solicitor?' If that is what happened, then this witness is about to learn something about the dangers of editing: 'Yóu, a trespasser in his house, giving him permission to ring up his own solicitor?' [92:92]. I quote no more, but there is something like half a page to show what can happen when archaic *may* gets mixed up in a serious transaction. The Judge intervenes, but it does little good; we just have to wait for the dust to settle.

The Germans have a technical term, *gesunkenes Kulturgut*, for the way the court dress of one epoch becomes the bourgeois finery of the next and the peasant garb of a century later. Fashions in speech are no different: 'If I may say so' (*74a*) consorts "genteelly" with the à-la-mode 'not terribly' when this witness is still trying to smooth and preen her ruffled feathers after being routed as we see presently. The same 'if I may say so' is functional, as functional as the wigs and the pronunciation *milud* for 'my Lord,' when Mr. Lawrence uses it at *200;* and 'May I say' causes us to listen with sympathy for a little to Dr. Douthwaite after *171*. We respond to the difference between ornament and sincerity.

But then at *108* the decent word would have been the doubly urbane *might;* isn't that what you would have said if you were honestly soliciting cooperation? Mrs. Bedford has told us, twice, what Mr. Lawrence was doing instead; once by his tone of voice, "very cold," and again by printing no '?' at the end of the ostensible question. The result is then one of our strongest imperative formulas; the assumption of the speaker's subservience is reversed: it is like a medieval blow with the *butt* of the knight's spear, reserved for inferiors. This is his beginning; but Nurse Randall is tough and the battle becomes long and bitter, and it ends not far from a draw.

He had almost too easy, swift, and thorough a success with that other witness; too thorough in that she becomes almost incapable of functioning, and he finally [37:43] has to offer her a chair. Mrs. Bedford gives the details almost lavishly, beginning a page before our reference; only part of it is printed in the Appendix, and the reference is to the spot where urbane *might* is replaced by *may: 72, 72a.*

We have to remember that Mr. Lawrence is defending his client on a capital charge and that the Judge is there to protect everyone; my guess is that Mr. Geoffrey Lawrence, Q.C., sought out Sister Mason-Ellis after the trial and apologized handsomely. He owed no apology to Detective-Superintendent Hannam, who knows the gimmick and can defend himself with it in turn: *135, 136, 138.*

Mr. Lawrence does nothing like this in cross-examining the witness Mr. Sogno, who is a lawyer too; after carefully procuring all he thinks he can get, he quits: "Counsel for the defence sits down, as well he might" [81:82]. This is not in the Appendix; it is purely literary.

Stable Modals

The casual modals, where English realism and pragmatism are at home, function in a political sort of scene, where everything changes from moment to moment and people just do the best they can; the stable modals do not function continuously but are constantly available for use when needed, like Constitutional Law. They have no tense, seemingly because they refer to what never changes; and again because what they refer to is everywhere and uniform and constant, it is impossible for it to be banished into unreality or softened with urbanity. The only escape is to just not mention it.

There are in fact long stretches of text, many pages together, with not one stable modal in *Trial;* and others with heavy concentrations. Not even *must*, occurring on the average nearly once every two pages, is used in Day Nine or the early part of Day Ten, sixteen pages in all; and the reason is that Mr. Lawrence, very cautiously cross-examining the dogmatic and self-righteous Dr. Douthwaite, succeeds in not once evoking the witness's characteristic moral certainty; and the Attorney-General, perhaps realizing that his witness had been alienating the jury, does the same in a brief re-direct examination. But then the Judge modestly intervenes and promptly gives us *183*. Then with careful maneuvering in the field of facts and competences, the Judge gets Dr. Douthwaite to commit himself to an untenable position in the world of facts and to reveal what is his favorite choice of minimal matrix. This ends with a striking paragraph at our reference *187;* note particularly the decisive value of *in these circumstances*, a phrase which itself identifies a minimal matrix which the Judge suggests is his own and Mr. Lawrence's too. The latter, taking up the challenge, continues in the same field of fact and polity, strikingly using mostly casual potentiality, until Mrs. Bedford can sum it up with the pregnant word in that category: where there *can* be a valid contrary view, there is reasonable doubt and therefore, *potentially*, acquittal. The Judge is not content, it would seem; he takes over and with occasional use of stable logic (*225*) but mostly with casual modals drives Dr. Douthwaite to the point of making a foolish casual assertion: 'He might well have' (*239*). And these are Dr. Douthwaite's last words in the case.

The Judge has the last words of all, and it is in this summing-up, as it is called in British usage, what we call the 'charge' to the jury, that the heaviest concentration of stable modals in *Trial* is found. According to the hypothesis which we are verifying, the meanings which the Judge must employ in making their duty clear to the jury are these:

MUST: adequate stable assurance: non-occurrence of the event is inconsistent with the actor's status as a proper member of the community: his failure to do the deed forfeits his status.

OUGHT TO: contingent stable assurance: failure to do the deed leaves the actor in danger of forfeiting that status, for it is consistent with the status of an improper member, contingently an outcast.

D<small>ARE</small>: adequate stable potentiality: the event is entirely consistent with status as a proper member of the community: doing the deed involves no jeopardy.

N<small>EED</small>: contingent stable potentiality: the deed is inconsistent with outcast status: the use of this modal is always negative, interrogative, or subordinate: the question is whether the deed is requisite for status as a proper member of the community.

The stable potentiality modals are each used three times in *Trial*, always in more or less formulaic sentences, as if they were on the verge of obsolescence: D<small>ARE</small> (*57, 103, 353*); N<small>EED</small> (*241, 326, 348*).

Dare is ancient; as with the other two adequate modals (the casual ones), its shift from the archaic to the modern meaning-structure has made hardly any noticeable difference in its employments. It may seem to be in competition with the 'ordinary' verb-base D<small>ARE</small>, again with no conspicuous difference in meaning but only the familiar grammatical differences.

Need is not citable as an archaic modal and seems in fact to have been absent from the modal family in the days when the archaic meaning-structure prevailed: it came to occupy its present position in the system just at the time when the modern meaning-structure came to prevail, late in the seventeenth century. It is not truly in competition with the verb-base N<small>EED</small>, which carries only technical messages: 'You don't need to wait' means that your waiting is not technically requisite: the state of the factual world will be just as good if you don't wait. 'You needn't wait' carries two social messages, either 'I'm indulgently excusing you' or 'I'm firmly dismissing you.' Both are analogous to the *archaic* meaning of M<small>AY</small> and correspond respectively to the straightforward and the ironic use of clauses like 'if I may ask.' Confusion between this and the verb-base N<small>EED</small> can, I think, quite fairly be said to be absent from mature usage, admitting that in a time and place of 'great upward mobility' as the sociological jargon puts it there is a plentiful supply of immature usage and confusion. But this historical stage cannot last indefinitely; I may turn out to be rashly optimistic, but I look for the firmness and symmetry of the English modal system and with it the mature usage to prevail as the community norm. I hasten to resolve a seeming contradiction in two uses of the term *archaic* above: my point now is that the opposition between archaic and modern meanings is absent here among the stable modals and the analogy of *needn't* to MAY is illuminating but trivial: it means no more than that English-speaking people are social animals.

The entrance of OUGHT TO into the modal system was simultaneous with that of NEED, as near as we can make out at this distance. Before, there were six modals; in the modern period there are eight. What the abstract shape of the archaic system was is something that baffles me for the present; the only thing certain is that it was not a cube like the present-day one. The most I feel able to say is that research into the modals in nineteenth-century standard German, and into as much of contemporary usage as does not conflict with that (there seems to be a new meaning for *ich will*, for instance, roughly 'I mean to'), seems to me at present to offer the best hope of finding a close parallel to Shakespeare's modal system, perhaps even the identical system: there must, after all, be a deep-seated reason why the Germans are so fond of Shakespeare.

The adaptation and adoption of OUGHT TO as a modal is known to lie between Shakespeare and the Junius political letters, and I suspect that the political prose of Milton would show an early transitional stage, Defoe perhaps a late one. While waiting for the research to be done, and at the risk of seeming like a fanciful realist instead of a proper nominalist, I offer a reconstruction which I hope will turn out to be trivial. The shift from archaic to modern meaning-structure in the casual modals had established, or was establishing, the polarity adequate–contingent there; and now OUGHT TO was put to work to provide a contingent partner for MUST, NEED to provide one for DARE. The pressure was so strong that old *ought to* was taken over as it was, complete with its *to* that had been the infinitive-marker, without pausing to reconstruct its shape. To this day, its negation is marginally various: in England (especially in the North?) *didn't ought to* is usual and can be heard on all social levels; in the United States, *oughtn't to* and *hadn't ought to* used to divide the map of the United States more or less neatly but now are in competition almost everywhere.

Both *didn't ought to* and *hadn't ought to* are traditional, survivals from the days when everybody reading the Book of Common Prayer, "We have left undone those things which we ought to have done," took *ought* in its original value (past indicative of OWE) and knew how to relocate the perfect marker: it had to be relocated because the meaning of perfect phase was shifting or had shifted to its present-day meaning, no longer fairly comparable to the French meaning but rather like that of classical Greek. Nowadays, with traditional values retreating, giving way to what David Riesman has taught us to call 'other-directedness,' *ought to* is being replaced by *should*, as *must* also is; it is sure to survive as long as the abstract semological cube retains its orientation, but I can't guess how long that will be. Meanwhile, *Trial* can be called upon to verify the cube as I have presented it, now specifically the *stable* face of it.

All 15 occurrences of OUGHT TO are in the Appendix, and 30 of the 110 occurrences of MUST. We begin with the latter. It sorts itself out promptly according to whether the 'actor' that is in danger of forfeiting status is or is not designated by the subject of an active verb and analogously with a passive one: (1) *5, 30, 74, 90, 97, 122, 144, 307, 308, 328, 329, 332, 334, 344, 365;* (2a) *76, 120, 158, 183, 225, 240, 280;* (2b) *53, 101, 102, 111, 121, 320;* (3) *38, 137.* Group 2*a* is in the current phase; Group 2*b* is in the perfect phase; Group 3 cannot be placed immediately.

Group 1 is always in current phase, and the actor is personal. At first glance, the use and meaning are transparent; that will turn out to be an illusion, but we can use it for a while to get started with. The first (*5*) is perfectly obvious: being a proper jury, they *must* etc. Others of this sort are: *30, 74, 97, 144, 307, 308, 328, 329, 332* (taking this, of course, as a literary transformation of 'You must have that attitude'), *334, 344, 365*. The epitome of them all is *74*. Sister Mason-Ellis is not asking whether she is going to be commanded to answer that. She is asking for information with reference to the very moment of her speaking the question; she means, 'Here I am, a loyal member of the community; what is the relation between me and answering that? Supposing I don't answer that, is my failure inconsistent with me being what I am?' I have worded this as two questions for a sufficient reason: the first question establishes the maximal social matrix as the frame of reference; the second question selects among the four stable modals.

This is the modal for binding duty; it will turn out to be also the modal for binding logic; and that will mean that within the modal system English does not distinguish between duty and logic. And if not there, English can't do it anywhere within the whole grammatical system: it will have to be done with the lexicon, with the dictionary because the grammar has not provided for the distinction. But that comes a bit later; let us finish this group. All that remains now (*90, 122*) is the first-person statement 'It is my duty to' corresponding to that question; no problem.

Before finishing with MUST, I ought to indulge in a couple of excursus. Like other relative assertions, this has no truth-value with respect to the event. Yet, on its own assumption that the community is constituted entirely of loyal members it makes the strongest possible assertion in favor of the occurrence. This has induced the illusion that it means the same thing as HAVE TO, which has been explained under the heading *Quasi-Auxiliaries* in Chapter II. That does have truth-value with respect to the *event*, of course with the understanding that the *having to* is the main event and that the rest of the predicate only specifies the event more particularly; and what else could we expect of the grammar of this language? In *Trial* there is no manifestation of any confusion between the two; and I think you ought to agree that the parent who evaded defining *must* by saying, 'Well, for instance your duty is what you must do,' was manifesting mature usage. The statistics for the rest of the population are not known to me.

The lexicon of English offers a facile description of the difference between adequate MUST and contingent OUGHT TO in this
form: it is the difference between *duty* and *office*, the latter allowing
that the occupant of an office does occasionally evade a duty without vacating the office; life is like that, and circumstances alter
cases; for that matter, so do whims and human frailties: they have
no effect on the matrix here, whereas for the casual modals they
determined it, but they do determine the historical course of events:
we'll see: *106*. The 15 *Trial* occurrences are: *79* (thought it was our
office to provide her with some sleep), *106*, *153*, *242*, *258*, *298*, *305*
(we ought to allow you to consider), *313* (the occupant of this office
is conscientious, so he does), *321*, *323*, *324*, *335*, *347*, *354*, *362* (is
this indeed our office, or would it be officious?). The reader can
sort this out further with ease; it will be observed that the perfect
phase is here deflected from its factual-assertion meaning to its
usual modal one. Contingency, we see, is the same thing as possible
evasion; here it differs from casual contingency only as the two
matrices differ, or in other words, according to what the event is
related to, in the basic (symbolic) definitions.

Now it will turn out that it is the office, or duty, of *the order of
nature* to see to it that events duly occur; and the order of nature
never evades its duty. This is also known as logic; but I give the
effective actor this name, *order of nature*, to point up the fact that
English treats it as a member of the community like you and me.
It is the actor, since Dr. Douthwaite cannot be held personally
responsible, at *158;* and similarly at *76*, *120*, and others. Is it not
clear it is not the jury's duty to feel satisfied, to get to feel satisfied,
to get into a state of being satisfied in any way they can, at *183?*
Rather, it is the duty of the community to satisfy them; but that
is not what the sentence says either. It says that somebody or
something must satisfy them first, and on that basis this could be
put into Group 1. Let us leave it and continue. At *225* there is
the specifically English sort of appeal to logic: the order of nature,
I submit, is being called upon to do its duty. Before jumping to
conclusions about *240*, we ought to look at *241*. It does *not* say,

'*He* need not necessarily be aware'! It may very well be true that each general practitioner has that duty, but this sentence does not say so; it says that *it must be true* that every G.P. is well aware. Now *280* is easy; and likewise Group 3.

Group 2*b* is in the perfect phase; and then the actor is *always* the order of nature, and its performance is logic. We get the feeling that the primary effect is that we are convinced, that something has convinced us. Well? Now Group 1 can be run through again, and there is no need for me to do it for us. I suggest only that as soon as emotional involvement fades sufficiently, we are likely to admit that the order of nature is the effectual actor each time.

Now we can examine anew, and for the last time, the difference between the stable and the casual modals, between the maximal and the minimal matrix of events. The crucial difference is that between consistency and randomness. When the circumstances are taken for granted, not challenged as to their regularity, casual modals are used; on perceiving that they are as they are by virtue of uniformity, one is ready (though never compelled) to shift to some stable modal. If one does not shift, *should* is used for both MUST and OUGHT TO.

A tendency to use *should* in this way, and correspondingly to use the stable modals less than in former times, would seem to be a manifestation of Riesman's 'other-directedness.' It is noticeable in *Trial* as well as in American usage.

Modal Negation

This is our last topic. In a sense it is clean-up work after either neglecting negation or taking it for granted; but in a way it is a natural conclusion to the more recent pages. For convenience, I repeat the tabulation of symbolic definitions of the eight English modals from an earlier page. The symbols are defined on page 152; and at this point I particularly remind you that the bar counts as a sign of negation every time, and that the fact that there is an even number of them (zero counting as an even number) in each definition means that the relative assertion is favorable to the

event: that it is an affirmative assertion. Then NOT must alter the
count to make it an odd number, and our topic must deal with
which of the alternative ways of making it so are realistic: what
each would mean if anything, and which of them are idiomatic. It
will not be an idle exercise, but the symbolic results will be left to
the reader and only the necessary discussion will be presented here.

$$\overline{E} \ \overline{o} \ A = \text{MUST} \qquad \overline{E} \ o \ \overline{A} = \text{OUGHT TO}$$
$$E \ o \ A = \text{DARE} \qquad E \ \overline{o} \ \overline{A} = \text{NEED}$$
$$\overline{E} \ \overline{o} \ C = \text{WILL} \qquad \overline{E} \ \overline{o} \ c = \text{SHALL}$$
$$E \ o \ C = \text{CAN} \qquad E \ o \ c = \text{MAY}$$

An odd number emerges from an even number by adding any
odd number to it. Here we can add either one or three bars. There
are three places to add just one; or three can be added, one of them
in each place; that makes four ways to do it. When a bar is com-
bined with a bar, both vanish: 'two minuses make a plus.' But
no bar can be imposed on either C or c; that is to say, there are
only *two* ways to negate a *casual* modal, while there are *four* ways
to negate a *stable* modal. Through this chapter we have been
verifying the modal definitions as expanded into discursive wording; here we are returning to their symbolic form to see how they
can be verified, if they can, rather directly by taking advantage
both of our discursive experience and of the special clarity of a
negated symbolic definition. If this success emerges, our *hypothesis*
becomes a *theory* that has been verified by all the 1340 modals in
Trial, or rather by the roughly one-fourth sample of them actually
cited. This is not a proof: we have stipulated that no hypothesis
can be proved, in exchange for the stipulation that only one hypothesis can or must be verified at a time.

Imposing either one or three negation-bars upon the symbolic
definitions, we find them passing over into each other freely:
imposing one upon the first symbol for MUST gives the same result
as imposing one upon the second symbol for DARE, and again the
same result as imposing three of them on the OUGHT TO definition
or one on the last symbol for NEED. Completing the exercise, we

find exactly four symbolic definitions for negated stable modals, each serving equally for all four negated modals; and four casual negations, each serving equally for two of them: which two depends on the difference between *C* and *c*.

But then the negated definitions sort themselves out again to form two major classes: *strong* negation with 'inconsistent with' as the middle symbol, and *weak* negation with 'consistent with' as the relation between the event and the circumstances or the actor. Among the casual modals, this tells us immediately that *can't not* ought to be equivalent to *will* and also to *won't not;* but that seems to be the end of that, for *shan't not* and *mayn't not* are unidiomatic, apparently because only the *weak* definitions of *shan't* and *mayn't* feel right and these are substantially worthless, not worth deeming equivalent to anything else.

Finally, I remark that 'not show' as a unit has been taken as an axiom above. Let me paraphrase that into 'omit to show' so as to get rid of the negative adverb. This will be called *eventual negation,* meaning that the eventual occurrence of the posited event is negated. The other extreme is *relative negation,* meaning that only the force of the modal is reversed while the event itself is presented positively.

I take it that *relative* negation can be adequately paraphrased by prefacing 'It is false that' to an affirmative relative assertion: 'I can't show it to her' is then equivalent to 'It is false that I can show it to her.' And 'I can't not show it to her' is equivalent to 'It is false that I can omit to show it to her.' Native speakers of English will all agree that this is true with respect to CAN.

The syntactic rules for NOT as given in Chapter III, under the heading *Negation,* tell us that NOT placed before the modal (so that by morphophonemic rule it becomes a zero-stressed suffix to the same) ought to give always and only relative negation; and this turns out to be true of CAN at least. With WILL, usages differ; some addressees take 'I won't show it to her' and 'I'll not show it to her' as essentially different, the second being *eventual* negation instead, while others react identically to both—which to me means that they have, so far in their lives, found no practical use for the difference—for reasons which emerge on inspection of the technical definitions of WILL. I am one of a minority, roughly 30 percent of the mature population in my area, with a good use for the distinction; still, if my percentage guess is roughly correct, the result is that there is only about one chance in ten that two of us will get together on this sort of transaction:

I had procured an air travel ticket, with its price charged to my account, and used it three weeks earlier; while awaiting reimbursement from my principal for expenses on that earlier journey, I now procured a second ticket and inquired: "I'm giving you a check now for one ticket; shall we say it's for this ticket or for the other one?" The clerk not only speaks my language but my dialect too; he answered, "Let it be for this one, and as for the other ticket we'll not bill you again," and I rather impertinently cross-questioned him and found that, sure enough, he meant to omit billing me for the first ticket on the regular day of billing clients for outstanding debt, rather than to make a negative prediction.

I suppose this is rare enough so that our 30 percent is likely to dwindle to zero in a generation or two, for lack of verification of the difference. That has evidently happened already with respect to all those modals whose -*n't* forms are rare or lacking today. Thus nobody ever says *mayn't* in my area, though *may* is common; *shan't* is obsolete; *must* is holding firm though perhaps decreasing in frequency (being replaced more and more usually by *should*) but *mustn't* is rather rarer; the same is true of *ought to;* contrarily, *daren't* and *needn't* are far firmer than affirmative *dare* or *need:* the modals, that is, for the verb-bases DARE and NEED are as alive as ever.

Technically speaking, all this is a sort of degeneration from the ideal of what English negation is fitted to accomplish. What is left in my area today is this, each grammatical formula either conventionally confined rather arbitrarily (in defiance of the basic grammar) to just one of the two possibilities, or else split according to the context or the tone of voice:

I won't show it to her: either relative or eventual negation.
I'll not show it to her: either relative or eventual negation.
Shall I not show it to her? eventual negation.
I cân't shów it to her: relative negation.
I cǎn nôt shów it to her: eventual negation.
I may not show it to her: archaic sense: relative negation.
I may not show it to her: modern sense: eventual negation.
I must not show it to her: eventual negation.
I mustn't show it to her: eventual negation.
I ought not to show it to her: eventual negation.
I oughtn't to show it to her: eventual negation.
I dare not show it to her: relative negation.
I daren't show it to her: relative negation.
I need not show it to her: relative negation.
I needn't show it to her: relative negation.

Now if my understanding of all this is somehow close to the truth, these peculiar idiomatic specializations ought to emerge easily from the hypothetical definitions of the several modals. The verification of this can safely be left to the reader. As the Judge said, "I do not think I need say more about it than this—that if you find a theory which the other doctor for the prosecution is not prepared to support and which the doctor for the defence says is wholly wrong—if indeed Dr. Ashby did not equally say it was wrong—you might think that it would be far too dangerous to adopt the theory of Dr. Douthwaite, whatever his qualifications may be and however impressed you may have been by the way in which he gave his evidence . . . "

APPENDIX

INDEX

Appendix

Page 40. On Formal Criteria

Here the sorting-out of the gerund from other types of words is being done according to 'formal criteria,' as linguists say. What I usually say is 'by form' if I say anything at all; I must admit to a tendency to take this sort of thing for granted, as if all my readers were professional linguists or at least apprentices. This habit is dangerous; a normal reader is apt to misunderstand 'form' as meaning *shape*, and that gets him into real trouble.

There is no denying that the *shape* of a gerund (namely that its first or only word ends with *-ing*) is identical to shapes encountered in at least *three other places in English grammar:* (*a*) the *bedding* that gets sent to the laundry, (*b*) the *bedding* down *of* the animals, (*c*) I've been *bedding* down the animals. This identity of shape is not what any linguist means by *form*.

Why not? Because if he got into the habit of treating *shapes* as linguistic *forms* he would have no place to stop short of the six-year-old child's interpretation of a certain hymn: Asked why she had given the name Gladly to her teddy-bear, she said it was because he was cross-eyed, and cited the song she had learned in Sunday School: "Gladly my cross I'd bear."

A shape is only *evidence* of form; the context has to be cross-questioned before we can be sure of the form that the shape testified to—for it too often happens that the evidence offered by shape is incompetent, irrelevant, or immaterial.

In sorting out *gerunds*, we start out from the shape: the first or only word ends with *-ing*. It is a great convenience, in fact, to be able to start out from a *single* shape before sorting words out according to form. But it must not be taken for granted. It just happens that all English gerunds have the same shape. Elsewhere in the English verb system, things will be more like what we are accustomed to in European languages: not only one shape for several forms, as in our gerund against other forms, *but also* several shapes for one form, for instance *took, sang, put, granted* among many other shapes of the single 'past tense' form of the English finite verb. We just happened to be lucky in starting out with the gerund instead of something hard like the tenses.

Being able to start out from the single shape (*-ing*) makes the search for form very easy, in principle, but hardly automatic. What is first needed is to notice somewhere—anywhere at all, just so the spot is not too far away (how far is too far? when the fishing is disappointing: all science is circular in this sense)—a *pair* of contextual phenomena: *two* things that so to speak happen *at once* in the neighborhood of some *-ing* words but not the neighborhood of certain *other* words of the same shape. Finding such pairs assures us that our explanation is not *ad hoc.*

Here is what we find this time: not only one but two obvious pairs: (1) *the* or an adjective, or both, close before the *-ing* shape, paired with *of* close after the *-ing* shape; (2) an adverb—to play safe, let's say a *-ly* word that is not *fatherly* or the like—close before the *-ing* shape, paired with the familiar sort of object of a transitive verb—*me, them,* etc.—close after the *-ing* shape. Conversely, we never find in standard English such a mixture as an adverb close before the *-ing* shape and *of* close after it.*

---

* This is a sort of tautology too: when we find that mixture we call it something other than standard English. For instance, in British novels we find it presented as typical of the London charwoman: 'carefully scrubbing of the floor.' This sort of 'for instance' is very often misunderstood. The point is *not* that there is anything essentially vulgar or incompetent about this particular mixture—adverb before, *of* after—but something quite different: where we happen to find it situated in the abstract map of the social structure of the community. After all, it ought to be obvious that *hisself* is a neater and essentially more competent word than *himself*— we all say *myself, yourself,* don't we?—it just happens to be located, in our map of the community, in a vulgar neighborhood.

Well, isn't that what grammar is all about? Oh yes, it is; look: in principle, *no single word* can be ungrammatical; it is only in the fitting-together that grammar is at home. What we have found here is something that only has numbers so far; next we do something *essentially trivial:* we replace the numbers with names: (1) *verbal noun* and (2) *gerund.*

No, this is what I really mean. You expected me to give those two names to the *shapes;* you expected me to say that there is a verbal noun *bedding* and that there is also a gerund *bedding.* Well, I've tried that—or rather, slipped into it inadvertently—only to be met with an alert editor's note: "Is this necessary here? The distinction is so fine that it seems to require an immediate substantiating argument. . . . Can they be treated as separate words?" The answer is that they not only can but *must* be treated as separate *forms;* otherwise I'd have to pack up and go home: without doing that, we'd never be able to describe English grammar at all. The technical term *gerund* does not refer to the shape *-ing* but instead to an employment of that shape.

What was it that the editor overlooked? A pregnant word of only one syllable, as crucial here as the word *the* in the third line of Coleridge's "In Xanadu did . . . " It was used three times. It is a preposition. There are two other prepositions that are used more often in English than this one, namely *of* and *to.* You'll just have to get used to this linguist's practice of saying exactly what is meant. All scientists do it, and it makes scientific writing exactly as hard and exactly as easy to read as poetry.

As far as I know, the main reason why linguists have more fun than people is what keeps happening next after some pairs have been found. For instance, once the gerunds have been sorted out, we discover that a gerund can be three words long, while a verbal noun can't in normal usage. And so we keep on; and if we push on boldly (keeping the members of the party roped together at suitable intervals) we may eventually find out a little something about *meaning.* But it would be forever impossible to find out anything about meaning if we were to use meanings as starting-points.

Page 65. On Contractions

The *h* sound started dropping out before vowels and *w* and *y* (as in *what* and *humor* [pardon me: *humour*]) in London and the Home Counties shortly before Shakespeare's day; that is why the King James Bible prints *my son* but *mine hand* according to the old pattern that called for *mine* before a vowel. Before *w* and *y* the *h* is gone in that region; in educated English it is coming back before *y* but not before *w*, and there is no room here to explain where it comes from so that it can get back. Before vowels the present-day situation is very simple: when that vowel has *weak* stress there can't be a spoken *h* in any kind of English today, American English or the Queen's English or any other; when the vowel has tertiary or major stress, the *h* is spoken in all standard English and in most provincial English—and in Cockney it has been coming back in recent generations with the help of school pressures and the like though with hyperurbanisms of course; we'll know that it has finally arrived by the vanishing of the hyperurbanisms: *h* where it doesn't belong, which I am told is rare today in the speech of Londoners born since the First World War.

The interesting point here is what happens to words that begin with *h* in the spelling (except for *honest* and the others that have lost it permanently if they ever had it: not all spelling is honest) and have both weak-stress uses and other uses; these are notably the forms of HAVE and the pronouns *he, him, his, her*. The latter have weak stress, so that there can't be any spoken *h*, in sentences like 'Give her another one' [197:180], so that what is spoken can never be, in genuine spoken English, different from the noun *giver*. Another rule of grammar has come in here: when *h* drops out in this way, the word is attached firmly and without a break to the preceding word. This is true in *all* English.

But now another factor comes in when English is printed. The novelists have the convention of printing the genuine pronunciation *give 'er* only when the sentence is spoken by a generally vulgar speaker; the vulgarity may be audible elsewhere in the sentence but there is no way to print it elsewhere; accordingly, it is printed here where it is inaudible, for everyone says *give 'er* in such a sentence, including all the speakers whose speech the novelist represents by printing *give her*, as Mrs. Bedford did in *Trial*.

This much for background; now we come back to *negation* and how it is represented in print. In teaching English as a foreign language, supposing that English and not reading-aloud pronunciation is to be taught, we simply have to explain to adult learners how the conventions of English print work. For instance, normal print uses *won't* only to represent *won't;* but uses *will not* to represent both *won't* and *will not*. The pedantic printing rule is that *Won't* is to be printed only at the beginning of a clause (which is usually the beginning of the sentence too), but that *won't* is represented by printed *will not* inside the clause. Accordingly, the adult foreign learner of English has to be taught enough English grammar so that he can sort out *won't* from *will not* when he sees *will not* before him in print. One rule of thumb is that the odds are better than ten to one that it means *won't*. The rest comes from experience guided by clear discriminations among the various patterns of English clauses. The crucial facts are all in this chapter (meaning Chapter III), though many details are missing.

Natives are not deceived until some teacher deceives them. Up to the age of nine, my daughter used to love to read aloud to me, and it was a delight to observe how accurately she sorted out *won't* from *will not* in reading from a book that printed *will not* every time; and why not? there are worse irregularities in English spelling, and after sorting out *cough* from *though* and *through*, this *won't* disguised as *will not* was child's play to her. She didn't know it was supposed to be hard. Or that it was supposed to be wrong. But then came her next year in school, under a teacher with a different sort of conscience; and promptly she quit reading aloud at home. The rest is silence; and that, I am told, means that she is an adult-type reader.

Or take Johnny, the mythical average American child, under an average teacher at age six to eight; my daughter was lucky to have exceptional teachers through that period. In his book he sees "Dick is not going to school today because it is Saturday." My daughter used to read such a sentence as English: 'Dick isn't going to school today—because it's Saturday.' When Johnny's teacher forces him to take the book's spelling seriously, she is flouting what every normal child knows at that age: the fact that such a sentence taken at face value is either ungrammatical or else has too far-fetched a message to be contemplated soberly. The alternative theory that a six-year-old doesn't know that much grammar is preposterous. For more of the theory, see my article, "Language and the School Child," *Harvard Educational Review*, March 1964.

Page 71. On Journalistic Inversion

The words *as* and *than* may, in some marginal usage—especially in journalistic and scientific writing—be followed by 'question word-order' when the finite is or resembles a propredicate; I can't always decide whether it is meant as one or not:

> In dropping the activity San Jose noted that the University of Wisconsin, the last major college to keep boxing going, had dropped it, *as did* Sacramento State of California. [Editorial, *The Capital Times*, Madison, Wisconsin, 19 November 1960]

> the enormous backlog of twentieth-century technology . . . Once this backlog is exhausted, Russia will have to rely, *as does* the United States, upon current discoveries. [*Atlantic Monthly*, January 1961, p. 66]

> The liver enzyme converts glucose-*l*-phosphate to glycogen more rapidly *than do* preparations from other tissues. [Advertisement of Schwarz Bio-Research, Inc., *Science* 132.1450 (1960)]

> it did not have the characteristic base-pairing *as did* normal host cell DNA. [*Science* 132.1492 (1960)]

There is no example in *Trial*. Nevertheless I would have dealt with this when 'question word-order' was first discussed (see pp. 58–59) if I had thought of it as normal English. For a handsome display of examples, see Fowler, *Modern English Usage*, article *Inversion*.

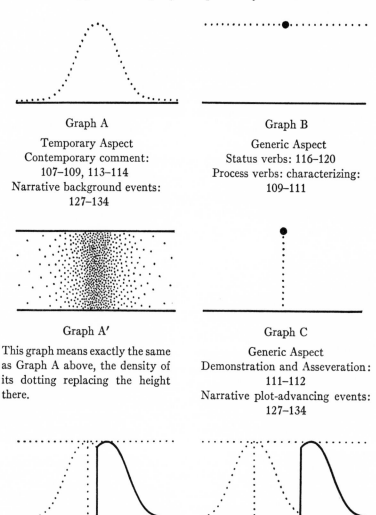

Graph A

Temporary Aspect
Contemporary comment:
107–109, 113–114
Narrative background events:
127–134

Graph B

Generic Aspect
Status verbs: 116–120
Process verbs: characterizing:
109–111

Graph A'

This graph means exactly the same
as Graph A above, the density of
its dotting replacing the height
there.

Graph C

Generic Aspect
Demonstration and Asseveration:
111–112
Narrative plot-advancing events:
127–134

Graph D

Perfect Phase: 140–144

Graph D'

Perfect Phase: 141

The greatest height in a graph represents perfect validity of the predication. In all graphs, time runs from left to right: Earlier or previous time is to the left, and later or subsequent time is to the right.

Page 148. On Busybodies

If there were such a danger of weakening our language, then by the same token there would be all the greater certainty of putting it back together again without the adventitious gimmicks that busybodies have been trying to install in the English modal system for two centuries and more, under the pretext of improving or adjusting it but in every case hampering its operation to the extent that they succeed in influencing innocent citizens.

I am going to leave those gimmicks where I find them, simply because there is nothing else I *can* do. The community is in control of the language, not me, nor for that matter any other grammarian. But I have an equivalent hope with a better foundation. Each such gimmick that seems to retain its place in the language is rather regaining it again and again, against the continual pressure of all the symmetries in the structure of the English assertion category. If we find one there in 1850 and the same one again in 1950, it is because those busybodies, not merely the professional but decisively the amateur ones—the English-speaking world is thoroughly well provided with the latter, and without them the professionals would accomplish nothing—have been laboriously re-installing them generation after generation. Otherwise they would drop out promptly. My hope is that the present-day fad of paying attention to descriptive linguistics will last long enough to prove an effective countervailing force, which it can do only by recruiting amateurs too.

Not a force working directly to improve the language, no. I say this not out of overweening modesty but rather because it is what all researchers are committed to do: we keep hands off so as not to spoil the data. We get more fun out of watching the language take care of itself (this is what is called *homeostasis* in medical theory) than we ever could out of tinkering with it. Medicine is farther advanced today than any other science concerned with humanity, and the reason is principally that it has left the busybody attitude behind. That is more important than the details of the wonder-drugs that were able to emerge once that attitude had vanished. The abandonment of bloodletting and purging was decisive. Today the physician knows that no drug readjusts the body—it could not in any case, for the homeostasis of the body is far more complex than the total of all the drugs that could be administered at one time—but that it only countervails some particular interference so that homeostasis can prevail again.

What I hope will attract the amateur recruits is the very thing that attracts the professional researcher: the sheer beauty of the mechanism in any language, awesome in its combination of ultimate simplicity with intricate efficaciousness in coping with the multifarious concerns of the community life that goes on heedless of grammarians. It is a system of habits; and a system is not merely a list. Habits never persist very long singly; they subsist as members of systems of habit. It is in language that we see the extreme of something that is true of all systems of habits: they tend towards symmetry, balance, homeostatic equilibrium.

If at any epoch a sub-system within a language were lopsided or contained vacancies, the normal transmission from generation to generation would promptly cure that. The reason is that the greater part of what we utter is not parroting but reconstruction by analogy. We learn parrot-wise hardly more than enough to ascertain the trends in what we have heard; the rest we create, and the only way we have for doing that is by analogies which continue the trends towards full symmetry. Hardly any subsystem within any language seems fully symmetrical when we come to analyse it, but that does not weaken the principle and has its own explanation. Many irregularities survive because they are used too many times in the course of a normal day to be overwhelmed by analogy; once they have become rare, they vanish: how many people know the traditional plural of *cow?*

Most apparent irregularities survive only as the visible peak of an iceberg does, by being continually supported by the buoyancy of unnoticed completions; when the analyst finally discovers the submerged structures, he regularly finds that the combination of the submerged with the visible part is as a whole perfectly firm and tolerably symmetrical. Gender in English is such a submerged supporter of an apparent irregularity: it maintains the -s of the traditional 'third person singular present tense' of the verb, though the verb has no gender of its own. Stress is another, as has been pointed out in Chapter III; and in Chapter VI near its end we find stress sorting out the apparent ambiguities of modal nega-tion. There are many other examples of this phenomenon in Chapter VI; but I must not cheat the reader of the fun of observing them.

Page 156. *Citations for the Modals*

Here I am making rather full use of the contextual information, especially the bracketed notes in *Trial*, to assign stress-markings to the crucial words. For example, nearly every occurrence of *shall* appears here as 'shăll,' and for sufficient reason each time. The reader is urged to check on this under *Stress* in Chapter I. Americans are very likely to go wrong on this, for a number of reasons. One is that the traditional uses of *shall* in American Eng-lish employ other stresses than weak; another is that when *shall* is forced upon us in 'grammar' lessons, the teacher customarily pro-nounces it with emphasis to drive the lesson home.

It is altogether likely that I have occasionally guessed wrong, but I am confident that my marking always represents a very common stressing in British English and nearly always the com-monest one. Where I was uncertain, I have left the stressing un-marked; and I do not mark what is not within quotation-marks in *Trial* unless compelled to.

A loquacious man, then, under evident pressure to make himself heard; and how many among those present who do not simply hope that the burden of his plea may[1] be true. [3:13]

A male voice droning: "May[2] it please your Lordship—" and the case is opened. [4:14]

A trial is supposed to start from scratch . . . The members of the jury listen. They hear the tale corroborated, and they hear it denied . . . they all but hear it backward again through a fine toothcomb. BUT THEY SHOULD[3] NEVER HAVE HEARD IT BEFORE. When they first walk into that court, sit down in that box, they are like people before the curtain has gone up. And this, one is conscious from the first, cannot[4] be so in the present case. [4:14]

addressing the jury in a full voice. The beginning is a warning. They must[5] try to dismiss from their minds all they may[6] have read or heard of this before. [5:15]

And how much is a grain of heroin in terms of what should[7] or could[8] be given? [6:16]

"Perhaps," a hint of complacency in the delivery, "perhaps yôu mày[9] thínk that the answer lies in the changes made in her wíll." [6:17]

"Mr. Sogno proposed that they mìght[10] wáit until Mrs. Morell's son came at the week-end, but the Doctor suggested that Mr. Sogno shŏuld[11] prepare a codicil and that the codicil cŏuld[12] be executed and later destroyed if it did not meet with Mrs. Morell's son's approval." [7:17]

"Perhaps you mìght[13] thínk it significant and sinister" [7:17]

"Whether he knew of the codicil executed while he was on holiday and what happened to it, you may[14] perhaps discover in the course of this trial. The Doctor may[15] have thóught shè shŏuld[16] háve no further opportunity for altering her will!" [8:18]

"She wanted to die—that cannŏt[17] be murder. It is impossible to accuse a doctor." [11:21; here the Attorney-General in his opening address to the jury is quoting Detective-Superintendent Hannam quoting Dr. Adams, who surely said *can't*]

" 'Murder—can[18] you prove it was murder?' Superintendent Hannam said, 'You are now charged with murder.' And the Doctor said, 'I do not think you could[19] prove it was murder—she was dying in any event.' As he left the house he gripped the hand of his receptionist and said to her, 'I will[20] see you in heaven.' " [11:21; same as above; this *will* is counted just once in my statistics, though quoted over and over again later in *Trial*]

The Judge courteously puts a question. It is the first time we hear him speak, and at once he reveals both grasp and charm. Could[21] it not be stated, he asks, how many grains a 5 c.c. syringe would[22] hold? [12:21]

other items bear the stamp of the committee-room, while the benches of the press-box might[23] have come from a Victorian school. . . . The prisoner can[24] look across the well at the Judge; the Judge sees him. . . . In court few members of the press or public can[25] see the prisoner and none can[26] see examining counsel ánd his witness at one time; and there are some low rows of seats behind the dock from which no one can[27] see anything at all. All can[28] see the Judge; which does not mean that he can[29] be heard by everyone. [13:22]

The facts connected with the alleged event are spread in open court by counsel and their witnesses, and re-assembled by the Judge; but it is the jury alone who must[30] come to the conclusion, Yes or No, it was like this or it cannot[31] have been; without their verdict no man in England can[32] be punished for any of the great offences, and their verdict, if it is acquittal, is irreversible. [12:23; author's comment]

On these points, so far, would[33] seem to rest the weight of the whole case, and not on the weak motive or the answer given on a form, or the Doctor's utterances to the police, wild though they may[34] be. — The motive, as presented by the prosecution, is bewilderingly inadequate. Can[35] they be suggesting that a—sane?—man in the Doctor's circumstances would[36] commit murder for the chance of inheriting some silver and an ancient motor-car ironically enough no longer mentioned in the will? Unless some sense or strength can[37] be infused into the motive it must[38] become the sagging point of this unequal web. [14:23; author's comment]

"Cheap. Not what you wóuld[39] expect to get in a British court." — "Chap hås got to put sómething in his case." — "Shsh . . . " — "Would[40] nót you think he cóuld[41] håve tåken his pick?" . . . — "WE WÌLL[41a] SEE." [15:24; conversation]

"You have told us that the Doctor used to visit Mrs. Morell at about 11 p.m. and give her an injection?" — "Yes." — "That would[42] be after you yourself had given her a quarter of a grain of morphia at 9 p.m.?" — "Yes." — "And at 11 p.m. Mrs. Morell would[43] be fairly dopey and half-asleep because of your earlier injection?" — "That is so." [17:26; the Attorney-General]

Mr. Lawrence . . . "Nurse Stronach, how many patients . . . do you think you have attended since Mrs. Morell died?" — "I could[44] not possibly tell you." [18:27]

"It was due to the injuries to the arteries of her brain?" — [Click] "Not only that." — Mr. Lawrence [covering] "That for a start. To what else?" — "I shóuld[45] say a great deal to the amount of drugs she was having." — [Dryly] "I thóught you were going to say that." [19:27]

"It is the usual thing when you are nursing. It is the proper thing to do." — "All experienced nurses do it?" — "They shóuld[46] dò." — "That is what yóu did?" — "Indeed we did. Every time we gave an injection we wrote it down—what it was, and the time, and signed our names." — [Gravely now, weight on every word] "And whatever you wrote in that book would[47] be accurate because it would[48] have been done right at that very moment?" — "It would."[49] — ... [speed again] "As distinct from your memory of six years later, these reports would[50] of course be absolutely accurate." — [Sturdily] "Oh yes, they would[51] be accurate from each one of us." — "So that if only we had these reports now we còuld[52] sêe thĕ trúth of exactly what happened ... when you were there?" [20:28]

[Very bland] "What this entry shows is that your memory was playing you a trick, does it not?" — "Apparently so." — "Óbviously so." — "It múst[53] hăve dòne. I cânnòt[54] remémber. It is a long time to remember these things." — "That [very pleased] is exactly what I suggested to you. It was a long time ago and mistakes of memory cân[55] bè máde. This was one of them." [24:32]

Whatever else Mr. Lawrence may[56] require of his witness, he expects her full attention. [25:33; author's comment]

The regulars of the national Press keep themselves to themselves and only the very brave dare[57] go near the pressroom. [28:35; author's narrative]

Did the Doctor ever write the prescriptions in her presence? — Nurse Stronach: "He often did." — The Judge: "Was that because someone had told him that the supply was running out, or because he found out himself?" — "He wŏuld[58] pròbably ásk and wê wòuld[59] téll hìm how the drugs were going." — "He would[60] write out a fresh prescription and would[61] give it to the nurses?" — "Yes, and we wŏuld[62] give it to the chauffeur, Price, who took it to the chemist. And when he bróught thèm, thêy wŏuld[63] bè tâken ín by the cook; she would[64] bring them to the dining-room to the nurse on duty who would[65] put them away. The nurses had charge of the locked cupboard in the dining-room where the drugs were kept. If the Doctor wanted drugs from the cupboard he would[66] ask for them and we would[67] produce the key; but he usually had his own drugs from his bag." [29:36]

"I think wê shăll[68] fínd that for months and months and months that routine sedation went on without any alterations?" [31:38]

We adjourn. The jury, too, goes home—by another door, down other stairs—unapproachable, unapproached. What may[69] be their reflections? [31:38; author's narrative and comment]

[Very slow] "Did one or the other of you say something to this effect, 'Don't you say that or you will[70] get me into trouble?' " — Sister Mason-Elllis: "I cannot[71] answer that." — ... "Perhaps I did not make my question clear. Let me try again. [Loud and clear] In the course of your discussion in the train this morning did one or the other of you—it may[72] have been you, it may[72a] have been Nurse Stronach or Nurse Randall— say words like these, now listen: . . . " — [Very distressed. Shallow voice] "Yes, I think one of them did say that, but which one I'm afraid I cannot[73] say." — "Was it yóu?" — [Full voice] "Oh no." — "Then it was either . . . [Quick whip] Which of those two was it?" — [Looking about her] "Must[74] I answer that?" — The Judge at once, "Yes." — [Faintly] "Then it was Nurse Randall. . . . [genteelly] I was not terribly interested if I may[74a] say so." — Mr. Lawrence [taking none of that] . . . Nurse Randall can[75] hardly have said those words in quite that voice. [33:39; last sentence is author's comment]

This new proof of Mr. Lawrence's omniscience must[76] be most bewildering. [35:41; author's comment]

" 'May 11th, very difficult and depressed from 3.30 to 5 p.m. Very weepy and accused me of leaving her alone the whole afternoon to die. Told me I should[77] be dismissed when the Doctor returned' " [36:42; Mr. Lawrence reading aloud from the nursing record]

" 'Wished she was dead and that she knew a doctor who would[78] put her to sleep forever' " [36:42; same]

"And this time it was plain that she was rapidly going downhill?" Yes. "And the Doctor thought that she ought[79] to have some sleep?" [37:43]

"One step backwards, two steps sideways, we wîll[80] be here next month at this rate . . . " — "If they côuld[81] nôt sew it up any better than that, they should[82] nôt have brought the damn case at all." [40:46; conversation]

"Would[83] you mind reading us out the whole of the completed form?" [42:48]

"So anybody reading this form would[84] have all the material information supplied by the Doctor? . . . They could[85] go at once to any of the nurses— could[86] they not?—and ask them questions about Mrs. Morell's case?" — [Dully] "They côuld[86a] hàve." [43:48]

The Judge says something, but dearly though one should[87] have liked to hear them, both question and answer are inaudible and the witness steps down. [44:49; author's narrative]

Each nurse can[88] only be examined on her own spell of duty. [46:51; author's comment]

Mr. Lawrence is on his feet before Nurse Randall can[89] give her answer. "I must[90] ask the Attorney-General not to lead in that form." — The Attorney-General [remaining urbane] "I will[91] put the question in another way—had you had any similar instructions before . . . ?"   [46:51]

"Did you perceive any jerks?" — "Yes, they were very bad." — "How bad? Could[92] you give an indication?" — "They were so bad I côuld[93] nŏt léave her . . . " — . . . "When this 5 c.c. injection was given what was her condition?" — "She wâs nŏt cónscious. She míght[94] hăve bèen sémiconscious."   [48:52]

[Mournfully] "What was the effect?" — "She became quieter and I called the other nurse because I côuld[95] sée she was passing out." — "Did she pass out?" — "At about 2 a.m., as far as I căn[96] remémber."   [49:53]

"You now understand," straight at Nurse Randall, "that you must[97] not discuss with anybody at all the evidence you have given or are going to give, and if you are wise you will[98] avoid the company of the other nurses in this case so that there can[99] be no grounds for complaint. Because if I do have any grounds for complaint I shall[100] take a very serious view of it."   [49:54]

"Nurse Randall, when you recorded paraldehyde 5 c.c. as given by the Doctor on the night of Mrs. Morell's death, how did you know it was paraldehyde?" — "I must[101] have been told." — . . . "Where did this paraldehyde come from?" — "I think the Doctor must[102] have brought it."   [51:55]

"And I dare[103] say you know this, don't you, that for months and months the regular treatment . . . hardly varied?"   [53:57]

"And the next question you were asked was whether you had ever given a routine injection of morphia and heroin . . . and you said, 'No,' and that would[104] not be quite right, and again for the same reason, would[105] it not?" — Nurse Randall [resigned tone] "No."   [56:60]

"And thât òught[106] tŏ bè thát for Pelion on Ossa." — "Shôuld[107] nŏt côunt on it; a fact in law has nine lives."   [56:60; conversation]

Mr. Lawrence: "I want to ask you about . . . [Very cold] May[108] I ask you to look again at your record for two nights befóre. Do you see that . . . you have written 'Twitchings more pronounced'?" — "Yes." — "That was the word you used—in the best way you could[109]—to describe the condition?"   [58:62]

Nurse Randall: "I just dô nŏt knów. I suppose I wrote it down quickly." — One would[110] give a good deal by now to learn the whole truth.   [59:62; ending with author's comment]

"Do you want to withdraw or alter those answers?" — "I must[111] have meant heavy sleep . . . [Blurring it again] She wôuld[112] nôt respônd to líght or have her mouth cleaned, whereas if she was not in a coma she would[113] have sucked a swab." [61:64]

"Is that the sort of memory you have?" — "No. But if I did nôt say it [pause] I wôuld[114] nôt remémber it, wôuld[115] I?" — "Nurse Randall, are you being frank with me over this business in the train?" — "I ám as far as I cán[116] bè." [64:67]

The Attorney-General [speaking fast, gulping his words] "I do submit that they were given deliberately and that they accelerated the death of the patient, but I will[117] not elaborate, my Lord, I adhere to that and I have medical evidence which leads me to say that." [66:68]

"The prosecution wants to finish by Wednesday." — "Yeah, and our boys will[118] be home for Christmas." — "Lawrence's going to call the Doctor and no one else." — "He wîll[119] talk his head off!" — "Hê mûst[120] bè lónging tò; wôuld[120a] nôt yóu?" [72:75; conversation]

Here, however, the flow is halted. Mr. Lawrence, who must[121] have been in ambush, puts in very hurriedly, "My Lord, I must[122] make a submission in the absence of the jury." — . . . Mr. Lawrence submits that the next part of the detective-inspector's evidence is damaging to his client while irrelevant to the case, and should[123] not be heard. The Attorney-General submits that it should.[124] [76:78]

Mr. Lawrence: "My Lord, I object. I do not think, with respect, that the contents of the earlier wills can[125] be evidence unless they are properly proved." — The Attorney-General: "Very well. I shãll[126] not ask about the contents of the earlier wills." [78:80]

Mr. Lawrence, in cross-examination [*parlante*, easy] "Mr. Sogno, when the Doctor talked to you on Mrs. Morell's behalf, had he made a point to you that he wanted, AS A DOCTOR, that you should[127] go without delay and deal with the matter so that her mind was at rest?" [79:81]

The superintendent, who has been waiting almost to attention in the box with an expression as if butter wôuld[128] nôt mélt in his cheek, is off again. "In my conversation . . . reference was made to the chest of silver. [*Vivace*] The accused told me, 'Mrs. Morell was a very dear patient. She insisted a long time before she died that I should[129] have it in her memory. I never wanted it.' " [82:84]

"I said, 'Doctor, I have no medical training myself, but surely the quantity of dangerous drugs obtained for Mrs. Morell during the last week of her life would[130] be fatal? and is pain usual with cerebral vascular accident?' The accused replied, 'There may[131] have been a couple of these final tablets left over, but I cannot[132] remember. If there were, I would[133] take them and destroy them. I am not dishonest with drugs.' " [85:86; so far, it had been an investigation under the Dangerous Drugs Act]

[Level voice, smooth. But the smile is somewhere] "It is impossible to understand what the coincidences were unless you help me to help you." — Mr. Lawrence [quite hard] "I will[134] certainly help you. I may[135] interpret the phrase 'unplanned casual meeting' that the meeting was entirely by chance?" — "Yôu máy."[136] [89:89]

The Judge: "I think you are right, this witness was a trespasser, but does that matter in this case if he was?" — There is a feeling that it does. The means making good the ends. At the back there is an exchange of looks. The degree of scrupulosity in the conduct of an investigation must[137] be a pointer to the validity of the results obtained. [92:92]

"He asked me if he might[138] do so and I gave him permission." [92:92]

"They were very staggering words to me. I recall them quite plainly." — "To whom were they addressed? Not to you police officers?" — [Dryly] "I should[139] not think so for a moment. They were addressed to Miss Lawrence . . . I would[140] say I heard those words, sir." [95:94]

It is not far from one, and the court is beginning to watch the clock, when who should[141] walk into the box again, Nurse Randall. [98:97]

"You recollected it is the usual thing to do to ring up the doctor in the morning and tell him of the patient's death?" — "Yes." — "You did not remember this at the time {when testifying last week}?" — "No." — "You remembered you were the chief nurse and you were the person who would[142] normally do that?" [98:97]

He is not, though, as it turns out, one of the expert witnesses, volunteers paid a daily fee whose function it will[143] be to analyse the facts, but a witness who is here because he must.[144] It is the Doctor's partner. [99:98; this is written; spoken: 'who has come' *or* 'he múst bè']

"A doctor who was selecting drugs for this type of case would[145] be likely to select them from the barbiturates?" — Dr. Harris [mind on the subject] "I shŏuld[146] imágine that wŏuld[147] probably be a first choice, except if the patient had acute cerebral irritation, and then he might[148] have to use stronger drugs to cover that period." — . . . "By stronger drugs you mean—?" — "Preferably morphia." — "Heroin is a stronger drug than even morphia?" — "Yes; I have not used it much myself, so I can't[149] speak from great experience." — "In considering your choice of drugs . . . would[150] you have regard at all as to what the after-effects might[151] be, the long-term effects of the drug?" — Dr. Harris [quite at ease now; almost with animation] "One would[152] have to consider the long-term effects, but . . . " — . . . "It has been suggested that because of the after-effects of morphia and heroin they ought[153] only to be used in cases of severe pain?" — "That is the usual indication for the use of these drugs." [107:104]

The Judge: "Yes, yes. [Trying again] But suppósing you came to the conclusion—leaving aside for the moment what steps yóu would[154] tâke—that the treatment was harmful and likely to shorten her life, would[155] you have done something about it or would[156] you have just said, that is not my affair, I will[157] carry on?" [108:105]

Dr. Douthwaite must[158] be six foot six. He is a most handsome man . . . and the most striking thing about it is his height. [109:106; author's narrative]

[Casually dogmatic] "Within a few days, as soon as one is able to obtain co-operation of the patient, one should[159] at once try to mobilise the patient and encourage movement of the body. [Hearty] Massages, exercises and so forth." [110:107; yes, this is Douthwaite]

"Would[160] you expect a patient suffering from stroke to exhibit signs of irritability?" — "I would[161] expect a woman of her age to be suffering to some extent from arterio-sclerosis and this would[162] lead to a degree of irritability." [112:108]

"What can[163] one do about this acquired tolerance?" — "There are two courses. [Resting his back against the box] You can[164] stop the drug and the tolerance will[165] disappear in a week or two; or you can[166] increase the drug and immediately you will[167] overcome the tolerance and satisfy the craving." — The Attorney-General: "What are the results of stopping the drug?" — Dr. Douthwaite: "The patient will[168] be terribly ill and have acute pains in the limbs and collapse." [114:110]

"It's a walkover all right!" — "Do you think there is a doctor in England who will[169] go into that box and stand up for heroin?" — "Dr. Douthwaite was véry sure." — "Yes—I slept on it, too." — "Can[170] any man know that much?" — "Well, he is the great narcotics wallah." [117:113]

Mr. Lawrence: "A short expectation of life very substantially minimises or mitigates the dangers of addiction?" — "Yes. [Warming] May[171] I say this is a problem which often confronts us, and my practice in teaching has always been that if a patient is obviously dying it is ridiculous to worry about addiction. If the strong probability is that the patient will[172] not live for more than a month or two, yŏu cânnŏt[173] wôrry abòut addíction. If the prognosis is very doubtful about time, say, six months to five years, addiction should[174] be carried in mind." — Mr. Lawrence [rounding it off] "So in the case of Mrs. Morell one of the most prominent circumstances would[175] be that a reasonable expectation of life at the time of her stroke was about six to twelve months?" [124:119]

"You, in fact, led a deputation to the Home Office asking there should[176] be no ban placed on the manufacture of heroin in this country?" [125:120]

"Would[177] you take it from me that the special injection in November is contemporaneous with . . . ?" — "I will[178] certainly take it from you if you say so." [126:120]

Mr. Lawrence: "If this sleeplessness would[179] have been allowed to go on, she would[180] have collapsed eventually?" [127:122]

The Judge [modestly] "I would[181] like to ask the witness some questions." — Dr. Douthwaite turns to the bench. — "Before the jury can[182] convict they must[183] be satisfied that there is an act of murder. In the circumstances of this case it means . . . If the case of the Crown is right, then one or more of these acts was attempted murder, and I should[184] like to be able to assist the jury by pointing out to them precisely what in relation to each act it is that forces you to postulate murder was being committed or attempted." — Dr. Douthwaite: "I may[185] have to postulate it in relation to the doses that had gone before . . . Clearly this was not an attempt to wean her from addiction . . . If it had been so, why shôuld[186] nŏt the héroin be reduced first rather than the morphia?" [132:125f]

The Judge, always alert to the unresolved, speaks to Mr. Lawrence: "You have heard me . . . I was struck by certain divergences between some of the answers given to me and answers given previously to you. If in these circumstances you were to make application to cross-examine further, I would[187] be inclined to grant it." [137:130]

"What I am putting to you is this—if this had been a case of a patient suffering from spinal carcinoma for example, the picture of that dosage complete over those days would[188] have been one well within the experience of the profession?" — Dr. Douthwaite still surprises by saying, "It would[189] have been a dosage suggesting a desire to terminate life." — Mr. Lawrence [blinking] "You would[190] be driven into the witness-box to say that the G.P. who followed that course was a murderer, wóuld[191] yòu?" — "I would[192] say he was giving large doses of drugs and those drugs wòuld[193] hăve câused déath." — Mr. Lawrence: "Would[194] you mind facing the question and giving me an answer?" [141:133]

The Judge takes over for a minute and skirts, very lightly, one of the undercurrents of the case. "I am anxious there should[195] not be introduced into this now questions that may[196] be partly questions of law. It may[197] be a matter of law, I don't know, and it may[198] be a matter of medical practice, that if a doctor gives drugs knowing that they will[199] shorten life, but gives them because they were necessary to relieve severe pain, he is not committing murder." — Mr. Lawrence: "Let me follow, if I may[200] say so with respect, that very helpful comment from my Lord." [142:134]

"Dr. Douthwaite, there is no reason at all then to postulate there was any accumulation in the body of this person?" — [Negligently, contemptuously] "Yes, there is every reason." — "Can[201] you ever say precisely what accumulation of morphia there may[202] be in a body?" — "No." — "It is all speculation?" — "The nearer a patient is to death, the more accumulation will[203] occur . . . I cannot[204] say more." [143:135]

"The Doctor deliberately withdrew morphia on October 31st so that the patient should[205] be rendered more vulnerable?" [144:136]

It no longer holds water, and the spectacle of the witness clinging to it is disconcerting. — Mr. Lawrence [not letting up] "We can[206] see from the nursing reports, can[207] we not, that over the first three or four days of no morphia there are no withdrawal symptoms? Bearing in mind that you would[208] naturally search for some innocent explanation before you went to the other, you cannot[209] say that you were forced inescapably to place a sinister interpretation on this alteration in the drugging, cán[210] yòu?" — "Well, I căn[211] ônly sáy I see no explanation for it." — . . . [Cruising] "But that is your personal view. You can[212] conceive it quite possible that a reasonably minded physician of equal eminence might[213] by no means find it necessary to postulate an intention to terminate life on the same evidence?" — "I have always agreed that there might[214] be contrary medical opinion. [Grim smile] I am expecting it." — "And that would[215] be medical opinion entitled to as much weight as yours?" — "I do not question that." — Mr. Lawrence [setting the seal on it] "You therefore admit the possibility of a skilled genuine view to the contrary of your position?" — This is no idle dotting of i's; for where there can[216] be a valid contrary view, there is reasonable doubt and therefore, potentially, acquittal. — Dr. Douthwaite [deadpan] "Yes." — Mr. Lawrence sits down. It is over. [146:138]

"I meant by that, my Lord, that doctors frequently disagree. I wóuld[217] in fact be surprised if an eminent doctor disagreed with me on certain points." — The Judge: "If another doctor were to say he disagreed entirely with your views on accumulation, would[218] that be a skilled genuine view to the contrary?" — Dr. Douthwaite [with a touch of his cheerful certainty] "I căn[219] ŏnly sáy I really would[220] be astonished if he does." — ... "Could[221] a view contrary to yours on the subject be due to error, ignorance, or incompetence, but be hónestly held?" — "Yes." — "Then why do you postulate an intent to kill?" — "I cânnŏt[222] concéive a man with the Doctor's ... qualifications having ignorance of this sort." — "You mean that in the case of a G.P. it might[223] be due to error, ignorance or incompetence, but in the case of a G.P. wíth an anæsthetist's qualifications it could[224] not be due to these?" — "That is my view." — "It must[225] follow then that if the Doctor were to go into the witness-box and say, 'I disagree entirely with this view,' he would[226] be guilty of perjury—he would[227] be saying he held a view which he cannot[228] honestly hold?" — "You have put me a very difficult point, my Lord. Nó—the Doctor could[229] not honestly say so."   [147:139]

The Judge: "One more point. You said that it was clear to the Doctor that she was a dying woman on November 1st. Now this is quite outside your province, but I am telling you so that you follow what is in my mind: the jury may[230] have to consider what motive the Doctor had. One motive that has been suggested is that if she had lived long enough she might[231] have altered her will ... So would[232] you review the position at the end of October, if you can,[233] to help the jury? If a man had that sort of motive would[234] he have said, 'Well, she has only a month to live anyway ... '? How far would[235] a doctor, seeing the medical picture as you see it, have felt it worthwhile to shorten her life for a purpose of that sort?" — "From the medical picture I would[236] have expected her to have lived only for a matter of a few weeks, and probably no more than two months." — "Is the Doctor saying to himself, 'She can[237] only live for three weeks anyway'? And would[238] he be embarking then on a course that in fact took thirteen days to bring about her death?" — "He might[239] wéll have." And these are Dr. Douthwaite's last words in the case.   [149:140]

Dr. Ashby ... thinks that every G.P. must[240] be well aware of the facts of morphia as it is a drug in almost universal use, but this need[241] not necessarily be the case with heroin.   [150:141; reported speech]

Dr. Ashby: "I think there was just a faint chance of weaning her during the first week of November—it was a matter of either inevitable death or a faint chance. Speaking personally, it was a chance which ought[242] properly to have been taken."   [151:142]

The Attorney-General: "On what do you base your view that after November 8th she was a dying woman?" — Dr. Ashby [cautious, weary, grey] "Well, even that may[243] be wrong. There may[244] have been a faint chance even beyond that. I think we shăll[245] have to examine the books for these last five days." [152:143]

"Can[246] you see any reason why this lady should[247] have died on November 13th if the heroin and morphia had nót been administered?" — Dr. Ashby's answer is hardly conclusive. — "I do nót thínk she would[248] have died. I can[249] see no reason in these reports to have expected her to die." [155:145]

Dr. Ashby [lucidly] ". . . I am not saying that is what happened, but this single entry is explicable on either ground and I would[250] not care to say which is the more likely . . . " — . . . Mr. Lawrence [on the spot] "It ís very often the thing that carries them off?" — Dr. Ashby [meditatively] "Yes—I think they are more likely to die of another stroke than of heart failure. [Making his decision; clearly] Yes, I will[251] accept that." [159:149]

One would[252] like to know under what circumstances a patient was given a hundred and twenty grains of morphia by mouth. Dr. Ashby may[253] ask after hours; we shall[254] never know. [161:150; author's comment]

"Mr. Lawrence," the Judge interposes mildly, "you have considered, have you not, Dr. Douthwaite's evidence? The jury will[255] have to consider whether they prefer the evidence of Dr. Douthwaite or Dr. Ashby." — Mr. Lawrence: "My Lord, I would[256] submit, not." [168:156]

The Judge [sitting back] "Your submission contains two points which to me seem to present difficulty. . . . The second difficulty is this [talking voice], suppósing that we can[257] take the evidence of Dr. Douthwaite and Dr. Ashby to be something like this, 'We know the treatment was wrong, we think a doctor with his qualifications ought[258] to have known it was wrong, but we concede as an alternative that he might[259] not have known,' if the evidence rested there, then it might[260] be said that I shŏuld[261] hâve tŏ diréct the jûry that it was not strong enough; but if one finds that a doctor has in fact benefited by death . . . " [169:157]

The Judge [no mistaking short shrift this time] "Mr. Lawrence, my conclusion is that the two doctors' evidence does give rise to questions which can[262] only be properly determined by the jury." — It is dismissal. Mr. Lawrence stands as if lost. There is an immediate resumption of rustling. The Judge, in his other voice, adds a few words to say that it is not desirable that he should[263] comment at this stage. [170:158]

Mr. Lawrence gabbles on, innocent and businesslike, "My first witness will[264] be Dr. John Bishop Harman and I think I should[265] tell your Lordship that the defence have decided in the circumstances of this case not to call the Doctor." [171:159]

Mr. Lawrence: "I will[266] begin at the beginning. You have seen the Cheshire reports? . . . And what do you say about the introduction of heroin later on by the Doctor?" — [Crisply] "I shŏuld[267] sáy it was unusual . . . It is not a drug commonly given." [172:159] "If this had been envisaged, would[268] she have had to have some substitute drug?" [173:160]

Dr. Harman [full self-possession] "There are several points to consider. . . . Semi-consciousness càn[269] équally wêll be produced by drugs or by a stroke." — "Supposing it was a stroke, what would[270] you expect from a patient of that age and history?" — [With abandon] "If it was a stroke, I shŏuld[271] expêct fúrther trôuble . . ." — As simple as that. . . . The Doctor sits unbudged. But the Doctor is now discounted. He will[272] not be called. . . . The explosive was a dud, the oracle has renounced its voice, the fountain will[273] stay in the sand . . . Wè shàll[274] nôt knów what was in this man's heart. — It is his good right of course, right human and in law, that goes without saying. Or does it? The prosecution cannot[275] comment on the chosen silence of an accused; a judge may;[276] as far as the overt acts and words of men can[277] go, there will[278] be a fair trial. [174:161]

Yet this curiosity, as we call it, is it not one of man's oldest, deepest longings? the desire to hear the tale, to know the truth and meaning, the solution and the cause? The wanting to see the wheels go round, the little boy and the watch, man and his maker, the need for pattern and design: only connect. And with it there is that other longing for what the pattern seen, the design revealed should[279] be—must[280] be! that longing, too, is as young as hope—the desire for symmetry, sense and justice, the absolute and the answer. [175:162]

"Yóu would[281] never prescribe doses of that quantity for a lady of that age?" — "I have never prescribed them." — "And you wóuld[282] never?" — Dr. Harman: "I am not prepared to say what I would[283] do." — The Attorney-General [thudding] "Do you think you would[284] ever prescribe doses of that magnitude?" — "I do not think I would."[285] [183:169]

[Declamatory] "Routine injections of the character described in the nursing notes. Routine injections of morphia and heroin. [Lower gear] Would[286] these be beneficial to health?" — They might[287] be; they might[288] be neutral and they might[289] be deleterious . . . It depends on how they are used. He cannot[290] see anything that suggests this drugging was deleterious. — The Attorney-General [rising note] "I am asking you, as a consultant, if you were told that a lady in her late seventies had this course of medication over two years, would[291] you have expected that to be good for her general health?" —Dr. Harman: "I shŏuld[292] inquire into the circumstances before

I expressed an opinion." — "And having inquired?" — "It would[293] depend on what the circumstances were." — The Attorney-General turns away. "Well, if you do not want to answer, I will[294] not press you." [186:171f]

". . . The burden resting upon counsel defending a man accused of murder is a very grave and heavy burden. We stand here as the Doctor's shield at all the stages of the case; and there is no more grave moment of anxiety than when the question arises, shall[295] the accused go into the witness-box?" [194:178; Mr. Lawrence to the jury]

"You are not judging whether the Doctor was a good doctor or not. There are good doctors, better doctors, and there are not so good doctors, but all are honest men doing their best according to their individual skill." What they do may[296] not commend itself always to the grand ones at the top of the profession, but that doesn't mean that they are murderers. [195:179; same; the last part as reported speech]

"The utterly fantastic hypothesis is put before you that this doctor . . . for the sake of getting a Rolls-Royce which he côuldn't[297] gêt ányhow because the son is still alive (I don't know whether the prosecution are suggesting he ought[298] to have killed the son first?), that this doctor, instead of standing back and letting nature take its course, suddenly embarks upon a course of murder. It is too ludicrous!" [199:182; same]

{The Judge charging the jury} "I shǒuld[299] like to say this, and I say it with the approval of the Lord Chief Justice—it is not desirable that on matters of this sort judges shòuld[300] express what are merely their personal views—I think it would[301] have been wiser in this case if the preliminary proceedings before the magistrates had been held in private. Because when you have a case which arouses widespread discussion it is inevitable that reports shòuld[302] appear in the Press which are read by the public and consequently by members of the public who might[303] be asked to serve on the jury . . . " [209:193; from this point on, all further citations are from this summing-up except for the very last; and then a new notice will be printed]

"You may[304] feel you ought[305] to be allowed to consider all the material that might[306] seem to you to be relevant and not to be restricted to what is put before you in this court. But, members of the jury, whether you like the rules or not, they are the rules which you must[307] accept and must[308] be bound by." [210:194]

"You heard Mr. Lawrence . . . tell the reasons . . . why . . . the Doctor had not gone into the witness-box. You may[309] have found those reasons convincing, or you may[310] have not. I am not going to deal with them. What

I am going to tell you is simply this—that it does not matter. . . . The Doctor has a right not to go in the witness-box . . . I shall[311] elaborate on that at the end because it is so important . . . Let me tell you that it would[312] be, in my judgment—and indeed as a matter of Law—utterly wrong if you were to regard the Doctor's silence as contributing in any way towards proof of guilt." [213:196]

"a jury in court has to rely on the sense of fairness of the police to give a fair summary of the conversations and not to twist phrases that were used. That is why it is always relevant to consider the conduct of the police. . . . Therefore I ought[313] to deal shortly with the criticisms that have been made." [218:201]

"If the doctors could[314] point to any injection about which they can[315] say, 'Well, we cânnôt[316] understánd how she had symptoms of that sort if the dose is as small as is recorded here,' then you might[317] have a genuine case which you could[318] begin to investigate. But short of that, members of the jury, you have nothing except mere conjecture." [223:205]

"You may[319] say, if you like, that there must[320] have been some careless-ness on the Doctor's part, that he ought[321] to have noticed when these prescriptions were being made that he was prescribing for quantities that were far larger than the quantities which the nurses' books show to have been given. You might[322] think that you ought[323] to go further, and that in some way these drugs were disappearing in a way in which they ought[324] not to." [224:206]

"I hope most sincerely that no one will[325] think that I am making accusa-tions against anybody." [224:206]

"I do not think I need[326] say more about it than this—that if you find a theory which . . . " [227:208]

"We convict only if the witness can[327] clearly supply from the witness-box the evidence to the jury who, as I say, have not got the transcript in front of them. If therefore you come to the conclusion that Dr. Ashby's evidence on this vital point was border-line evidence . . . well then, you must[328] leave it. Unless you go the whole way with Dr. Douthwaite on this point, you must[329] say that Dr. Ashby's evidence was border-line. [Still without the slightest truck with oratory] And in the matter of murder you cannot[330] act upon border-line evidence, and therefore you would[331] not be safe in convicting. That must[332] be your attitude in the end." — And the court adjourns at the usual hour. [228:209]

"Wéll, yòu cán[333] îf yòu líke, put that view together with the certainty—I do not think that is too high a word—almost certainty, at any rate, of Dr. Douthwaite, and say the prosecution case is proved. But you mùst[334] álso consider whether you ought[335] not to put Dr. Ashby's view together with the evidence of Dr. Harman." [230:212]

"If the Doctor had calculated that, he would[336] have said to himself, would[337] he not, 'Well, she may[338] be dead in two or three weeks and then I will[339] get the chest I have been waiting for so long.' " [232:214]

"Perhaps that was a lapse of memory and quite understandable. But, again, you might[340] have liked to have heard his own explanation about it. You might[341] have liked to have heard, too, his own explanation about 'easing the passing,' a phrase which might[342] be used quite innocently, but, on the other hand, a phrase which might[343] perhaps go further. However, you mùst[344] tâke into accóunt not isolated phrases but the trend of his statements on the whole, . . . Take the chance interview last October. At the end of it the superintendent said to him, 'I hope I shăll[345] fínish all these inquiries soon, and we will[346] probably have another talk.' . . . And when he was asked at the time of the search about drugs, there was that key sentence at the end, 'I am not dishonest about drugs.' It shows—does it not?—that what he thought he was being confronted with was some suggestion that he had been engaged in some sort of illicit traffic—prescribing more than he ought[347] to have prescribed, or something of that sort—but not murder. . . . — I think there is only one other matter to which I need[348] refer you . . . , and that is the point made by the Attorney-General on Friday about the nurses' note-books." [234:215]

"[With a measure of fervour] I hope that the day will[349] never come when that right is denied to any Englishman. It is not a refuge of technicality: the law on this matter reflects the natural thought of England. So great is our horror at the idea that a man might[350] be questioned, forced to speak and perhaps to condemn himself out of his own mouth, [for the first time without detachment] that we afford to everyone suspected or accused of a crime, at every stage, and to the very end, the right to say: 'Ask me no questions, I shăll[351] answer none. Prove your case.' — . . . And so this long process ends with the question with which it began: 'Murder? Can[352] you prove it?' — I dare[353] say it is the first time that you have sat in that jury-box. It is not the first time that I have sat in this chair. And not infrequently I have heard a case presented by the prosecution that seemed to me to be manifestly a strong one, and sometimes I have felt it my duty to tell the jury so. I do not think, therefore, that I ought[354] to hesitate to tell you that here the case for the defence seems to me to be manifestly a strong one . . . But it is the same question in the end, always the same—is the case for the Crown strong enough to carry conviction to your mind? It is your question. You have to answer it. It lies always with you, the jury.

Always with you. And you will[355] now consider what that answer shall[356] be." [236:217; end of the Judge's charge to the jury]

But why did the grace of God choose thus? Life, one might[357] say, has a way of throwing up strange twists—who can[358] tell?—without this piece of bad luck, without that loss, that outright catastrophe, I might[359] never have seen, have met, have known; I would[360] not have had that chance; I should[361] not now be hére . . . It was all for the best. Do we really say that, and how often? Ought[362] we to say it for another? "Nous avons tous assez de force pour supporter les maux d'autrui." Always fortitude enough, words enough to explain away another man's misfortune . . . Can[363] we let it go at that, can[364] we turn now from the Doctor's fate with the sense that, somehow, in some way, all is well; or must[365] we accept that his entanglement was another tale told by an idiot? [239:220; author's comment]

Page 164. On Documentary Shall

For typical American manipulations of *shall*, two citations will suffice. The first displays the purely cosmetic employment. Since the United Nations Charter, in its English version, was drafted by Americans, it uses *shall*, but of course not in the place where we find it in the first citation. Anybody who understands the Charter will naturally say 'loses, is going to lose, will lose, its vote as the U.N. Charter provides that it shall'—but there is a certain art and mystery about the placement of a beauty-patch:

Whether a member nation which fails to pay its assessment shall lose its vote in the General Assembly, as provided in the U.N. Charter, is a matter likely to be tested this year. [*The Reader's Digest*, March 1964, p. 67]

. . . who explained the following changes in the document since it was brought to the December meeting of the Faculty. — 1. The use of "shall" and "will" has been standardized throughout. "Must" was changed to "shall" and except where simple futurity was intended, every "will" was changed to "shall." . . . 3. In 10A.06 the phrase "full-time" has been added in the first sentence, and "shall be designated as temporary" has been added to the second sentence. . . . the faculty unanimously voted its appreciation to . . . the Codification Committee for their work on the codification of the appointment and tenure rules. The action was greeted with applause. . . . it was voted that . . . This motion shall supersede any or all prior Faculty action inconsistent therewith. [*Minutes* of the January 1964 meeting of the University of Wisconsin Faculty]

The preposterous use of *prior* (in normal English it means 'superior because earlier') for *previous* is standard in amateur drafting; it provides a final beauty-patch after the substitution of *shall supersede* for *supersedes.* The rest of the procedure is more complex, but I will do my best with it.

First, under the principle *suum cuique* we give a Codification Committee the task of redrafting a document which was formerly an Administration document, subject to ratification in Faculty meeting.

Second, the committee ascertains what the old wording means, an easy task because it is in English and precedents have accumulated.

Third, the committee decides that *suum cuique* has gone far enough; if not checked in time, it might even lead to interpretation of the document by a jury of one's peers, in case a tenure dispute gets into court *deo volente:* see *Trial,* modal citations *195–200.*

Fourth, 'no injury without a remedy' (I seem to have mislaid the Latin for that, but never mind), the committee turns to standard grammars to ascertain the wording *for* the document, a *volte-face* (our Latin has slid, *facilis descensus averni,* right through Italian into French, I'm afraid, which just goes to show you what can happen when you let a language have its way) involving reinterpreting *ascertain* from 'the only current use' [*Shorter Oxford Dictionary* sense 3, cf *Webster's Third New International Dictionary* sense 2] into what Jonathan Swift meant in saying "some effectual method for correcting, enlarging, and ascertaining our language" [*SOD* 'obsolete since 1789,' *TNI* 'archaic' with the same Swift citation].

Fifth, since we are now on solid ground at last—correcting is proper to a committee of professors, as it was to Swift, and enlarging can be done in our document's 10A.06—we correct by rule and compass.

Sixth, if the document ever goes before a jury, we can be sure (since 'correct' is an axiom in our culture) that *magna est veritas et prevalebit* over the jury's bafflement.

Seventh, we return to *suum cuique* and get it all ratified in Faculty meeting, *nemine contradicente* and *magna cum laude*.

I was too fascinated at the time,* but I think I've got it all straight now with the aid of that distinguished jurist W. S. Gilbert.

Page 178. On Scarecrows

In quoting Fowler *ad nauseam* I make certain typographical changes for the convenience of readers. (1) I replace boldface type with small capitals, and boldface numerals with Roman numerals; (2) I use roman for his italic citations, and italics for his single words in roman within them; (3) I spell out his &; (4) I paragraph his citations and prefix key-numbers to them, so that they can be referred to by number in the discussions which I add.

SHALL and WILL, SHOULD and WOULD. I. Plain future and conditional. II. I would like. III. Indefinite future and relative. IV. Elegant variation. V. *That*-clauses. VI. Decorative and prophetic *shall*.

'To use *will* in these cases is now a mark of Scottish, Irish, provincial, or extra-British idiom'—Dr Henry Bradley in the OED. 'These cases' are of the type most fully illustrated below (see I), and the words of so high an authority are here quoted because there is an inclination, among those not to the manner born, to question the existence, besides denying the need, of distinctions between *sh.* and *w.* The distinctions are elaborate; they are fully set forth in the OED; and no formal grammar or dictionary can be held to have done its duty if it has not laid down the necessary rules. It will therefore be assumed here that the reader is aware of the normal usage

* Duly published as the handbook on Appointment, Tenure, and Dismissal Procedures, the document now contains several survivals of modern English. The Regents have provided one: "These rules and regulations are promulgated in the conviction that in serving a free society the scholar must himself be free." Others were left in the section headings, unaltered by the Committee: "10A.07 Divisional committees must advise on certain appointments" is the heading over the sentence that includes "the dean shall ask"; "10A.15 Nature of non-faculty appointment [is] to be stated in writing" is the heading over "the nature of such an appointment shall be specified in writing"; and "10B.10 Copies of tenure rules [are] to be supplied" over "The Secretary of the Faculty shall send . . ." I have supplied in brackets the copulas which drop out in headline-writing based on normal English; but document-drafting does not shorten: it replaces. I expect to have retired before the next Codification Committee is selected. Meanwhile, let us give thanks for small mercies.

so far as abstract statement can bring it home to him; and the object will be to make the dry bones live by exhibiting groups of sentences, all from newspapers of the better sort, in which one or other principle of idiom has been outraged. The 'Scotch, Irish, provincial, or extra-British' writer will thus have before him a conspectus of the pitfalls that are most to be feared.

I. Plain future or conditional statements and questions in the first person should have *shall, should;* the . . . *will*s and *would*s in the following examples are wrong:—

1. It is impossible to exaggerate the terrible consequences of this proposed act; in Egypt, in India, in every country from the Mediterranean to the frontiers of China, we *will* teach the lesson that no reliance can be placed on the word of England.
2. This is pleasant reading; but we *won't* get our £2,000 this year.
3. Perhaps we *will* soon be surfeited by the unending stream of 'new' literature, and *will* turn with relief to . . .
4. We might not be able to get all the oil we wanted from our coal, but we *would* always get enough to prevent . . .
5. What exactly was the total of the Turkish forces in this area we do not know—and probably never *will*.
6. He was plain to read from the beginning, and could hardly, we *would* have supposed, have made an appeal to a girl of this character.
7. But the late King Edward brushed aside all such nonsense; and where *would* we be today without the French 'entente'?
8. If we traced it back far enough we *would* find that the origin was . . .
9. If we permit our contribution to be substituted for a part of the building programme, we *will* be casting our vote with the 'little navy' people.
10. If we compare these two statements, we *will* see that so far as this point goes they agree.
11. I *would* not be doing right if I were to anticipate that communication.
12. If it were true the Germans would be right, and we *would* be wrong.
13. If British trade interests are to be revived, we *will* stand in need of these men who know Russia.
14. But if the re-shuffling of the world goes on producing new 'issues', I *will*, I fear, catch the fever again.
15. To the average citizen it would appear that in forestalling this plot we *would* in fact be rendering the German people no less service than . . .
16. I think I *would* be a knave if I announced my intention of handing over my salary to . . .
17. It is quite clear that when Home Rule is being fought in the Commons I *will* have to devote all my time to it.
18. Reports of fighting in China are as conflicting as we *would* expect.

19. I am confident that within three years we employers *will* be reaping benefit from it.
20. We have collected more in consequence of that valuation than we *would* have done without it.
21. We never know when we take up the morning paper, some of us, which side we *will* be on next.
22. The whole story of the rescue of the men from Kerrig Island is a heroism of the sea which we *will* do well to realize.
23. Mr J. H. Thomas's vision of the Utopia in which we *will* live 'When Labour Rules'.

In all these the idea of intention, volition, choice, etc., which goes with *will* or *would* in the first person, is plainly out of the question. Two examples follow in which such an idea is precluded not by the actual words quoted, but by the unquoted context; in such cases the offence against idiom is aggravated by the possibility of misinterpretation:—

24. We *would* thus get at once the thing wanted; an opera open practically all the year round (idiomatic sense, We aim at getting thus: intended sense, This, if it were not unfortunately impossible, would give us).
25. 'Who's Who' is entirely without a competitor; and there is perhaps no book on our reference shelves that we *would* miss sooner (idiomatic sense, There is no book we should be so glad to be rid of: intended sense, There is no book we should so quickly feel the want of).

Two other examples will provide for a common exception to the rule as given absolutely above. In sentences that are, actually or virtually, reported, a verb that as reported is in the first person but was originally in the second or third often keeps *will* or *would:*—

26. People have underrated us, some even going so far as to say that we *would* not win a single test match (the people said *You,* or *They, will not,* which justifies, though it by no means necessitates, *we would not* in the report).
27. He need not fear that we *will* be 'sated' by narratives like his (his fear was *They,* or *You, will be sated,* which makes *we will* not indeed advisable, but defensible).

II. The verbs *like, prefer, care, be glad, be inclined,* etc., are very common in first-person conditional statements (*I should like to know* etc.). In these *should,* not *would,* is the right form. 'I would like to say' is no more idiomatic English than 'I would find it hard to say'; but hundreds of people who would be horrified by the latter are ready to write the former. The explanation is to be found in confusion between two posssible ways of speaking, the modern 'I should like to say', and the archaic 'I would say'; in the modern form the desire is expressed in the verb *like* and requires no other expression; in the archaic form the desire had to be given in *would* because otherwise it was not expressed at all. The . . . *would*s and *will*s, then, are all wrong:—

28. In regard to the general question, I *would like* to speak today with a certain amount of reserve.
29. The other argument upon which I *would like* to comment is as follows.
30. We must shut our ears to the tales of some of the lame dogs we *would like* to help over a stile.
31. We cannot go into details, and *would prefer* to postpone criticism until . . .
32. Nor has he furnished me with one thing with which I *would care* to sit down in my little room and think.
33. I, as Chief Liberal Whip, *will be very glad* to place them in touch with the local secretary.
34. If we should take a wider view, I *would be inclined* to say that . . .
35. In this month of 'grey rain and silver mist' we *will be glad* to keep within our average rainfall of a little over 2 in.

An example less patently wrong is:

36. We *would be the last* to argue that publication in this form commits our contemporary to agreement with the views expressed.

This is defensible if the writer will assure us that his meaning was We should wish to be the last, instead of, as it doubtless was, We should be the last.

We are more than halfway through the article here, and can stop because in the remainder Fowler for the most part makes sense. For the benefit of readers who possess his unquestionably valuable book—for example, his treatment of the split infinitive is a classic of good sense and good taste applied to facts—I will specify: III. The trouble is that those writers tried to write documentary English with the requisite archaisms, and failed. IV. Same deal, complicated by local inconsistency. V. Same again, now complicated by flouting the established *should* (standard in American too) in favor of *will*. VI. One specimen will suffice:

You *shall* have watched, it may be, the ways of birds and beasts in a garden or wood for half a lifetime; and your friend, the first time that you show him your preserves, *shall* straightway walk up the leverets, or point out the gold crest's nest which you have always wanted to find.

Now Fowler and Bradley were only the last and second-last in a chain of re-copiers that began about two and a half centuries ago when the schools of England first began to offer a ready market for authoritarian grammars of English. Before that, school grammar tradition was only the tradition for teaching Latin, which had to be done on the authoritarian principle for self-evident reasons. When school teaching of English grammar began, it naturally continued along exactly the same line: what else could grammar be, after all, but the correcting of errors? It was established that the impulse of nature could only issue into bad Latin; it was assumed that it would surely create bad English too. Contemporary usage varied, as good usage always does; those people didn't know that as we know it now, and they sought to ascertain the best English for teaching as the only English. There was a political parallel, just at that time, and it was something of a general cultural parallel too. It is surely no coincidence that the leading writers of English school grammars just then were Scots, and I believe the majority of them were Jacobites: legitimists in grammar as in politics and in culture-theory generally.

Latin could not sort out SHALL and WILL for them, and they were incapable (except for Buchanan, an early and little regarded grammarian, the clearest head of them all) of sorting them out from actual usage; the task would have been beyond all ordinary powers anyhow, because it was still within the period of transition from the archaic to the modern meaning-structure for all modals. What the successful school of English grammarians did was to go behind all contemporary and recent usage and to base their SHALL and WILL rules on the traditions of legal document drafting and bolster them with etymology. Hence the justification that Fowler still gives: because WILL (ultimately because of its etymology) resembles the *will* in 'Where there's a will there's a way' and in 'Barkis is willing,' Fowler speaks of "the idea of intention, volition, choice, etc." which had actually been absent from the modal WILL since somewhat before Shakespeare's day, and supposes that it must be the basic meaning even today. He was not alone in supposing this: he had all the chain of grammars, copied from earlier grammars, stretching behind him all the way back to the beginning of the eighteenth century.

All the same, it is an odd thing—I don't know what else to call it —that the amazing performance which I have quoted is the work of the same man whose sapient words at the beginning of his article on *Pronunciation* could stand without retouching in any modern linguistic treatise. Our knowledge, then, that Fowler was capable of clear thinking on other occasions can furnish a certain justification for scrutinizing his list of SHALL and WILL examples from the identical point of view that he took for his treatment of pronunciation.

The root of his error in the SHALL and WILL article is simply his assumption that the choice between them is not a choice of meanings but is merely an obedience to grammar, either obedience to true grammar or to false grammar. If saying *I* (or *we*) mechanically entails saying SHALL, then the SHALL is redundant to the *I* or the *we* and conveys no message of its own. This is as elementary as anything in logic; it is, in fact, the same argument that I used in establishing the status of meaningless DO in Chapter III, and Fowler's theory can fairly be called the theory of meaningless SHALL and WILL. In contrast, the basic principle of my discussion in Chapter VI is that Englishmen generally mean what they say and say what they mean. I could proceed to cite the arguments and again cite the examples by number, here as in Chapter VI; instead, and simply to obviate dragging this out over a vast number of pages, I will merely allude to what Chapter VI has established.

1. Foreseeing terrible consequences gives an Englishman adequate assurance for being categorical: we *will* teach the lesson.
2. We *shall* get our money in English, right enough, for good things are awaited with diffidence because of the contingencies; but certainly we *won't* get it *this year*.
3. *Perhaps* we *shall* be surfeited; very well; score one for Fowler. But wait: an Englishman has a right to dismiss *Perhaps* as a conventional preface, and to be guided rather by the *soon;* meaning 'without (undue) delay' this assures him adequately to say *we will*. Finally, he is going to say

and will turn under the strong stylistic rule against repeating *shall* in suc-
cesive clauses, and this almost automatic second *will* can be anticipated
with the first.

4. We *would always* get enough oil: the *might* clause eliminates contingency.
5. We do not know—and never *shall:* we have met this in *Trial* too. But
   with *probably*, the *Trial* word is not *shall* but *will*.
6. We are expert at supposing rightly, and unreality can substitute for
   contingency.
7. We'*d* be in the soup for a dead cert. See below, items 8, 11, 16.
8. *Far enough* gives adequate assurance by definition.
9. This one would be ruined by using *shall*, for it could only mean '*After*
   we permit that, sooner or later we *shall be casting* our vote unless some
   contingency intervenes.'
10. If we compare *these two* statements—how could a condition be clearer?
11. Utterly remote unreality still need not make a condition unclear; it's a
    question of who is boss, as Humpty Dumpty said.
12. The Germans would be right *if William came*, and we *would* be wrong
    by definition: ghost-stories have to be taken seriously or they wouldn't
    be any fun—that was the point of the Saki play.
13. Who says we aren't all that good at reviving British trade interests?
    When they are revived, we *will certainly* stand in need, so why not say
    so? We *shall* stand in need? I though you agreed.
14. An Englishman can say 'I fear' easily, though he has never felt genuine
    fear. This is British understatement for 'I *will certainly* catch the fever
    again,' and *shall* is not citable with *certainly* in *Trial*, or I dare say, any
    unedited present-day sample.
15. We *would indeed* be rendering them a service if it comes to that.
16. So you think I *should* be a knave? I though you knew me better.
17. Since it is so clear, there is nothing for me to do but admit it.
18. We are always clear about what we *would* expect of China.
19. When I am confident I always say *will*, since that is what it means.
20. Do you imagine we don't *know* how much we have collected? We are
    adequately assured against the unreal case of what we *would* have done.
21. But we know we *will* be on one side or the other.
22. We always realize what we *will* do well to realize.
23. At least Mr. J. H. Thomas is sure we *will* live there.

In all these the idea of intention, volition, choice, etc., which anciently went with *will* or *would* in the first person (or in any person:
Would God!) is plainly as dead as Geoffrey Chaucer. Even Fowler
knows exactly what is meant by saying (24) 'we *would* thus get at

once the thing wanted', and (25) 'that we *would* miss sooner'; for if he didn't know, how could he pretend so accurately?

II. 'I would like to say' is exactly as idiomatic English as 'I would find it hard to say'—each is said when that is what is meant, and their parallels are easy to find in *Trial*.

28. I *would like* to speak with a certain amount of reserve if I had any, but I can't conceal what *Trial* has revealed: The Judge modestly says, '*I would* like to ask the witness some questions,' not despite the fact that his modesty will not delay the proceeding but *because* of that; then when he realizes that he may yet be helpless to assist the jury he is forced to say, 'I *should like* to be able to assist the jury.'

29. The other argument which I *would* like to comment on is as follows: Voilà! Didn't take me long, did it!

30. If it were not true that we *would like* to help them over a stile, nothing would be clear and definite enough for *must*.

31. If we *could* by some odd chance go into details, *perhaps* we *should* prefer to postpone it; but in this clear case . . .

32. It is hardly conceivable that he *should* furnish me with such a thing, so I *shouldn't care* to depend on it; but I *would care* to if he did.

33. If I couldn't be sure enough to say 'I *will be very glad*' I *wouldn't* be a competent Chief Liberal Whip.

34. If we *should* take a wider view, we *would* hear our Judge say, 'If *in these circumstances* you *were to make* an application to cross-examine further, I *would be inclined* to grant it.'

35. Of course we *will be glad;* who *wouldn't*?

36. So we *should be the last, should* we? Not us, not half.

Now just a minute, friends and neighbors. I'm not a murderer. He was a scarecrow. To stuff his straw man, Fowler had to rake through a number of tons of the national Press. Nearly everything he read conformed both to *Trial* and to Dr. Bradley. This is a pattern which has been explained before; see *Verification*, page 154. Let us not fall into confusion about this. *Trial* was not edited as the "newspapers of the better sort" are edited, much of their content—the leaders, the book-reviews, and so on—pretty thoroughly edited in the way R. A. C. described for us: page 163 here. Then the competent witness for modern English is to be found in print only rarely: *Trial* seems to be unique in its bulk and quality as well.

Index

A : 'actor,' 152
ABLE TO, BE, 26, 185
ABOUT TO, BE, 23; negated, 24
absolute logic, 154, 195, 197
abstract representation of verb form, 47
accent-marks (*ó, ô*, etc.): to show stress, 12
accepted reality, 122, 150
active voice: infinitive, 19; 'non-passive' and, 92, 94; meaning of, 96, 98
actor: named, 44; unmentioned with non-finite if identical with subject of governing verb, 44; for gerund, 45; described by participle, 50; with stable modals, 151 196f
actual tense: in finite schema, 81; meaning of, 125; futurity with, 134ff
additive meaning, 82ff, 99
adequate modals, 150, 157f, 178, 180
adjective: infinitive as, 19; participial, 51
advancing the plot. *See* plot-advancing
adverb: infinitive as, 18, 19; interrupting a finite, 62
'affirmative': defined, 153
after: with gerund, 42
ain't, 76
Allen, W. Stannard, 45, 114f
am, 55, 76
ambiguity: of neutral voice, 98; of the aspects, 136f
American English, 6f, 13, 65, 170ff, 214; NOT TO BE ABOUT TO in, 24
analogy, 213
anaphoric questions, 59
archaic modal meanings, 148, 166ff, 180, 192
archaisms, 31, 171
are, 55
aren't: printed *are not,* 64

arithmetic: binary and decimal, 73
as: as I, as they, etc., 71, 73, 76; *as if, as though,* 124; *as far as,* 184
aspect: of infinitive, 19; temporary, from *on* with gerund, 44; in finite schema, 81; tense, phase, and, 101ff; English, 107ff; Portuguese and Spanish, 107, 113; Slavic, 107, 113, 126f; choice of, 111, 113, 133; privative marking of, 112; in narrative, 126, 131, 133, 135; tense, time, and, 127ff; in modal summary, 149. *See also* generic aspect; temporary aspect
assertion: preliminary definition of, 14, 17, 72; in finite schema, 81; defined symbolically, 153
asseveration, 111, 114, 127, 130
assurance, 150, 156ff, 191
astrology, 155, 177
atomic theory, 4
Authoritative Freedom, 167, 180
Authoritative Probity, 167, 180
Authority: acknowledged or imposed with *may,* 179, 188; as a scarecrow, 233, 238
auxiliaries: modal auxiliaries called simply 'modals,' 21; meaningless DO and parts of the finite markers, HAVE and BE, 76. *See also* quasi-auxiliaries

background events: temporary aspect for, 127, 129f, 133f
base. *See* verb-base
BE (*auxiliary*): followed by *I, we, he, she, they,* 73; in finite schema, 76; uses of, 86ff
BE (*the verb-base meaning* 'exist'), 88
BE ABLE TO, 26, 185
BE ABOUT TO, 23; negated, 24
beauty in language, 213

be... being: not found in *Trial*, 75, 79

Bedford, Sybille: as observer and writer, 7, 8, 9, 131; biography of, 122*n*

been and *being:* formation of, 55

before with gerund, 42

BE GOING TO, 22, 141*n*, 160

BE -ING: in finite schema, 76; temporary aspect marker, 81

belief: definitions of modes of, 153

BE -N: in finite schema, 76; passive voice marker, 81

Best We Can Do, The, 9, 122*n*

BE SUPPOSED TO, 28

BE TO, 22

better had, 125

binary arithmetic, 73

Black Cat Book BA–21, 9

boundaries of signals, 5

boundary of minimal social matrix of events, 150, 183f

brackets: use of in *Trial*, 7f; in citations, 9, 10f

Bradley, Henry, 233, 237, 240

British English, 6ff, 13, 67, 214, 233; extended propredicate in, 68; short propredicates in, 75, 79

Brown, Ivor, 71

busybodies, 212

by: with gerund, 43; marking the actor with passive voice, 95

C: defined as 'all the circumstances,' 152; from *R* by trimming, 183ff

c: defined as 'some but not all the circumstances,' 152

CAN: compared with BE ABLE TO, 26, 28, 185; in finite schema, 76; in modal summary, 149f; defined symbolically, 153; defined discursively, 180; uses of, 180ff; negated, 199, 201

Can do!, 68

can't: printed as *cannot,* 8, 63, 181; used arbitrarily, 182

capitals, small. *See* small capitals

case, in, 38

casual assurance, 156ff

casual modals, 149ff; negated, 199ff

casual potentiality, 179ff

casual style, 57

categories and meanings, 14, 81f

causal (prior) hypothesis, 176

cause and effect in perfect phase, 140ff

center: of minimal matrix, 150, 183; maximal matrix has no, 152

chance: and casual modals, 149

characterizing: with *used to,* 29; with unmarked passive, 97; with generic aspect, 110f, 114, 130

Chaucer, Geoffrey, 239

children's grammar, 209f

circumstances: never excluded, 153; define casual modals, 156, 180; alter cases, 168

citations to two *Trial* editions: described, 9f

citations for modals, 214ff

clear conditions: 157ff

clipping: of infinitive, 16, 65; of finite, 66; of sentence, 66

Cockney, 206*n*, 208

Coleridge, Samuel Taylor, 207

Collation Table for *Trial* editions, 10, 251

Collins edition of *Trial,* 9, 251

come to think of it, 37

command: not meaning of MUST, 151, 195

comment. *See* contemporary comment

community: mores and membership, 150ff, 195; controls language, 212

complement: of infinitive, 17; infinitive as a, 18

components of meaning, 81, 149

conative form of verb, 21

conclusion: unreal, 176f

condition: provision contrasted to, 37; clear, 157ff; real and unreal, 175, 176

conditional form of verb, 176

confidence. *See* prudent confidence

confirmation question, 59; with *can,* 181

connotation: of perfect phase, 144f; of futurity in modals, 159, 185

constituency, immediate, 5

consultative style, 57

'contemporary': as label for present participle, 49

contemporary comment, 111, 113, 130ff, 135f

contemporary scene: and meaning of present participle, 49f; and unreal hypothesis, 176

context evidence: for stressing, 12; for

meaning, 26, 102, 112; for adequate assurance, 158

contingency: defined, 156, 196; as interpretation of hazard, 178; as equivalent to possible evasion, 196

'continuous': as label for temporary aspect, 106

contractions, 8, 12, 63f, 65

contrast, 67

copula, 86ff; its propredicate rule, 89ff; written English exception to propredicate rule, 90

cosmetic *shall*, 231

could. See CAN

countable circumstances with *can*, 180f

countable parts and relations, 4

court reporter, 8, 64

Cozzens, James Gould, 7

criteria, formal, 205

cube of modals, semological, 149

culture: and status verbs, 119

current phase, 139; in the infinitive, 19; in finite schema, 81

'd, 12

-D, in finite schema, 76; as tense marker, 81

DARE: in finite schema, 76; in modal summary, 150; defined symbolically, 153; defined discursively, 192; history of, 192; negated, 200f

daren't, dare not, 200f

Darwin, Darwinism, 3f

dashes, use of in citations, 11

data and verification, 6, 155

deletion of tense marker, 131

demonstration: and generic aspect, 111, 114, 130

denotation: of perfect phase, 140, 144; of futurity, lacking in modals, 159, 185

descriptive linguistics, 4f, 59, 87

desiderative form of verb, 21

dichotomies in finite schema, 79

did, 59

Diderot, Denis, 3

didn't, 63

didn't ought to, 194

diffidence: expressed as contingency, 161f

DO *(auxiliary). See* meaningless DO

DO *(the verb-base meaning* 'perform'*)*, 68

documentary *shall*, 161, 164, 170, 231f, 233n

does, 63, 72

does not or *doesn't*, 8

do so as misinterpretation of DÒ, 70

drafting of documents. *See* documentary *shall*

duty: identified with logic as the meaning of MUST, 148, 195

E: defined, 152. *See also* event

echolalia, 133

economy in language, 61, 90

edited English, 65, 124, 163f, 240

editions of *Trial*, 9

educated semi-formal English, 7

effects, delayed: and perfect phase, 140ff

Einstein, Albert, 154

elimination of syllable (ð), 12f

emphasis, 11f, 59, 61

English: selection of sample of, 6; written, 9, 90; native spoken, 12

evasion: contingency as possible, 168, 196

event *(key technical term here, signifying the sort of thing that is specified by verb-bases, thus perhaps relations* [RESEMBLE, *etc.*] *and states* [WORRY, BE COLD] *as well as deeds* [SHOW], *insofar as a base is being used to specify it; in Chapter VI especially, event is what is specified by the whole clause minus the modal if any)*: 149, 152, *and passim*

eventual negation, 67, 199, 201

extended propredicate, 68

factual assertion: in finite schema, 81; in modal summary, 149; defined symbolically, 152f

Fadiman, Clifton, 31

Fairley, Barker, 69

finite *(short for* finite verb or propredicate)*: defined by choice of subject, 14, 72; defined by form, 53ff, 76; defined discursively, 72; serial-numbered list, 77ff; defined symbolically, 152

Five Clocks, The, 57n, 164n

for: with subject of infinitive, 18f; with gerund, 43

force-feeding of SHALL, 172, 214

foreign learners of English, 5, 44, 97, 114

form: definition of, 48; meaning and, 81, 101; shape and, 205ff

formal chill: imposed by *may*, 188f

formal criteria, 205

formal style, 57, 63f

forms, latent, 75

Fowler, H. W., 31*n*, 177f, 179, 210, 233ff, 239f

Fowler, Murray, 75

framing: temporary aspect as, 113

Franklin, Benjamin, 166

freedom: BE ABLE TO signifying time-limited, 27; underlying archaic modal meanings, 167, 180

Free Will, 4, 127, 183

French: traces of, in British English, 122*n;* perfect tense, 144f; vivid present and conditional, 178

Fries, Charles Carpenter, 31*n*, 45

function: in finite schema, 81; base as privative marker of, 100; in modal summary, 149

futurity: with BE TO, 22; with BE GOING TO, 22, 134, 141*n*, 160; as a meaning of actual tense, 118, 134ff; as a connotation of modals, 151, 159, 185; defined, 160

gender, 71f, 214

generalizing meaning of modal remote tense, 169

generic aspect: in finite schema, 81; characterizing, 109f, 114, 130; defined, 112; transformation rule, 130; futurity with, 134f

German: perfect tense, 144f; passive voice, 193; modal system and, 193

gerund: defined, 40, 205ff; prepositions with, 42; as source of temporary aspect, 44; subject of, 45; schema, 53

GET: past participle with, 51

Gilbert, William Schwenk, 233

gimmicks in language, 190, 212

give 'er, 208f

Glinz, Hans, 147*n*

GO TO: *I went to open my eyes*, 23

grammar: signals, 5; stressing and, 12; defined, 21; school impact on, 65, 177, 209f, 214

grammarians, 19, 179, 212

grammatical distinctions, 90

grammatical limits of form, 76

grammatical meanings, 14, 81

grammatical signals, 5, 12

graphing: of aspect and phase, 109, 211; of narrative events, 130

group-modifier: infinitive as, 18

Grove Press edition of *Trial*, 9

h, dropped out: weak-stress rule, 208

habits: and language, 213

had, 52, 55; as *håd*, 12

had better, had rather, 125

hadn't ought to, 194

Halsted, George Bruce, 177*n*, 178

hardly, 180, 184

has, 72

HAVE (*auxiliary*), 52; spelled *of*, 65; in finite schema, 76

HAVE (*the verb-base meaning* 'possess'): with *to* or *got to*, 25, 195; past participle with, 51f; as status verb, 118

HAVE -N: in finite schema, 76; perfect phase marker, 81

hazard: and expression of contingency, 178

headlines: aspect in, 132; copula omitted in, 233*n*

he'd, 12

high time, 124

historical present, 126

hitchhikers on speech, 8

homeostasis, 212ff

hyperurbanisms, 122, 172, 208

hyphened bit: defined, 55; vanishes before zero, 55, 76; NOT as a, 63

hyphens in American editions of *Trial*, 9

hypothesis: scientific, 154f; as background to a *would* clause, 175ff

Iberian aspect, 107, 113

'idiomatic': as label, 93f, 96

idiomatic specializations: modals and, 201

if it be, 37

if it were, 122

immediate constituency, 5

immediate future, 135

imperative, 31, 35f

'imperfect': as label for temporary

aspect, 107
in: with gerund, 43
in case, 38
infinitive: marked with *to,* 14, 16; clipped, 16, 65; as a noun, 17ff; as object or complement, 17ff; as subject, 17; meaning of, 17ff; subject of, 17ff; anticipated by *it,* 18; voice, aspect, and phase of, 19; split, 30f; unlike presentative, 31; in competition with gerund, 40
information question, 59, 181
-ing, -ING: in various sorts of words, 40; as gerund marker, 40, 53; in finite schema, 54, 76
insistence, 61, 82
intensity as meaning: status verbs and temporary aspect, 116, 118
interrogative intonation, 59
intransitive verb-bases, 74, 94
inversion, 36, 58ff, 210
irregularities: of past participles, 48; within a language, 213f
irresponsible styles, 64
is, 72
it: with infinitive or gerund, 18, 41
italics: for emphasis, 11; in citations, 15; marking words to be disregarded, 15, 38

jeopardy: and choice of modals, 151, 191f

KEEP: past participle with, 51
Kennedy, John F., 51, 146
Kipling, Rudyard, 57
knowledgeability, 151, 157

language: finite nature of, 4; a system of habits, 213
Latin: subject lacking in, 56; passive verbs in, 93, 95
learners of English: foreign, 5, 44, 97, 114; and modals, 147
LET: and presentative, 36
let's and *let us,* 12
lexical meaning, 14, 81, 87, 101
lexicon, 5, 74
linguistic change, 164
linguistic results, 5
linguistics: as young science, 3; descrip-

tive, 4; as fad, 212
linguistic theory, 5, 59
linguists, 5, 147, 205, 207
'll: will, not *shall,* 156, 162f
logic: symbolic, 152; absolute, 154; identified with duty or order of nature, 195, 197

major stress, 12
MAKE: past participle with, 51
marked categories in finite schema, 81
marker: of infinitive, 16; of gerund, 53; finite list, 76; of meaning, 81; privative effect on meaning, 99, 112; statistics of use, 101, 143
matrix. *See* maximal matrix; minimal matrix
maximal matrix: described, 150ff; contrasted with minimal matrix, 197
MAY: in finite schema, 76; in modal summary, 149f; defined symbolically, 153; defined discursively, 180; in modern sense for indeterminate probability, 186; in archaic sense for Subservient Freedom, 187ff
may: arbitrary for *might* or *can,* 188ff
May it please your Lordship, 36
mayn't, 200
meaning: of signals, 5; lexical and grammatical, 14, 81; of finites, 14, 17; categorical, 17, 82; of infinitive, 19; from context, 26, 102; of presentative, 34; of participles, 49f; base or referential, 82ff; additive and privative, 82, 84, 98; of passive voice, 93, 95f; of temporary aspect, 107, 129, 131, 133ff; of remote tense, 121ff; of perfect phase, 140ff; of BE GOING TO, 141*n;* of modals, 148, 166, 167, 180, 192ff; of modal remote tense, 169; search for, 207
meaningful form, 101
meaningful items in schema, 73
meaningless DO, 59; *do not* or *don't,* 8; in extended propredicates, 68; and propredicate rules, 71; in finite schema, 73, 76
might: for urbanity, 187; literary, 190. *See also* MAY
mind: Would you mind?, 174
minimal matrix: described, 150; bound-

ary of, 183ff; contrasted with maximal matrix, 197

minor stress: described, 12; unspoken words with, 57

misspelling: and schools, 65

mixed tenses, 126, 131

modals: listed, 76, 147; learning of, 147; modern meanings of, 148, 167, 180, 192ff; preliminary discussion, 150ff; defined symbolically, 153; Shakespearean modal meanings, 166f; negation of, 197ff; citations, 214ff

moral certainty and morality: and stable modals, 154, 190f

mores, 150; not consciously learned, 151

MUST: does not mean HAVE TO, 25; in finite schema, 76; in modal summary, 150; does not express command, 151, 195; defined symbolically, 153; defined discursively, 191; replaced by *should*, 194, 197

mustn't, 200f

-N: in participles, 48, 56; in gerund schema, 53; in finite schema, 76

narrative aspects, 126ff; in both tenses, 132, 133

native speech, 12

natural history, 3f

nature. *See* order of nature

NEED: in finite schema, 76; in modal summary, 150; defined symbolically, 153; anciently not a modal, 167; defined discursively, 192; history and prospects, 192f

needn't, 200f

negation using NOT, 63f; with auxiliaries, 30; of whole clause, 63; relative and eventual, 67, 199, 201; defined, 153; of modals, 197ff; strong and weak, 199; in print, 209f

neutral voice: in finite schema, 81. *See also* passive voice

newspaper headlines, aspect in, 132

Newton, Isaac, 154f, 181

Nixon, Richard, 51

non-passive verbs, 92ff

normal speech, 64

NOT: as a hyphenated bit, 63; placement of, 63f; meaning of, 198

NOT BE ABOUT TO, 24

nouns in *-ing*, 40, 205ff

numbering of finites, 73f, 76

object: infinitive as, 17f

Occam's Razor, 34, 87

occasional relation: prepositions with gerund, 42ff

OED. *See* Oxford Dictionary

of: with gerund, 42; spelling for *'ve*, 65

office: as meaning of OUGHT TO, 196

Old Bailey, 7

omission: of subject, 56f; of base, 66

on: with gerund, 42; omitted to form temporary aspect, 44

oratorical style, 64

ORDER: past participle with, 51

order of nature: as member of the community, 152; as actor, 152, 196; as logic, 196

Ota, Akira, 116

other-directedness, 194, 197

oughtn't to, didn't ought to, hadn't ought to, 194

OUGHT TO: does not mean BE SUPPOSED TO, 28; in finite schema, 76; in modal summary, 150; defined symbolically, 153; replaced by *should*, 170, 194, 197; defined discursively, 191; history of, 193f; meaning 'office,' 196

Oxford Dictionary, 3, 46, 232, 233

paradigm, 80, 120

paralinguistic events, 8

participial adjectives, 51

participle, 40; meanings, 49f. *See also* past participle; present participle

passive voice: of infinitive, 19; of participle, 49; in finite schema, 81; with fake subject, 88; terminology, 92; meaning of, 93, 95f; primary, secondary, and tertiary, 94f

past: with gerund, 43

past participle: form of, 48; meaning of, 49; as adjective or noun, 50f

past tense: used for perfect, 142, 145f. *See also* remote tense

pedantry, 10, 65, 163. *See also* edited English

Penguin edition of *Trial*, 9f, 122n

perfect phase: of infinitive, 19: of participles, 49f; in finite schema, 81;

meaning of English, 140ff; graphed, 140f, 211; unlike French or German, 144f; instability of, 146

phase. *See* perfect phase

pitch, extra-high, 11, 61

PLEASE, 36

plot-advancing events, 127, 129f, 133

Poincaré, Henri, 177f

polarity in modal meanings, 151

Portuguese aspect, 107, 113

positing with presentative, 34ff

possessive as gerund subject, 45

posterior (teleological) hypothesis, 176

potentiality, 149f, 179ff

pragmatism, 153, 190

predication: defined, 71f, 152

prepositions with gerund, 42f

presentative: contrasted to infinitive, 31; meaning of, 34ff; subject of, 34f; as object or complement, 35; as imperative, 35; as provisional, 37

present participle: not contained in temporary aspect, 44; subject of, 46f; used as adjective or adverb, 46f; form of, 50; meaning of, 50

present tense: and time, 106; historical, 126f, 131f. *See also* actual tense

primary passive, 94ff

primary stress, 12, 61

prior (causal) hypothesis, 176

privative marking: of voice, 98f; of tense, 99; of function, 100; of aspect, 112; of phase, 145f

privative meaning, 82ff

probably, 158, 239

probity, 167f, 169

process verbs, 116ff, 130

'progressive': as label for temporary aspect, 106

propredicate: form of, 65ff; British short, 67, 75, 79; British extended, 68ff; function, 81; copular, 89ff

provisional sentence, 37

prudent confidence: and choice of modals, 157f, 178

psychic-state verbs, 118ff

psychiatrists and language, 8

Ptolemaic astronomy, 155

quasi-auxiliaries, 20ff, 160

question: word-order, 58, 59f, 71, 210;

information, 59; confirmation, 59; wording of, 60; reverse or tag, 64, 184

R: defined, 152; trimmed to leave *C*, 183ff

R. A. C. (R. A. Close), 163, 172, 240

rather, had, 125

reading-aloud style, 64

real condition, 122, 176

realism, 153, 190

reality: accepted, 122; learned continuously, 150; defined, 152

referential meaning, 81ff

refutation of hypothesis, 154f

relation verbs, 118f

relative assertion, 149, 168

relative negation, 199, 201

remote tense: in finite schema, 81; meaning of, 121ff; of modals, 169; adequate assurance, 172ff; unreal hypothesis, 176

Riesman, David, 194, 197

-s, 53, 63, 72f, 76, 214

Sayers, Dorothy, 33, 69, 75

says [sez], 72

schema: as slot-and-filler display, 5; defined, 53ff; gerund, 53; simplified finite, 54; complete finite, 76; marker use and non-use as dichotomies, 79; labeled for meanings, 81, 101, 147; items as components of form and markers of meanings, 81f

schools: impact on English, 65, 172, 179, 209f, 214

science: of language, 4; verification in, 154f; simplicity in, 182; necessary circularity in, 206; pregnant wording in, 207; language of, 210

scientific hypothesis and theory, 154

secondary passive, 94f

secondary stress, 12, 63f

semi-formal English, 6, 8

semological cube of modals, 149

Shakespeare, William: supplementary clauses with DO quoted from, 68; modal meanings, 166f

SHALL: in finite schema, 76; in modal summary, 149f; defined symbolically, 153; defined discursively, 156; in modern sense for diffidence, 161ff;

American folklore on, 161, 163; pronunciation of, 163, 214; documentary, 164, 231ff; normal American use of, 164; in archaic sense for Subservient Probity, 167ff; school force-feeding of, 172, 214; H. W. Fowler on, 233ff. *See also* should

shan't, 200

shape: form and, 205ff

should: differing in meaning from BE SUPPOSED TO, 28; replacing *would* in edited English, 124; replacing MUST and OUGHT TO, 170, 194, 197; American traditional use of, 170f; modern British use misunderstood by Americans, 171. *See also* SHALL

signalling, expressive, 11, 61

signals: grammatical, 5; of meaning, 81f

signals grammar, 5

Simon and Schuster edition of *Trial,* 9

Slavic aspect, 107, 113, 126

slot-and-filler display. *See* schema

small capitals: in *Trial,* 11; for bases and markers, 20*n*, 47f. *See also* schema

Smith, Henry Lee, Jr., 8, 11, 138

Snow, C. P., 69, 94, 122

social matrices of events. *See* maximal matrix; minimal matrix

Southern American English: NOT BE ABOUT TO in, 24

Spanish and Portuguese aspect, 107, 113

speech: native, 12; normal and special, 64

spelling: of Penguin edition of *Trial,* 10; concealed from schoolboys, 65

split infinitive, 30f

square brackets: uses of in *Trial* citations, 8, 9, 10

stable modals, 150ff, 190ff, 198, 201

status verbs, 116ff, 130

stress (*technical term for significant degree of force in speaking one syllable in comparison to neighbors, popularly called* 'accent'): English, 12; marked in citations, 12, 68f, 214; on participles and adjectives, 51; grammatical significance of, 52, 63f, 68f; irresponsible, 64; reduction of, 68

strong negation, 199

structure, submerged, 213f

style: casual, 57; normal, special, formal, oratorical, 63f

subject: infinitive as, 17f; of infinitive, 18f; of presentative, 34f; of gerund, 45f; of present participle, 46f; unspoken, 57; identification of, 71; with gender, 71f; of finite, 72; fake, 88

subjunctive, 37

Subservient Freedom, 167, 180, 187ff

Subservient Probity, 167ff

suffixes, 47f, 53, 55, 74, 87

suppose, supposing, 36, 184

SUPPOSED TO, BE, 28

Sweet, Henry, 45

Swift, Jonathan, 232

symbolic definitions, 153

teleological (posterior) hypothesis, 176

temporary aspect: origin of, 44; in finite schema, 81; meaning of, 107ff; as time-framing, 113; in narrative, 129ff

tense: in finite schema, 81; and time, 106, 121, 125; mixture of tenses, 126, 131; of modals, 169

tertiary passive, 94ff

tertiary stress, 12

than: than I, than they, etc., 71, 73, 76

theory and verification, 154f

thère: as fake subject, 41, 88

third person, 37, 72

This is she, 73

time: BE ABLE TO and clock or calendar, 27, 184f; and tense, 106; and aspect, 109ff, 113f

time: It's time, about time, high time, 124

Time Reading Program edition of *Trial,* 10, 251

to: as infinitive marker, 16; with gerund, 43

tone of voice, 7f, 61, 188ff

Trager, George L., 138

transcript of trial, 7ff; flaws in, 64

transformations, 5, 18, 59, 72, 127, 130

transitive verb-bases, 74, 94

Trial of Dr. Adams, The: as normal English, 8, 240; editions, 9f; as adequate small sample, 79f

trimming of *R* to leave *C,* 183ff

truth-value, 17, 71, 82, 147, 149

Tuckett, Captain Harvey, 69

universal time, 109f
unreal conditions and conclusion, 124f, 176f
unreality, 121ff
urbanity, 173ff, 188f
USED TO, 29, 137f
usen't to, 30

've: misspelled *of,* 65
verb (*the use of this word both as a technical term and as an ordinary word in the same book is not entirely avoidable; in its narrowest sense it is opposed to* propredicate; *in its broadest technical sense it includes* non-finites; *in its popular sense it can mean* base; *in any case, it can consist of more than one word within the clause, perhaps in a sequence interrupted by other words*): as one constituent system of English, 5; governing infinitive, 20, 30; governing presentative, 35; governing past participle, 51; finite derived from complete schema, 76
verbal noun, 205ff
verb-base (*often called simply* verb): cited in small capitals, 20*n*, 47f; meaning is both additive and privative, 82ff, 98ff; BE X as a, 87ff; as marker of verb function, 99f
verb function: in finite schema, 81
verification: theory of, 154f
victim: described by participle, 49f; defined, 93; in passive voice, 95, 97f
voice. *See* active voice; passive voice
voice, tone of. *See* tone of voice
vulgarity: how represented in printed speech, 208f

vulnerable statement: scientific hypothesis as, 154

wasn't, 64
Waugh, Evelyn, 69
weak negation, 199
weak stress, 12
went to open my eyes, 23
weren't, 63
what wh...ever, 60, 73
whim: and casual modals, 149, 196
WILL: negated, 64, 199f, 209; in finite schema, 76; in modal summary, 149f; defined symbolically, 153; defined discursively, 156; meanings same with all subjects, 157; has no denotation of futurity, 159; archaic and modern meanings of, 166f; mistreated by H. W. Fowler, 233ff. *See also 'll; would*
Wilson, Angus, 69
without: with gerund, 43
won't, 63, 64, 199f, 209
word-order: question, 58ff; with finite, 72f; passive, 95
would: in unreal condition (and conclusion), 124, 176f; editorially replaced by *should,* 124; real-past use of, 137f, 173; in British and American English, 172, 178; H. W. Fowler on, 233ff
wouldn't, 63, 64
writing: conventional, 8, 90; journalistic, 210
Wyndham, John, 70
Wyndham-Smith, Cecily, 69

zero (ð, etc.), 12

COLLATION TABLE

See pages 9–10. To use either of the other two editions, take the second of our twinned numbers, the Penguin page-number, and enter the table under P. Then under C will be found the Collins page-and-line number for the first line of that Penguin page, and under T the Time Reading Program numbers.

P	C	T	P	C	T	P	C	T
13	17.01	1.01	82	95.03	96.26	152	176.11	193.03
14	18.10	2.23	84	97.14	99.20	154	178.01	195.01
16	20.23	5.13	86	99.33	102.24	156	180.14	198.03
18	22.33	8.06	88	102.01	105.01	158	182.25	200.29
20	25.08	11.01	90	104.13	108.03	160	185.05	203.24
22	27.20	13.23	92	106.21	110.24	162	187.13	206.11
24	29.32	16.19	94	108.31	113.16	164	189.24	209.02
26	32.01	20.01	96	111.09	116.14	166	192.01	211.28
28	34.12	23.01	98	113.17	119.07	168	194.01	214.01
30	36.21	25.29	100	115.25	121.30	170	196.14	217.01
32	38.34	28.20	102	118.01	125.01	172	198.29	219.26
34	41.11	31.13	104	120.12	127.29	174	201.08	222.24
36	43.19	34.02	106	122.26	130.22	176	203.18	225.17
38	45.32	36.26	108	125.03	133.16	178	205.05	227.21
40	48.06	40.20	110	127.12	136.06	180	207.17	230.18
42	50.15	43.13	112	129.23	138.28	182	209.31	233.10
44	52.24	45.32	114	132.07	141.19	184	212.06	236.04
46	54.35	48.19	116	134.16	144.11			
48	57.09	51.13	118	136.31	147.05			
50	59.16	54.06	120	139.05	149.27	190	218.06	242.19
52	61.26	57.01	122	141.14	152.15	192	220.17	245.15
54	63.34	59.23	124	144.01	155.01	194	222.31	248.10
56	66.06	62.20	126	146.14	158.06	196	225.06	251.06
58	68.16	65.08	128	148.26	161.01	198	227.14	253.27
60	70.25	67.31	130	150.33	163.24	200	229.31	256.27
62	73.07	70.20				202	232.06	259.23
64	75.14	73.12	134	156.08	168.21	204	234.19	262.20
66	77.26	76.05	136	158.19	171.13	206	236.31	265.12
68	79.33	78.25	138	160.25	174.01	208	239.07	268.09
70	82.09	81.17	140	162.33	176.22	210	241.19	271.04
72	84.19	84.11	142	165.07	179.15	212	243.06	273.20
			144	167.01	182.01	214	245.16	276.12
76	88.08	88.19	146	169.11	184.29	216	247.29	279.09
78	90.17	91.09	148	171.22	187.18	218	250.06	282.01
80	92.25	93.32	150	173.32	190.10	220	252.17	284.23